COMMONWEALTH CARIBBEAN CORPORATE GOVERNANCE

Edited by Suzanne Ffolkes-Goldson

Routledge
Taylor & Francis Group
LONDON AND NEW YORK

First published 2016
by Routledge
2 Park Square, Milton Park, Abingdon, Oxon, OX14 4RN

and by Routledge
605 Third Avenue, New York, NY 10017

Routledge is an imprint of the Taylor & Francis Group, an informa business

British Library Cataloguing in Publication Data
A catalogue record for this book is available from the British Library

Library of Congress Cataloging-in-Publication Data
Commonwealth Caribbean corporate governance / edited by Suzanne Ffoakes-Goldson. — First edition.
pages cm
Includes bibliographical references and index.
1. Corporate governance—Law and legislation—West Indies, British. I. Ffoakes-Goldson, Suzanne C.
KGL5328.C66 2015
346.729′065—dc23
2015017470

ISBN: 978-1-138-79470-2 (hbk)
ISBN: 978-1-138-79469-6 (pbk)
ISBN: 978-1-315-75905-0 (ebk)

Typeset in Baskerville
by Apex CoVantage, LLC

COMMONWEALTH CARIBBEAN CORPORATE GOVERNANCE

Corporate governance initiatives have been developing at a rapid pace in the Commonwealth Caribbean through legislation, case law and codes. *Commonwealth Caribbean Corporate Governance* offers an overview of current practice and legal developments in corporate governance, highlighting the interpretation of the legislation through case law and the codes of corporate governance which have now been implemented. It also considers the challenges which emerging markets face in an attempt to adopt the corporate governance initiatives of developed markets.

This text explores the emergence and development of corporate governance in the region from a range of angles, including the protection and empowerment of shareholders, the impact on government agencies, and the role and responsibilities of directors and officers in companies and in government agencies.

Written by a panel of academics, legal practitioners and experts working in business, this book will be an invaluable resource for judges, lawyers, corporate executives and students of business, corporate law and corporate management.

Suzanne Ffolkes-Goldson is an Attorney at Law and Lecturer and former Deputy Dean for Graduate Matters & External Affairs in the Faculty of Law at the University of the West Indies Mona Campus. She specialises in Corporate Governance, Criminal Law, Company/Corporate Law, and Corporate Management, and is the course director for the LLM course on Corporate Governance.

COMMONWEALTH CARIBBEAN LAW SERIES

The Commonwealth Caribbean Law Series is the only series of law books that covers the jurisdiction of the English speaking Caribbean nations. The first titles in the series were published in 1995 to acclaim from academics, practitioners and the judiciary in the region. Several editions followed, and they have now become essential reading for those learning and practising Caribbean law.

This must have series is required holdings for any law library specialising in Caribbean legal information.

Titles in this series include:

Alternative Dispute Resolution
Albert Fiadjoe

Commonwealth Caribbean Business Law
Rajendra Ramlogan and Natalie Persadie

Commonwealth Caribbean Company Law
Andrew Burgess

Commonwealth Caribbean Civil Procedure
Gilbert Kodilinye and Vanessa Kodilinye

Commonwealth Caribbean Constitutional Law
Sir Fred Phillips

Commonwealth Caribbean Land Law
Sampson Owusu

Commonwealth Caribbean Law and Legal Systems
Rose-Marie Belle Antoine

Commonwealth Caribbean Public Law
Albert Fiadjoe

Commonwealth Caribbean Tort Law
Gilbert Kodilinye

Commonwealth Caribbean Law of Trusts
Gilbert Kodilinye and Trevor Carmichael

Judicial Review in the Commonwealth Caribbean
Rajendra Ramlogan

Commonwealth Caribbean Administrative Law
Eddy Ventose

Commonwealth Caribbean Contract Law
Gilbert Kodilinye and Maria Kodilinye

Commonwealth Caribbean Practice and Procedure
Dana S. Seetahal

Commonwealth Caribbean Employment and Labour Law
Natalie Corthésy and Carla–Anne Harris-Roper

Commonwealth Caribbean Tort Law
Gilbert Kodilinye

Commonwealth Caribbean Property Law
Gilbert Kodilinye

Commonwealth Caribbean Business Law
Natalie Persadie and Rajendra Ramlogan

Forthcoming titles:

Commonwealth Caribbean Intellectual Property Law
Eddy Ventose

Commonwealth Caribbean Civil Procedure
Gilbert Kodilinye and Vanessa Kodilinye

CONTENTS

NOTES ON CONTRIBUTORS

CELIA BLAKE

Celia Blake is a Senior Lecturer at the University of the West Indies where her teaching assignments include corporate law. She has served as a Commissioner of the Financial Services Commission, Jamaica's securities, insurance and pensions regulator, and has also been a board member of the country's central bank. In addition to her body of research and publications in language and the law/forensic linguistics, she has written on issues involving financial regulation in the Caribbean, including judicial oversight of financial regulatory action and regulatory aspects in cross-border insolvency. In this volume, she considers the legal position of the directors of financial regulators in the Commonwealth Caribbean and provides an insight into their role in institutional and regulatory governance.

JANET DINE

Janet Dine was educated at King's College, London, 1969–1972 (LLB) and 1979 (PhD) and at the Inns of Court of Law, 1973, and practised as a barrister dealing with criminal and commercial cases. She became a lecturer at King's College London between 1978 and 1992 in charge of the London LLM, coordinating the courses at all of the London Colleges, and became Director of the Centre of European Law at King's and taught on Criminal Law, European Law, Conflict of Laws and Company Law. In 1990 she was appointed legal adviser on the European Company Statute in the House of Lords' Committee on the European Communities. Professor Dine was appointed as a Reader at the University of Essex in 1992 teaching Company Law, Criminal Law and European Law. From 1992 to 2001 she was a Commissioner for Friendly Societies (a government appointment). She was promoted to a Chair at Essex University and became the Head of the Law School in 1994 until 1997. She took an MA in Theology and Society (2002) at the University of Essex.

In 2003 Professor Dine was appointed as a commercial law expert in a project funded by the World Bank, the EU and the Deutsche Gesellschaft für Internationale Zusammenarbeit (GIZ) GmbH which aimed to assist the Balkan states to join the EU. She drafted laws and advised governments in Kosovo, Serbia, Montenegro and Albania to align their law with the EU *acquis communautaire*. With Michael Blecher she drafted 'Albanian Law 9901 on Entrepreneurs and Companies' of 14 April 2008.

In 2005, Professor Dine was appointed as the Director of the Centre of Commercial Law Studies at Queen Mary College, London.

SUZANNE FFOLKES-GOLDSON

Mrs Suzanne Ffolkes-Goldson is an Attorney at Law, Lecturer and former Deputy Dean for Graduate Matters & External Affairs, in the Faculty of Law at the UWI Mona Campus. She specialises in Corporate Governance, Criminal Law, Company/

Corporate Law, and Corporate Management, and is the course director for the LLM course on Corporate Governance.

Mrs Ffolkes-Goldson has a degree in Economics from York University, Canada, an LLB from the University of the West Indies and a BCL from Oxford University. She is called to the Bar in Jamaica and Barbados.

Mrs Ffolkes-Goldson has been an adviser to the CARICOM Committee on the Reform of Company Law in the Commonwealth Caribbean and the Joint Select Committee of Parliament on the Jamaica Companies Act 2004. Mrs Goldson is also a member of the Corporate Governance Committee of the Private Sector Organization of Jamaica, responsible for the drafting and dissemination of corporate governance principles for Jamaica and the Commonwealth Caribbean. She is also a member of the Implementation Oversight Committee for the Corporate Governance Framework for Public Bodies, Ministry of Finance. She is certified under the Global Corporate Governance Forum/World Bank, International Finance Corporation, Caribbean Training of Trainers Programme in Corporate Governance Board Leadership.

Mrs Ffolkes-Goldson has presented extensive research on Company/Corporate Law, Corporate Governance, Corporate Insolvency and Corporate Social Responsibility at numerous seminars, workshops and conferences, locally, regionally and internationally. She has published a number of articles in regional and international journals on these subjects. Her upcoming book, *Corporate Business Principles*, provides a guide for practitioners and scholars to the Companies Act and the development of the law in Jamaica and in the Commonwealth Caribbean region.

SANDRA GLASGOW

Sandra AC Glasgow is the Founder and Managing Director of BizTactics Limited, a consulting company dedicated to nurturing growth-aspiring firms and promoting best-in-class corporate governance. She is a Founding Member of Jamaica's first Angel Investor Network, FirstAngelsJA. She was Chief Executive Officer of the Private Sector Organisation of Jamaica (PSOJ) where she led a project funded by the Canadian International Development Agency to update the PSOJ's Code on Corporate Governance, published in 2009, along with a companion *Handbook and Tool Kit on Good Governance*. Prior to joining the PSOJ in 2007, she was the Senior Vice President for Corporate Services at the University of Technology, Jamaica and the Founder of UTech's Technology Innovation Centre (TIC), having successfully transformed the operations of its precursor, the Entrepreneurial Centre, into a world-class business incubator for start-up technology ventures and a provider of a wide range of training, consulting and business services for entrepreneurial Jamaican firms.

A graduate of the University of the West Indies, she holds a Bachelor of Science Degree in Applied Zoology and Applied Botany and a Master's Degree in Business Administration, with a specialisation in the Management of Technology, University of the West Indies (UWI), Mona campus

She was certified as a Director in 2003 by the now defunct Commonwealth Association for Corporate Governance (CAGC), as a Trainer of Trainers in Corporate

Governance Board Leadership by the International Finance Corporation in 2008 and a Trainer of Trainers in Business Ethics by the Inter-American Investment Corporation and the US Department of Commerce in 2011.

DERRICK McKOY

Dr Derrick McKoy is a Senior Lecturer and Dean in the Faculty of Law at the University of the West Indies (UWI), Mona campus. He holds doctorates in Business Administration and in Law, and he is a graduate of the Norman Manley Law School. He was Contractor-General of Jamaica from 1998 to 2005, and has served as Chairman of the Fair Trading Commission, Chairman of the Antidumping and Subsidies Commission, member of the Disciplinary Committee of the General Legal Council, and as a member of the All Island Electricity Appeals Tribunal. In addition to his teaching in the Faculty of Law, Dr McKoy has taught in the Institute of International Relations, the Mona School of Business and Management, the Norman Manley Law School, Barry University's Andreas School of Business, and Nova Southeastern University's Huizenga School of Business. He is a member of the Jamaican Bar and the Jamaica Institute of Management and writes a blog at www.derrickmckoy.net.

TABLE OF CASES

TABLE OF STATUTES

INTRODUCTION

Commonwealth Caribbean Corporate Governance

Suzanne Ffolkes-Goldson

The motivation for the publication of a book on Commonwealth Caribbean corporate governance is borne out of the observation that corporate governance initiatives have been developing in the region at a rapid pace, through legislation, case law and codes. These initiatives have mainly been adopted from the developed countries. Governments, the public sector, legislators, the judiciary, lawyers, accountants, auditors, the business community, local and foreign investors, scholars and multilateral agencies, have need to assess the impact of the legislation, case law and codes on the region given their specific and various roles and responsibilities. The book is therefore designed to highlight the legislation and the interpretation of the legislation through case law and the codes of corporate governance now implemented in the region.

In the wake of international crises, such as the Maxwell empire scandal in the UK in the early1990s, the Asian Financial Crisis in the late 1990s,[1] the Enron crisis in the US in the early 2000s and the financial crisis in 2008, robust corporate governance frameworks emerged worldwide. This is against the backdrop of the recognition or better yet, consensus, that one of the main reasons for the various crises was poor corporate governance as demonstrated in: (i) lack of transparency and accountability; (ii) weak regulation; (iii) limited shareholder and stakeholder involvement/empowerment;[2] and (iv) inattention to risk and risk consequences. Not only did these crises affect companies and their shareholders, but a much wider group of stakeholders including employees, creditors and the community in which the companies operated.

There exists a great deal of literature on, and analysis of, the various financial crises some of which have been mentioned above. The responses to these crises have included *inter alia*, the introduction of corporate governance codes and legislation and more stringent regulatory frameworks and enforcement strategies. In Europe, the responses to corporate governance failures have mainly been through soft law and moral suasion in the form of codes and principles, whereas in the US, the responses were decidedly in legislative form.[3] Multilateral organizations such as the World Bank and the OECD have established minimum corporate governance standards through their corporate governance codes. The preamble to the OECD Guidelines states *inter alia*:

> Increasingly, the OECD and its member governments have recognized the synergy between macroeconomic and structural policies in achieving fundamental policy goals. Corporate governance is one key element in improving economic efficiency and growth as well as enhancing investor confidence . . . Corporate governance is

---

1 Thailand, Malaysia, Indonesia and South Korea.
2 In particular that of minority shareholders.
3 Eg US Sarbanes-Oxley Act 2002.

> only part of the larger economic context in which firms operate that includes, for example, macroeconomic policies and the degree of competition in product and factor markets. The corporate governance framework also depends on the legal, regulatory, and institutional environment. In addition, factors such as business ethics and corporate awareness of the environmental and societal interests of the communities in which a company operates can also have an impact on its reputation and its long-term success.[4]

The Commonwealth Caribbean comprises a group of 18 independent territories, which were formerly under British rule.[5] Although these territories share a common history of slavery and exploitation through colonialism, they have experienced varied levels of economic development due to differences in, *inter alia*, resources, leadership, levels of corruption and local and foreign direct investment (FDI). Many of the territories in the region depend on the trade of their primary resources, tourism and FDI, which leaves them vulnerable to external economic shocks. Limited resources compound the problems, and/or changing demands for the resources which exist and which the territories hope to exploit (eg sugar, bauxite, bananas).

Professor Janet Dine[6] writes passionately about the economic challenges of emerging markets in the face of a brutal history and the 'neo-liberal agenda' which has at its core, the shareholder primacy model of corporate law. Professor Dine paints a picture of trade imbalance between developed and developing markets, and multinational and transnational exploitation of emerging markets, through, *inter alia*, an emphasis on the shareholder primacy model. She concludes, however, that the Commonwealth Caribbean, by abandoning the shareholder primacy model in favour of the stakeholder model of company law and corporate governance, has set the stage for a more equal society.

The development of an indigenous financial industry since independence has not been encouraging, as evidenced by the financial sector collapse in Jamaica in the 1990s during which many indigenous banks and insurance companies imploded,[7] and the CL Financial (CL) debacle in Trinidad and Tobago in 2009 when

4 www.acts.oecd.org.

5 Independent nations: Antigua and Barbuda, the Bahamas, Barbados, Belize (formerly British Honduras), Dominica, Grenada, Guyana (formerly British Guiana), Jamaica, St Christopher [hereafter, St Kitts] and Nevis, St Lucia, St Vincent and the Grenadines, Trinidad and Tobago and British overseas territories: Anguilla, the British Virgin Islands, the Cayman Islands, Montserrat and the Turks and Caicos Islands. www.thecommonwealth.org.

6 Janet Dine, Chapter 1.

7 'Between 1995 and 1998 six commercial banks (accounting for 60% of deposits in the population of nine commercial banks, five life insurance companies (accounting for over ninety per cent of premium income in the business), one-third of all merchant banks, and several building societies were found to be insolvent and closed.' G Bonnick, 'Storm in a Teacup: Crisis in Jamaica's Financial Sector' Adlith Brown Memorial Lecture Delivered at the Thirtieth Annual Conference of the Caribbean Centre for Monetary Studies held in Nassau Bahamas, October 1998 (Final version May 1999). See also J Daley and K Matthews, 'Efficiency and Convergence in the Jamaican Banking Sector 1998–2007' No E2009/30, Cardiff Economics Working Papers from Cardiff University, Cardiff Business School, Economics Section http://business.cardiff.ac.uk/sites/default/files/E2009_30.pdf.

CL Financial (which was the largest conglomerate in Trinidad and Tobago and the Caribbean), met its demise.[8] It has been argued that poor corporate governance, the weak regulatory environment, coupled with the financial policies of the day, were significant contributors to the financial sector failures in both Jamaica and Trinidad.[9] These epic failures resulted in huge government bailouts to prevent a liquidity crisis and a spread to the real economy. Apart from the heavy price paid by the taxpayers of those countries, the old shareholder primacy model of corporate law in Jamaica was of little assistance to those stakeholders who were left whistling for their money. It is little wonder that Jamaica led the charge for an emphasis on corporate governance initiatives, first through legislation, and then through the introduction of a private sector-led Corporate Governance Code. The recognition of a weak regulatory environment also informed the introduction of the Financial Services Commission in Jamaica in 2001, with broad powers for the regulation of the insurance, pensions and securities industries.[10]

The challenge, which many of the territories of the region face, however, is the fact that much of the legislation and codes adopted from developed countries may not be entirely appropriate for developing countries,[11] given the differences in, *inter alia*, the corporate culture, the regulatory environment (often due to lack of resources) and opportunities for corruption.

> The various codes, principles and legislation of the developed markets modeled in the Caribbean do not always take into account the predominance of closely-held companies, few listings of public companies on the local stock exchanges, the limited investment in shares by local and foreign investors, limited desire for shareholder involvement by the local shareholders; the limited involvement of institutional investors, the slow and limited supply of market information, and the predominance of debt financing as against equity financing. Moreover, in the context of the global financial meltdown, Commonwealth Caribbean territories and other smaller emerging economies, as

8 'CLICO is the largest insurance company in the country and the region, the flagship of the parent company, CL Financial (CLF), which is the largest privately-owned conglomerate in the Commonwealth Caribbean with operations spanning its core business of insurance, but which also includes financial services, real estate development, manufacturing, agriculture and forestry, retail and distribution, energy, media and communications . . . thus CBTT was "very conscious of the contagion risks that the financial collapse of an institution as vast as CLF could have on the entire financial system of Trinidad and Tobago and indeed, in the entire Caribbean region."' W Soverall, 'CLICO's Collapse: Poor Corporate Governance' (2012) 2(2) American International Journal of Contemporary Research http://www.aijcrnet.com/journals/Vol_2_No_2_February_2012/20.pdf.

9 S Ffolkes-Goldson and E Greenaway, 'Booms Needs Busts: Improving the Legal Framework for Insolvency' (2012) www.capricaribbean.com; N Girvan, 'The CL Financial Debacle: Big Companies Should Not Run Small Countries', www.normangirvan.info/the-cl-financial-debacle-big-companies-should-not-run-small-countries.

10 The Bank of Jamaica regulates deposit taking institutions. The Central Bank of Trinidad and Tobago regulates the banking, insurance and pensions industries and the Trinidad and Tobago Securities and Exchange Commission.

11 S Ffolkes-Goldson, 'Corporate Governance: A One Size Fits All?' in D Berry and T Robinson (eds), *Transitions in Caribbean Law: Lawmaking, Constitutionalism and the Confluence of International and Domestic Law* (Caribbean Law Publishing, 2013) 33–50.

> opposed to larger emerging economies such as China, India and Brazil, are faced with the challenge of the cost of assessing risk, the difficulty in accessing such information and the cost of enforcement of legislation and regulations.[12]

It has been argued that the OECD Principles cannot simply be applied universally:

> . . . while appreciating that the OECD has engaged in activities such as regional round-tables in order to take account of the local context, the Principles themselves are based on the corporate governance model of the OECD member countries not perfectly suitable for emerging markets.[13]

The challenge of rationalizing the adoption of codes and legislation is addressed directly and indirectly throughout the publication.

Sandra Glasgow[14] gives a history of the emergence of corporate governance in the region, the adoption of various principles and codes, and provides an analysis of where Jamaica and Trinidad stack up in terms of disclosure *vis-à-vis* other countries. She also looks at the growing trends in corporate governance with particular emphasis on gender. The fact that Jamaica has been at the forefront of corporate governance in the region suggests that the successes in Jamaica, such as they are, may well have resulted from increased moral suasion and awareness through the introduction of a code and legislation. It remains to be seen whether there is also an impact in Trinidad, given the recent introduction of a corporate governance code there and increased regulatory oversight since the CL Financial debacle.

My chapter[15] on the duties and responsibilities of directors and officers of companies, trace some of the legislative changes in the last 20 years in a number of Commonwealth Caribbean jurisdictions which reflect corporate governance and the interpretation of the legislation through case law. The increased exposure of directors and officers, have been adopted *in pari materia* with the Canada Business Corporations Act, save for a few outliers, and reflect the corporate governance imperatives, emerging from the various corporate executive abuses reflected in Commonwealth case law. The provisions also provide safe-harbour for directors and officers, to ensure that qualified persons are not discouraged from taking up directorships. The legislation in the region stops short of legislating morality, but an analysis of the current Codes of Corporate Governance in the region (Barbados, Jamaica and Trinidad and Tobago), reveals that there is a clear attempt at moral suasion. In particular, the Private Sector Organization of Jamaica Corporate Governance Code 2009, reflects the increasing duties and responsibilities of the directors and officers of all companies and public listed companies, in particular, found in the UK, Australia, South Africa (King III) and

12 Ibid 38.

13 M Siems and O Alvarez-Macotela, 'The OECD Principles of Corporate Governance in Emerging Markets: A Successful Example of Networked Governance?' in M Fenwick, S Van Uystel and S Wrbka (eds), *Networked Governance, Transnational Business and the Law* (Springer, 2014).

14 Sandra Glasgow, Chapter 2.

15 Suzanne Ffolkes-Goldson, Chapter 3.

OECD Codes. There are, however, recommendations for a revision of this code to include recent international corporate governance developments such as: the board's responsibility for the long-term success of the company; an annual non-binding vote on 'say-on-pay'; increased risk management and internal control and corporate social responsibility.

My chapter[16] on the protection and empowerment of shareholders and other stakeholders highlights the shift from a shareholder primacy model to the modern stakeholder model of corporate governance through a survey of Companies Acts and Corporate Governance Codes in the region. The case law which has emerged so far in the region reflects a variation in the levels of stakeholder protection due to the wording of the provisions relating to it and/or the interpretation of these provisions, found in case law. These limitations, however, are ameliorated by the Codes of Corporate Governance introduced in Barbados, Jamaica and Trinidad which make broad recommendations for shareholder and stakeholder empowerment through increased disclosure and accountability.

Corporate governance principles have gone beyond the private sector, to influence public sector bodies, through the introduction of legislation, which has an impact on government agencies. The recently approved Jamaica Corporate Governance Framework for Public Bodies states, *inter alia*:

> The Government of Jamaica aims to improve accountability, probity, transparency among Public Bodies in order to achieve a more compliant, responsive, efficient and effective Public Service. In essence, its ultimate aim is to bring Jamaican Public Bodies, especially the operation and effectiveness of corporate boards in line with international corporate governance best practices and emerging trends.[17]

Celia Blake[18] discusses the duties and responsibilities of directors and senior officers of government agencies responsible for financial regulation/supervision in the region. Since the introduction of legislation to strengthen the governance of the financial sector entities, the watch-dog role of financial supervisors also demands a high standard of corporate governance within the supervisory agencies. This topic, has not attracted much attention in the region, however, it is accepted that corporate governance legislation and codes are ineffective where the oversight is limited or compromised.

Derrick McKoy[19] explores public sector governance as a whole by looking at: (i) change through public sector reforms in developed, developing and transitional countries under 'the new public management'; (ii) crisis as it informs public sector management, such as the global financial crisis of 2007 and 2008 and organized crime; and (iii) dysfunction, given the differences in the private sector and public sector, where public sector management systems must accommodate a demanding body of stakeholders, the uncertainty of administrative change and reform, international

16 Suzanne Ffolkes-Goldson, Chapter 4.
17 www.ocg.gov.jm.
18 Celia Blake, Chapter 5.
19 Derrick McKoy, Chapter 6.

crises, complicated measures of success and failure and a different standard from the private sector as it relates to corruption.

It is hoped that this publication will provide a resource for the assessment of the state of corporate governance in the private and public sector, through analysis of legislation, case law and codes in some of the territories of the Commonwealth Caribbean region, while highlighting the challenges which emerging markets face in an attempt to adopt the corporate governance initiatives of developed markets.

CHAPTER 1

CORPORATE GOVERNANCE, EMERGING MARKETS AND DEVELOPMENT

The Commonwealth Caribbean

JANET DINE

INTRODUCTION

When I was invited to write a chapter in *Commonwealth Caribbean Corporate Governance*, I was hopeful that the situation that I depicted in *Companies, International Trade and Human Rights*[1] would be healthier. In some ways, I argue, it is, and on the other hand it is worse. It is better because many people understand what is happening although they are not able to change the situation easily. It is worse because of the debt situation in some Caribbean countries.[2] There is a proliferation of Bilateral Investment Treaties (BITs) and Multilateral Investment Treaties (MITs) involving the Caribbean countries. The grip of the neo-liberal economic paradigm is pervasive as shown by the interference of the International Monetary Fund (IMF).

The brief of this chapter was to update some of the chapters in the 2005 book especially as far the Caribbean countries were touched on. This is an ambitious brief because the Caribbean area is enormous with about 7,000 islands,[3] different political systems, different cultures, histories and corporate governance regimes.[4] The remit of this chapter is narrower because the book only includes the Commonwealth Caribbean countries;[5] however, it is a large task and inevitably I will only be able to touch on

1 J Dine, *Companies, International Trade and Human Rights* (Cambridge University Press, 2005).

2 For example, in Jamaica the GDP–debt ratio is 140% and in 2013 the IMF approved a $932 million four-year 'Extended Fund Facility', their conditions. The rate of unemployment is 16.5%. See The World Fact Book, 'Central America and Caribbean: Jamaica' <https://www.cia.gov/library/publications/the-world-factbook/geos/jm.html>, accessed 9 November 2014.

3 Worldatlas, 'Caribbean' <http://www.worldatlas.com/webimage/countrys/carib.htm> accessed 9 October 2014.

4 R Antoine, *Commonwealth Caribbean Law and Legal Systems* (2nd edn, Routledge-Cavendish, 2008). See also A Foxley, *Groundwork for Inclusive Development, Responses to Emergent Challenges for Latin American and Caribbean Economies* (Center for Latin American and Latino Studies, American University, 2014): 'in late 2012, 20 countries already had per capita incomes of more than US$10,000, and in four of them (Antigua and Barbuda, Argentina, Chile, and Trinidad and Tobago) the figure was close to US$20,000. At the same time, another 11 economies are struggling to enter the middle income group, with very unequal performances, ranging from Haiti to countries like Jamaica and the Dominican Republic, which will have crossed the US$10,000 threshold by 2015.'

5 This is difficult because there are different definitions of 'The Caribbean Commonwealth'. See The Commonwealth, 'Member Countries' <http://thecommonwealth.org/member-countries> accessed 9 October 2014 and 'Members of the Commonwealth Federation' <http://www.tntisland.com/countries.html>, accessed 9 October 2009. My understanding is that it extends to Antigua and Barbuda; Bahamas; Barbados; Belize; Dominica; Guyana; Jamaica; St Lucia; St Kitts and Nevis; St Vincent and Grenadines; Trinidad and Tobago.

a few countries in any detail.[6] However, I am sad that the preface that I wrote in 2005 is still resoundingly true and I am still angry about the inequality between individuals and countries. I wrote:

> This book is written from a perspective shared with Thomas Pogge; We, the affluent countries and their citizens, continue to impose a global economic order under which millions avoidably die each year from poverty-related causes. We would regard it as a grave injustice if such an economic order were imposed within a national society. We must regard our imposition of the present global order as a grave injustice unless we have a plausible rationale for a suitable double standard. We do not have such a plausible rationale.[7]

First I must define the parameters of the chapter. Why is the chapter talking about 'corporate governance' while considering international trade treaties, the international financial institutions, economic theories, inequality and climate change? For this I will go back to an earlier text, *The Governance of Company Groups*[8] where I wrote:

> My colleagues have commentated frequently on my propensity to see company law illustration for (nearly) discussion, accusing me of expecting company law to 'take over the world'. This is the book where I discover that not company law but companies have all but done so and confront us with the frightening reality of polarisation of incomes and the globalisation of poverty.[9]

I have now broadened the focus because of the prevalence of the recent phenomenon of 'corporate governance' a term that cannot be easily defined:

> One would think that the issue of corporate governance would be a purely technical and slightly legalistic one falling within the ambit of what we define rather strictly as company law. Therefore, the issue in question would fall within the interests of mainly academics or corporate lawyers. The truth however is very different. Corporate governance found itself at the very centre of a debate that relates to the very cultural identity and basic political choices made on the part of societies. The fact that corporate governance has provoked a debate, which effectively touched upon the fundamental ideological choices of the societies in question, clearly revealed the true parameters of the issue and its far-reaching effect. The reason behind the debate that has generated hundreds of academic articles and books,[10] a very lively exchange of ideas and

6 There has been efforts to promote an economic integration in the region, the latest agreement is the CSME, Caribbean, Single Market and Economy, 2006 but it is faltering. See Curtis Reynold, 'The Political Economy of Caribbean Regionalism in the Twenty-First Century: Rebirth or Resuscitation?' (2012) <http://ssrn.com/abstract=2297556> accessed 23 October 2014.

7 Thomas Pogge, *World Poverty and Human Rights* (2nd edn, Polity, 2007) 109.

8 Cambridge University Press, 2000.

9 Dine, *Governance of Company Groups* (Cambridge University Press, 2000) preface, xix.

10 A Riley, 'Understanding and Regulating the Corporation' (1995) 58(4) Modern Law Review 595, 595; J E Stiglitz, 'Multinational Corporations: Balancing Rights and Responsibilities' (2007) 101 Proceedings of the Annual Meeting (American Society of International Law); D Attenborough, 'Giving Purpose to the Corporate Purpose Debate: An Equitable Maximisation and Viability Principle' (2012) 32(1) Legal Studies 4; J E Parkinson, *Corporate Power and Responsibility: Issues in the Theory of Company Law* (Clarendon Press, 1993) 237; A Keyes, *The Corporate Objective* (Edward Elgar, 2011); B Cheffins, *Company Law: Theory, Structure and Operation* (Clarendon Press, 1997) 1999; S Bottomley, *The Constitutional Corporation* (Ashgate, 2007).

> opinions on the part of politicians, industry and society and sometimes a rather overt confrontation between important parts of the society such as the employees and the employers is the fact that corporate governance requires the effective engagement of actors that lie at the heart of the most important issues for humanity. To consider 'Corporate Governance' is also to consider competing models of capitalism and competing global economic models.[11]

The history and therefore the culture of the Caribbean countries are imbued by the tragic events around the transatlantic slave trade.[12] There is more and more research and evidence of the disastrous legacy[13] of the trade on people in the Caribbean countries and also in the black communities in the United States and in Europe ranging from hypertension in black individuals to the lack of confidence with makes some people whiten their skins.[14] Other colonised people have recognised 'cultural cringe',[15] a lack of confidence in their cultural heritage. These issues are wide ranging so this chapter will focus on the 'modern colonisation' of small 'developing' countries and emerging markets and what this means in the Caribbean. Ha-Joon Chang powerfully illustrates the way that rich nations are bullying less advantaged countries by a web of legal treaties which assumes that the only way that countries can develop is by opening their markets, which is the neo-liberal orthodoxy. This posits a free market, deregulation, a small state and privatisation.[16] Although Chang does not believe that there is a deliberate conspiracy to stop poorer countries developing, this is what is happening because of the rhetoric and implementation of the neo-liberal experiment aided by the international financial institutions, the 'Unholy Trinity',[17] the IMF, the World Bank (WB) and the World Trade Organization (WTO). Chang's thesis is that all of the developed nations historically used a set of instruments, which promoted 'infant industries' either by protecting those industries or by subjecting other countries by means of wars, colonisation and unfair trade practices. When the victorious, developed countries are ready they will open their borders because they are able to trade with other parties using their advanced technology.[18] Since the International Financial

---

11 J Dine and M Koutsias, *The Nature of Corporate Governance; the Significance of National Cultural Identity* (Edward Elgar, 2013).

12 J E Inikori and S L Engerman (eds), *The Atlantic Slave Trade; Effects on Economics, Societies, and Peoples in Africa, the Americas, and Europe* (Duke University Press, 1992).

13 See forthcoming Fernne Brennan, *Race Rights, Reparations, Institutional Racism and the Law* (Ashgate, 2015).

14 Fernne Brennan and John Packer (eds), *Colonisation, Slavery, Reparations and Trade; Remedying the 'Past'* (Routledge, 2013); C E Grim, 'The Possible Relationship between the Transatlantic Slave and Hypertension in Blacks Today' in Inikori and Engerman (eds), *The Atlantic Slave Trade* (Duke University Press, 1992) 239.

15 I am indebted to my colleague Richard Cornes for this term coined when we were researching whether the British Virgin Island (BVI) should build a Commercial Court. See Richard Cornes (Project Leader), Steve Anderman, Janet Dine, Lisa Jack, Paul Webster QC and William Wood QC, *The Judicial System of the Virgin Islands; Options for Reform* (Essex University, 2006).

16 Ha-Joon Chang, *Kicking Away the Ladder: Development Strategy in Historical Perspective* (1st edn, Anthem Press, 2003) and *Bad Samaritans* (Random House Business, 2007).

17 Ha-Joon Chang, *Bad Samaritans* (Random House Business, 2007) 36.

18 Ha-Joon Chang, *Kicking Away the Ladder* (1st edn, Anthem Press, 2003) and *Bad Samaritans* (Random House Business, 2007) and see also Ha-Joon Chang, *Economics; The User's Guide* (Pelican, 2014).

Institutions (IFIs) are dominated by rich nations other less advantaged countries are cowed by asymmetric treaties.[19]

The transatlantic slave trade was probably the largest 'free-market' experiment in the western world; it was only free for the rich slave owner, clearly not free for the slaves. Here there are resonance with what is happening in international trade, the rich nations are 'free', poor countries are bound with chains. Ironically at the time of slavery there were regulations, an insurance industry, laws about shipping the 'chattels' in the home countries and, laws in the colonised countries about suppressing rights for the slaves. Now the IFIs impose 'conditionality' on poor states. Small jurisdictions have always been at the mercy of the rules governing international trade and, in that respect, little has changed. In the light of the discussion relating to 'free trade' above it is worth reiterating that one of the key points made by those who opposed abolition of the slave trade was that such an abolition interfered with the 'freedom of trade' of the merchants involved. It is also interesting to note that the slave trade was 'free' from regulation but protected by a network of law, including company, contract and insurance law as well as 'international' laws such as the Navigation Acts.[20]

It is necessary to dissect the dominant 'free-trade' rhetoric and realise that the 'freedoms' are tilted to powerful and rich interests. 'The free market' doesn't exist. Every market has rules and boundaries that restrict freedom of choice. A market looks free only because we so unconditionally accept its underlying restrictions that we fail to see them.[21] *Laissez-faire* doctrines disguise power relations between individuals and countries. Free market economists, while claiming moral neutrality for their theories,[22] use a discourse, which has the effect of disguising power differences causing a sliding slope of perception from actual equality to formal equality. Formal equality is not real; economic theories positing equality rest on the concept of equal bargaining power (including equality of information) and the resultant 'efficiency'. The result of assuming equality of bargaining power means that there is no justification in intervening in the resultant property distribution. Such an intervention is an interference in the 'freedom to choose' to carry out a particular transaction. The defence of freedom may thus be prayed in aid of a market system, which is then free to create enormous inequalities. This concept of freedom of choice has considerable resonance both at national and international levels, applying to individuals, corporations and states. Assertions of freedom and equality disguise the real power relations.

> Every stable social system possesses an order of power and wealth, but unlike historically prior distributive schemes, the market order avoids the imposition of a detailed pattern. Instead of a structure of rank and privilege fixing entitlements to wealth and power, the distributive mechanism of the market allocates resources to those persons

19 BITs, MITs and Regional Treaties and Dispute mechanisms such as International Centre for Settlement of Investment Disputes (ICSID).

20 Dine, *Companies, International Law and Human Rights* (Cambridge University Press, 2005) 134.

21 Ha-Joon Chang, *23 Things They Don't Tell You about Capitalism* (Penguin, 2010) 1.

22 According to D Campbell, 'Reflexivity and Welfarism in the Modern Law of Contract' (2000) Oxford Journal of Legal Studies 477, a claim most powerfully made by F Hayek in *The Road to Serfdom* (Routledge, 1986).

> able and willing to pay the highest price for them . . . The market order avows blindness to claims of privilege or force, so it recognises no claims of an inherent right to govern or to possess superior wealth . . . The market order lets fly the centrifugal forces of radical individualism, permitting philosophers to celebrate the relative fluidity of its distributive outcome and to legitimate it by appeals to the impervious mask of market forces. No other order so successfully disguises the fact that it constitutes an order at all.[23]

Campbell agrees:[24]

> *Laissez faire* is a social structure facilitating economic exchange, but one which, by virtue of its radical individualism, paradoxically denies that it is a social structure . . . *laissez faire* is a framework so characterised by unconscious asymmetries of power as to make choice 'a very poor joke' for most citizens.[25] Weber wrote; 'pure economics is a theory which is apolitical', which asserts 'no moral evaluations' and which is 'individualistic' in its orientation . . . The extreme free traders, however, conceived of it as an adequate picture of 'natural' reality, i.e., reality not distorted by human stupidity, and they proceeded to set it up as a moral imperative – as a valid normative ideal – whereas it is only a convenient ideal type to be used in empirical analysis.[26]

These extreme 'moral deflection devices' used by the neo-liberal or free-trade moralists are supported by 'extreme economics', which are elevated into a 'science'.[27] This exacerbates the lack of transparency effect and cloaks political discourse: 'unlike the natural sciences, economics involves value judgments, even though many Neoclassical[28] economists would tell you that what they do is *value-free* science'.[29] Exploding the myth is crucial because it means that everyone should explore any 'common-sense' notions that have been propagated by the economists and used by powerful, rich special interests. It is important to consider the root causes of the problems, economically, philosophically and legally. It is not good enough to divide specialities into watertight compartments. Many scholars argue that powerful companies are a central part of a system, which exacerbates poverty and inequality.[30] The world has become a

23 H Collins, *The Law of Contract* (Weidenfeld & Nicholson, 1986), cited in D Campbell, 'Reflexivity and Welfarism in the Modern Law of Contract' (2000) Oxford Journal of Legal Studies 477.

24 ibid, 490.

25 Campbell, citing I R Macneil, 'Bureaucracy and Contracts of Adhesion' (1984) 22 Osgoode Hall Law Journal 5, 6.

26 M Weber, 'The Meaning of "Ethical Neutrality" in Sociology and Economics (1917)' in E Shils and H Finch (eds), *Max Weber on the Methodology of the Social Sciences* (Glencoe, 1949) 44.

27 T Picketty, *Capital in the Twenty-First Century* (Harvard University Press, 2013): '"economic science" . . . stricks . . . terrible arrogant because it suggests that economics has attained a higher scientific status that the other social sciences', 573–4.

28 In this chapter I use 'neo-liberal' economics, Chang uses 'Neoclassical' economics; I believe that there is little difference between these two terms.

29 Ha-Joon Chang, *Economics: The User's Guide* (Pelican, 2014) 112.

30 Dine, *Companies, International Trade and Human Rights* (Cambridge University Press, 2005), A Clapham, 'The Question of Jurisdiction under International Criminal Law over Legal Persons' in M Kamminga and S Zia-Zarifi (eds), *Liability of Multinational Corporations under International Law* (Kluwer Law International, 2000); J. Bakan, *The Corporation: the Pathological Pursuit of Profit and Power* (Free Press, 2004).

dangerous unequal place – even for the rich[31] in the major cities of the West. Debt services alone account for $200 billion a year in currency flows from the South to the North. While 1.2 billion people – nearly a fifth of the world's population – have to manage on less than a dollar a day.[32]

The first decade of this century has not revealed a better world for the poor; rather research shows that inequality has been rampant,[33] and studies suggesting that powerful companies should have responsibilities to the planet and to stakeholders other than shareholders are now legion.[34] However, there are comparatively few arguments[35] linking these problems to the structure of company law and corporate governance itself. The links between company law and corporate governance, deepening poverty and the structure of company law have not yet been fully drawn. Adding the multifaceted environmental[36] crisis, including climate change and pollution, means that we need to question all of our institutions, including companies and the related issue of corporate governance. Companies are not a natural phenomenon, they were crafted by societies whether by individuals or together in regional pacts (like the European Union (EU)) and influenced by global players like the 'Unholy Trinity', the IMF, the WB,

31 United Nations Development Programme (UNDP), *Beyond Scarcity; Power, Poverty and the Global Water Crisis* (Human Development Report, 2006).

32 Ulrich Beck, *Power in the Global Age* (Polity Press, 2005) 24–5. See also Duncan Green, *From Poverty to Power* (Practical Action Publishing in association with Oxfam GB for Oxfam International, 2008/9), J Stiglitz, *The Price of Inequality* (Allen Lane, Penguin, 2012), Richard Wilkinson and Kate Pickett, *The Spirit Level* (Penguin, 2009 and 2010).

33 World Hunger, '2015 World Hunger and Poverty Facts and Statistics' <http://www.worldhunger.org/articles/Learn/world%20hunger%20facts%202002.htm> accessed 28 July 2012, UNDP (Report 2010) <http://www.oxfam.org.au/refugee/public/issues/ . . . /statistics.php> accessed 28 July 2012.

34 For a few see: John Ruggie, UN Human Rights Council (HRC), 'Report of the Special Representative of the Secretary-General on the issue of human rights and transnational corporations and other enterprises' (11 March 2011) UN Doc A/HRC/17/31; Jennifer Zerk, *Multinational and Corporate Social Responsibilities: Limitations and Opportunities in International Law* (Cambridge University Press, 2006), Eroglu Muzaffer, *Multinational Enterprises and Tort Liabilities* (Edward Elgar, 2008), Nina Boeger and others (eds), *Perspectives on Corporate Social Responsibility* (Edward Elgar, 2008).

35 But see Alan Dignam and Michael Galanis, *The Globalization of Corporate Governance* (Ashgate, 2009); J Zerk, *Multinational and Corporate Social Responsibilities: Limitations and Opportunities in International Law* (Cambridge University Press, 2006); Eroglu Muzaffer, *Multinational Enterprises and Tort Liabilities* (Edward Elgar, 2008).

36 Mike Hulme, *Why We Disagree about Climate Change* (Cambridge University Press, 2009), Edward Barbier, *A Global Green New Deal* (United Nations Environment Programme (UNEP), 2010) <http://www.unep.org/> accessed 25 October 2012, Dieter Helm and Cameron Hepburn (eds), *The Economics and Politics of Climate Change* (Oxford University Press, 2009); Nicholas Stern, *The Economics of Climate Change* (Cambridge University Press, 2008); M Chossudovsky, *The Globalisation of Poverty* (Pluto, 1998); P Harrison, *Inside the Third World* (3rd edn, Penguin, 1993); M Hertsgaard, *Earth Odyssey* (Abacus, 1999); J Karliner, *The Corporate Planet* (Sierra Club, 1997); *Oxfam Global Finance, Tax Havens: Releasing the Hidden Billions for Poverty Eradication* (Oxfam, 2001) <http://policy-practice.oxfam.org.uk/our-work/aid-development-finance> accessed 25 October 2012; and *Oxfam America Oil Gaz and Mining: Poor Communities Pay the Price* (Oxfam, 2001); Michael Redclift and Ted Benton (eds), *Social Theory and the Global Environment* (Routledge, 1994); Naomi Klein, *This Changes Everything* (Allen Lane, 2014).

the WTO[37] or Organisation for Economic Cooperation and Development (OECD). Their behaviour and structures must be examined and scrutinised in understanding corporate governance.

THE NEO-LIBERAL PARADIGM: RATIONALITY AND SELFISHNESS

The neo-liberal economic paradigm was first invented by the Chicago University economists, the so-called Milton Friedman 'Chicago Boys' who were recruited by the Central Intelligence Agency (CIA) to help with the reconstruction of the Chilean economy following the Pinochet coup in 1973.[38] Although Milton Friedman is the author of the modern neo-liberal school, there is a long tradition of right-wing scholars who wanted to disparage the state and promote markets. The economic model that the neo-liberal doctrine promotes is predicated on 'rational human choice', specifically 'the pursuit of self-interests by individual economic actors'.[39] All of this selfishness magically provides a maximal social beneficial outcome. Robert and Edward Skidelsky[40] traced the history of the neo-liberal paradigm back to the enlightenment philosophers who believed that men were rational.[41] They propounded a theory of utilitarianism. Skidelsky and Skidelsky used the 'Faustian Bargain' fable to illustrate the point.[42] The issue was that utilitarian theories can be good for economic growth but often the instruments that are used are immoral, and in Christopher Marlowe's play *Dr Faustus*, the eponymous hero lost his soul.[43] Some other authors augmented the fable to allow Faust to go to heaven because he did good deeds; now this is what is meant by a 'win-win situation'!

> By the early nineteenth century, in Goethe's classic retelling (1808 and 1832) Faust has become a symbol of endlessly striving modern man, fallible but ultimately worthy of love. Goethe's *Faust* can be seen as the literary expression of the *felix culpa* of the political economist. With the help of Mephistopheles, Faust does all of kinds of terrible things, but at the end his soul goes to heaven because he has 'striven greatly'. Faust's elevation from wicked prankster to world-historic hero reflects the weakening of Christian orthodoxy and its absolute prohibition on evil. It insinuates the heretical thought that in our dealing with the Devil it is *we* who can come off winners.[44]

37 A Dignam and M Galanis, 'Corporate Governance and the Importance of Macroeconomic Context' (2008) 28 Oxford Journal of Legal Studies 201.

38 N Klein, *The Shock Doctrine: The Rise of Disaster Capitalism* (Allen Lane, 2007) 7, 25–38.

39 Ha-Joon Chang, *Economics: The User's Guide* (Pelican, 2013) 115.

40 R Skidelsky and E Skidelsky, *How Much is Enough? Money and the Good Life* (Allen Lane, 2012).

41 P A Schous, *Reasoned Freedom* (Cornell University Press, 1992).

42 See also George Monbiot, *Heat: How Can We Stop the Planet Burning* (Allen Lane, Penguin, 2006) using the fable to illustrate the catastrophe of climate change.

43 C Marlowe, *The Tragical, History of the Life and Death of Doctor Faustus* (CreateSpace Independent Publishing Platform, 2014) 1604.

44 Skidelsky and Skidelsky (n 40) 55.

John Maynard Keynes was also ambivalent about capitalism, saying that 'It was a civilization which unleashed bad motive for the sake of good results. Morality had to be put in cold storage till abundance was achieved, for abundance would, make possible a good life for all'.[45] Keynes also wrote:

> We must pretend to ourselves and to every one that fair is foul and foul is fair; for foul is useful and fair is not. Avarice and usury and precaution must be our god for a little longer still. For only they can lead us out of the tunnel of economic necessity into daylight.[46]

The Skidelskys show us that Christian theology had a simple dichotomy of evil and good, but this was lost when the Reformation softened the simple Christian orthodoxy.[47] After this, utilitarianism doctrines were more likely to be followed allowing the strong dichotomy between God and devil to be degraded:

> The Renaissance invented – or rediscovered – the idea of *using* human desires to govern societies rather than castigating them as wicked. The wise prince, wrote Machiavelli,[48] threats people as they are, not as they should be: he exploits their fickleness, hypocrisy and greed to attain his ends.[49]

Both doctrines are simplistic because we now know much more about the human brain and the complexity of the networks connecting the desires and emotions in the human mind.[50] However the dichotomy of evil and good continues to be a powerful narrative and, against this utilitarian principle, theories were propounded by a merchant class who found a powerful voice in Bernard Mandeville (1670–1733). The Skidelskys cite Mandeville's best-known work, *The Fable of the Bees, or the Private Vices, Publick Benefits*:

> Mandeville's bees are addicted to 'Fraud, Luxury and Pride', yet succeed, through 'State's Craft', in transforming these 'private vices' into the public benefit' of commerce and industry:
>
> The Root of Evil, Avarice,
> That damn's ill-nature's baneful Vice
> Was Slave to Prodigality,
> That Noble Sin; whilst Luxury

45 ibid 43.

46 J M Keynes, *Essays in Persuasion*, *The Collected Writings of John Maynard Keynes*, vol 9 (Cambridge University Press, 1078) 372, and see R Skidelsky, *Keynes; The Return of the Master* (Penguin, 2009).

47 Skidelsky and Skidelsky (n 40) 47.

48 N Machiavelli, *The Florentine History*, vol 2 (Forgotten Books, Nabu Press, 2010).

49 Skidelsky and Skidelsky (n 40) 47, and see T Sedlacek, *Economics of Good and Evil* (Oxford University Press, 2011) 36–38, citing Michael Novak, *The Spirit of Democratic Capitalism* (Free Press, 1993), saying that only democratic capitalism realises 'how deeply evil nature is rooted in the human soul . . . The system of democratic capitalism can "bring down the power of sin" – i.e. to retransform its energy into creative force (and in doing so the best way to get revenge on Satan)', 77–78.

50 D Eagleman, *Incognito: The Secret Lives of the Brain* (Cannongate, 2011), particularly Chapter 5: 'The Brain as a team of rivals' where the author posits the idea that the brain is similar to a democracy.

Employ'd a Million of the Poor,
And odious Pride a Million more:
Envy it self, and Vanity,
Were Ministers of Industry.[51]

The stage is set for Adam Smith's *The Wealth of Nations*.[52] The Skidelskys argue that the paradigm shift was possible because Adam Smith presents

> . . . humans as driven by natural desire from self-improvement, which under conditions of free competition leads them 'as if an invisible hand' to promote the public well-being . . . This was a revolutionary invention. Traditional morality had conceived of society as an enterprise devoted to the common good . . . Smith's doctrine of self-interest did more than just turn avarice into a virtue; it turned classical virtue into a vice . . . In Smith's political economy, asceticism becomes the virtuous form of self-interest, the efficient cause of capital accumulation. Alms-giving was discouraged because it promotes idleness.[53]

Sedlacek argues that this interpretation is simplistic; in fact Adam Smith's book, *The Theory of Moral Sentiments*, starts with:

> How selfish soever man may be supposed, there are evident some principles in his nature, which interest him in the fortune of others, and render their happiness necessary to him, though he derives nothing from it except the pleasure of seeing it.[54]

Sedlacek argues that Smith's legacy is narrowed into his famous book *Wealth of Nations*, which is necessarily his best work, although Smith himself preferred *The Theory of Moral Sentiments*.[55] For Smith 'moral teachings are based on mutual kindness (benevolence) and *restraint*';[56] Sedlacek argues that this means that he was a follower of a school which believed that 'any benefit destroys morality'.[57] Smith tried to find a way to measure behaviour using an impartial spectator, 'a reasonable man on the Clapham bus'.

> We suppose ourselves the spectator of our behaviour, and endeavour to imagine what effect it would, in this light, produce upon us. This is the only looking-glass by which we can, in some measure, with the eyes of other people, scrutinize the propriety of our own contact.[58]

---

51 Skidelsky and Skidelsky (n 40) 49.

52 Adam Smith, *The Wealth of Nations* (Prometheus Books, 1991, originally published in 1776).

53 Skidelsky and Skidelsky (n 40) 50 and see the recent debate in the UK, especially by right-wing Conservative politicians, K Kwarteng and others, *Britain Unchained* (Palgrave Macmillan, 2012), J Stiglitz, *The Price of Inequality* (Allen Lane Penguin, 2012) 229.

54 Adam Smith, *The Theory of Moral Sentiments* (H G Bonn, 1853, originally published in 1759) 3.

55 T Sedlacek, *Economics of Good and Evil: The Quest for Economic Meaning from Gilgamesh to Wall Street* (Oxford University Press, 2011) 195. See also Amartya Sen, *The Idea of Justice* (Penguin, 2009) 44–46.

56 Smith (n 54) 438.

57 ibid 438 and Sedlacek (n 55) 96; Smith cites Augustine, Plato and Aquinas.

58 Adam Smith, *The Theory of Moral Sentiments* (H. G. Bonn, 1853, originally published in 1759) 164.

This is very close to Sen's teaching on objectivity or a Rawlsian concept of society. Sedlacek argues that Smith was maligned 'using Smith's philosophy to support a pure laissez-faire economic system is simply not accurate. Smith never asserted that every market allocation benefits society'.[59] In fact Smith believed that society works due to sympathy between men, using the standard of the reasonable person. Smith himself believed that the government should distribute goods for the poor:

> . . . they [the government] divide with the poor the produce of their improvements. They are led by an invisible hand to make nearly the same distribution of the necessary of life, which have been, had the earth be divided into equal portions among all of its inhabitants . . . When providence divided the earth among a few lordly masters, it neither forgot nor abandoned those who seems to have been left out in the partition . . . the same regard to the beauty of order, of art and contrivance, frequently serves to recommend those institutions which tends to promote the public welfare.[60]

Smith's work is therefore more complex than many believe; the intense focus on the market is another misapprehension; however, it is very convenient for the rich and trickle-down theories. Smith's theories have been subverted.

Max Weber believed that the protestant ethics gave birth[61] to capitalism and he feared it. Weber understood that capitalism was likely to lead to secularism and he thought that this would debase society. His thesis was to research the culture of capitalists and capture their spirit via Calvinism, predestination, anxiety and savings.[62] Weber was critical of Marx's theory believing that it missed a particular element, which was the religious aspect of human and moral development. At the time of writing the essay *The Protestant Ethic and Spirit of Capitalism*, Germany was undertaking rapid industrialisation and Weber noticed that the new capitalists were overwhelmingly protestant and he linked this with the religious proclivities of this class.[63] This class were unable to serve in a public forum because of their minority status:

> National or religious minorities which are in a position of subordination to a group of rules are likely, through their voluntary or involuntary exclusion from position of political influence, to be driven with peculiar force into economic activities. Their ablest members seek to satisfy the desire for recognition of their abilities in this field, since there is no opportunity in the service of the State.[64]

Weber observed that although the Catholics in Germany were the minority in the population they were not significant entrepreneurs. Therefore Weber thought that there was a different interpretation for the lack of entrepreneurs in the Catholic population. He thought that Protestants had devised a strong culture of rationalism.[65]

59 Sedlacek (n 55) 197.
60 Smith (n 58) 264–265.
61 Sedlacek (n 55) 45–46.
62 Max Weber, *The Protestant Ethic and the Spirit of Capitalism* (Routledge, 1992, originally published in 1920 in German in *Gesammele Aufastze Zur Religionssoziologie*).
63 ibid 3.
64 ibid 6–7.
65 ibid 7.

Weber sought the explanation in the 'permanent intrinsic character of their religious belief'.[66] A simplistic explanation might be found in the nature of Catholic views especially the ascetic principles leading to shunning entrepreneurs. However the Catholic Church also believed that individuals could owe property and the quantity of goods allowed was fiercely disputed. On the other hand, the Puritans were particularly harsh in their views on a soft life.[67] Weber therefore had found a conundrum; the Protestants were rich even though their faith propounded intense aesthetic principles. However, Weber understood that the temptation involved in amassing wealth was clear, capitalism will not itself lead to selfishness but mixed with a strong rational impulse it is likely to derail ethical principles.

> Unlimited greed for gain is not in the least identical with capitalism, and is still less its spirit. Capitalism *may* even be identified with the restraint, or at least a rational tempering, of this irrational impulse. But capitalism is identical with the pursuit of profit, and forever *renewed* profit, by means of continuous, rational, capitalistic enterprise. For it must be so: in a wholly capitalistic order of society, an individual capitalistic enterprise (sic) which did not take advantage of its opportunities for profit-making would be doomed to extinction.[68]

It seems clear from this small portion of thinkers, rational thinkers, theologians and ethical philosophers that capitalism can have ethical principles embedded in its philosophy. However the temptations are also very clear, only significant principles can limit capitalism, the neo-liberal paradigm allows the worst enticement by the promotion of selfishness and the credence that selfishness is good for society. Undoubtedly the temptations of slavery were condoned by 'free-market' rhetoric, during one of the debates on abolition in 1789 a member for Liverpool, Lord Penrhyn, said that 'were the Commons to vote for abolition, "they actually would strike at seventy millions of property, they ruined the colonies and, by destroying an essential nursery of seamen, gave up the dominion of the sea at a single stroke"'.[69] One anti-abolition MP argued that the slave-traders were 'fellow entrepreneurs' and actually the 'greatest slaves-to their high responsibilities'.[70] In France in 1793 the 'trade was subsidised in the form of a bonus for every slave landed; Nantes in fact enjoyed its best year ever as a slave city in 1790, sending forty-nine ships to Africa. For the slave merchants in this politically radical city, the word "liberty" seems to signify the idea that the slave trade should be open to all'.[71] Simultaneously the revolutionary war started between France and Britain and meant that abolition could be attacked by linking the radical ideas of the revolution. Lord Abingdon argued that the abolition of the trade will ignite 'a disastrous obsession with abolition with the rights of man which had so damaged France'.[72] Later, in 1846,

66 ibid.
67 ibid 8.
68 A Giddens, *Introduction of Weber, Protestant Ethics and Capitalism* (Routledge, 1992) xxxi–xxxii.
69 Hugh Thomas, *The Slave Trade: History of the Atlantic* (W&N, 2006) 512.
70 ibid 513.
71 ibid 521.
72 ibid 530.

there was huge controversy about Brazilian sugar which used slave labour, the abolitionists were disconcerted when the Corn Laws were enacted, since the rhetoric was strongly free-trade based. In 1846, when the Sugar Duty Act passed, the abolitionists were unable to reinstate the duty even though it was clearly hypocrisy of a high order:

> We import the accursed thing [Brazilian sugar]; we bond it; we employ our skill and machinery to render it more alluring to the eye and the palate; we export it to Leghorn and Hamburg; we send it to all the coffee houses of Italy and Germany; we packed a profit on all this; and we put on a pharisaical air, and thank God that we are not like those sinful Italians and Germans, who have no scruple about swallowing slave-grown sugar . . .[73]

All of these concerns were aired during the struggle to abolish the slave trade and now new free-trade doctrines are subverted to argue for no regulation or only regulations which are convenient for the 'Bad Samaritans'.

THE RESULT: THE RISE OF MULTINATIONAL ENTERPRISES AND THE DIMINISHING POWER OF THE STATE

The neo-liberal utopian vision of a win-win situation is a rosy vision but it is not reality. Instead the neo-liberal theology has given us multinational enterprises (MNEs), which are so powerful that some governments are nearly powerless (especially the poorer countries).[74] Neo-liberal economic theory is also the dominant force fuelling the convergence theory which says that all company governance should be run on the Anglo-American, contractual model.[75] Muchlinski argues:

> The end of the first decade of the twenty-first century was a pivotal moment in the history of transnational corporate regulation. The decade began at the height of the neoliberal revolution with its emphasis on financialization, liberalization, privatization, and deregulation. Transnational corporate groups were given free choice of means in their global operations. They could move across borders and adopt whatever business form they wished when the economic case for doing so suited them. There were few regulatory burdens placed on them. In return, states opened their borders so goods, services, and investment could flow freely. At the same time, states offered prime, state-owned industries for privatization through foreign inward investment and reduced

73 ibid 734, echoing later arguments about garments from Bangladesh, Jason Burke, 'Rana Plaza: one year on from the Bangladesh factory disaster' (*Guardian*, 19 April 2014) <http://www.theguardian.com/world/2014/apr/19/rana-plaza-bangladesh-one-year-on> accessed 23 October 2014.

74 K Ainger, 'A Financial Coup d'Etat: The Spanish government may be happy to sacrifice sovereignty for a bailout. But not the Indignos' (*Guardian*, 26 September 2012).

75 J Dine and M Kousias, *The Nature of Corporate Governance; The Significance of National Cultural Identity* (Edward Elgar, 2013); H Hansmann and R Kraakman, 'The End of History for Corporate Law' (2000) Harvard Law School John M. Olin Center for Law, Economics and Business Discussion Paper Series 280 but see a powerful contra-argument by Andrew Keay, *The Corporate Objective* (Edward Elgar, 2011) and J Parkinson, 'The Socially Responsible Company' in M Addo (ed), *Human Rights Standards and the Responsibility of Transnational Corporations* (Kluwer, 1999).

barriers to foreign takeovers of privately owned firms. Furthermore, regulatory activity could be reined in, allowing the market to control the outcomes. Controls through competition, tax, and disclosure laws were minimized as they presented a burden for business.[76]

This system of economics is an efficient system, in monetary terms, for the few, but also significantly flawed, leaving many externalities in its wake. One of the externalities is the erosion of democracy. This is why Beck[77] realises that not only has power shifted from governments and people but also that ethical principles are absent, including justice.[78]

We have seen earlier versions of rational choice economics, these theories have been earlier elaborated by the scholarship propounded by the Austrian economist Ludwig Von Mises and social philosopher Friedrich Von Hayek.[79] Von Mises's axiom that 'egoism is the basic law of society'[80] led him to conclude that unrestricted *laissez-faire* free markets and governments that are confined to the defence of unhampered private property rights comprised the only viable policy for the human race.[81] The neo-classicist doctrine is that rational actors will, if left undirected, make maximally efficient economic decisions which will maximise their welfare, leading to an efficient economy where all will eventually benefit:

> For more than 20 years economists were enthralled by so-called 'rational expectations' models which assumed that all participants have the same (if not perfect) information and act perfectly rationally, that markets are perfectly efficient, that unemployment never exists (except when caused by greedy unions or government minimum wages) and where there is never any credit rationing.[82]

That this model is becoming increasingly discredited does not alter the fact that faithful adherents to this model are acting on the theory, and now it is the dominant economic paradigm for the world.

> At the time of writing, markets have assumed mythological proportions. Like the Gods of ancient days, their displeasure looms over popular protestations. In places such as Greece and Italy, governments stand or fall by their ability to respond to divine

76 P Muchlinski, 'The Changing Face of Transnational Business Governance: Private Corporate Law Liability and Accountability of Transnational Groups in a Post-Crisis World' (Summer 2011) 18 Indiana Journal of Global Studies 666.

77 Ulrich Beck, *Power in the Global Age* (1st edn, Polity, 2005).

78 See also A Kwa, *Power Politics in the WTO* (Focus on the Global South, Bangkok January 2003), J Dine, *Companies, International Trade and Human Rights* (Cambridge University Press, 2005) especially Chapter 3.

79 K Birch and V Mykhnenko, 'Introduction – A World Turned Right Way Up' in K Birch and V Mykhnenko (eds), *The Rise and Fall of Neo-liberalism: The Collapse of an Economic Order?* (Zed Books, 2010) 3.

80 ibid.

81 M N Rothbard, 'Biography of Ludwig Von Mises (1881–1973)' (Ludwig Von Mises Institute) <http://mises.org/about/3248> accessed 16 August 2012.

82 J Stiglitz, 'There is no invisible hand' (*Guardian*, 20 December 2002), and see Stiglitz, *The Price of Inequality* (1st edn, W W Norton & Company, 2012).

> dictates. Translated into modern discourse, what is being witnessed is the practice of neoliberal national and transnational governance.[83]

The consequences are dire for the populations of these countries:[84] the denigration of the environment and increasing inequality but also the decrease of democracy, including the hollowing out of national states.

> The neo-liberal regime provides for globally binding decisions against individual states' resistance, and a universally valid and application 'policy mix' is propagated accordingly. This means that political reforms should be oriented towards economic objectives – low inflation, a balanced budget, the removal of trade barriers and foreign currency controls, maximum mobility for capital minimum regulation of the labour market and a lean, adaptable welfare state that orders its citizens to work. These are *the* reform objectives of the neo-liberal regime . . . it is supposed to be apolitical but of course it is highly political.[85]

However, neo-liberal thought, wherever its original base, is reality in the western world. The theology of the beatitudes is eclipsed: 'Thou shalt love thy neighbour'[86] is now redundant. Utilitarian doctrines are very dangerous, as Pogge writes:

> . . . moral norms, designed to protect the livelihood and dignity of the vulnerable, place burdens on the strong. If such norms are compelling enough, the strong make an effort to comply. But they also, consciously or unconsciously, try to get around the norms by arranging their social world so as to minimise their burdens of compliance.[87]

PROMOTING THE NEO-LIBERAL AGENDA IN CORPORATE GOVERNANCE: STANDARDS, CODES AND TEMPLATES

The World Bank conducts corporate governance country assessments under the Reports on the Observance of Standards and Codes (ROSC) initiative at the invitation of country authorities. The World Bank uses a diagnostic tool – a Template – that it has developed to gather pertinent information for preparing the Corporate Governance ROSC.[88] It is very clear that the World Bank Template of Corporate governance is significantly tilted against stakeholders other than shareholders; the Template

83 Yonit Percival (DPhil thesis, Queen Mary, University of London, 2014).

84 Vassilis Monastiriotis, 'The Greek Crisis in focus, Austerity, Recession and the path to Recovery' (Hellenic Observatory, LSE, 2011) <http://www2.lse.ac.uk/europeanInstitute/research/hellenicObservatory/pdf/GreeSE/GreeSE%20Special%20Issue.pdf> accessed 21 August 2012; GlobalPost, 'Greek unemployment soars with one fifth out of work' <http://www.globalpost.com/dispatch/news/business-tech/debt-crisis/120412/greek-unemployment-soars-over-one-five-out-work> accessed 21 August 2012.

85 Ulrich Beck, *Power in the Global Age* (1st edn, Polity, 2005) 79.

86 The Bible (2014, New King James Version) Matthew 5:43, although the Puritans were ambivalent about capitalism; see the early section on Weber in P H Sedgwick, *Christian Ethics* (Cambridge University Press, 1999).

87 T Pogge, *World Poverty and Human Rights* (Polity Press, 2002 and 2008) 5.

88 World Bank Group, 'Reports on the Observance of Standards and Codes' <http://www.worldbank.org/ifa/rosc_cg.html> accessed 17 August 2012.

propagates the canard[89] that the shareholders are the owners[90] of the company. The Template considers the most important issues of corporate governance to be the rules about shareholders' rights and particularly their property rights. The Template is in a form of a questionnaire and the first section is entitled 'Ownership and Control', question 1 being about the 'ownership and its concentration'.[91] Later in this Template a key concept of neo-liberal axioms appears, that is the message that markets should be 'efficient' without properly defining efficiency: it is certain that the Template prefers a shareholder primacy or insider model.[92] On these terms many externalities are not included in the definition of 'efficiency', especially a fair wage for employees.

> A Corporate governance framework should be developed with a view to its impact on overall economic performance, market integrity and the incentives it creates for the market participants and the promotion of transparent efficient markets.[93]

Chapter II details the importance of shareholders' rights: 'The title is "The rights of shareholders and key ownership functions": The corporate governance framework should protect and facilitate the exercise of shareholders' rights'.[94] The questions in this section are extensive, involving questions 141–201, after this there is a wide-ranging set of questions about the market for corporate controls which is neo-liberal speak for takeovers which allows the powerful companies to dominate the international agenda and often dominate states:[95] 'Markets for corporate control should be allowed to function in an efficient and transparent manner'[96] (19 questions). Chapter III returns to the equitable treatment of shareholders' rights with (another 31 questions). The Template only mentions stakeholders at question 277 where Chapter V deals with stakeholders: 'Do any laws provide rights to stakeholders (employees, trade unions, creditors, customers, suppliers, consumers, and the community) to participate or have input in the corporate governance of the company?' Although the section is headed 'Stakeholders' it is telling in its definition; it 'includes constituencies *other than shareholders*,[97] such as employees, trade unions, creditors, customers, suppliers, consumers, and the community'.[98] The divisions between 'stakeholders and shareholders are

89 R Ireland, 'Company Law and the Myth of Shareholder Ownership' (1999) MLR 62(1), See also J Hill, 'Visions and Revisions of the Shareholder' (2000) American Journal of Comparative Law 39.

90 Keay, *The Corporate Objective* (Edward Elgar, 2011), considering this issue several times including when he cites the UK's Cadbury Committee in its Committee on the Financial Aspect of Corporate Governance, *Report on the Financial Aspect of Corporate Governance* (1st published Burgess Science Press and Gee and Co Ltd, 1992) 66. See also the ownership debate Chapter 2.

91 World Bank Group, 'Reports on the Observance of Standards and Codes' <http://www.worldbank.org/ifa/rosc_cg.html> accessed 20 August 2012.

92 See later on the definition of these terms.

93 ibid.

94 ibid.

95 See later on the takeover debate.

96 World Bank Group, 'Reports on the Observance of Standards and Codes' <http://www.worldbank.org/ifa/rosc_cg.html> accessed 17 August 2012.

97 My italics.

98 ibid.

very glaring. Shareholders are a privileged class, not part of the company's' community, the Template clearly classifies the lambs and the goats, and as well as this, evidently the shareholders are 'owners' and the rest of the stakeholders of the enterprise are not part of the polity. It is interesting that the term 'corporate social responsibility' is not included although many scholars believe that the convergence of corporate social responsibility and corporate governance is one of the ways that accountability and responsibility in companies could be fostered. Responsible capitalism and neo-liberal capitalism are at odds. Corporate Governance and Corporate Social Responsibility (CSR) is where competing philosophies divide. To illustrate this divide is to look at the OECD's Corporate Governance Code (2004) and the OECD Guidelines for Multinational Enterprises (2011) which are significantly different and, some would say, contradict themselves.[99] The OECD's Corporate Governance Code is about regulating the internal management of companies; the Guidelines are concerned about external pressures on companies including ethical, social and environmental issues.[100] This author believes Corporate Governance and Corporate Social Responsibility should be aligned, in particularly in the Caribbean where there is glaring inequality.

INEQUALITY

We have seen the seeds of inequality in neo-liberal doctrine, preaching selfishness, utilitarianism, a lack of ethics and importance of property rights and contractual models of companies.[101] Stopping these practices will only start if corporate governance is reformed, giving stakeholders a significant role in society. First, why is inequality important? Leaving the ethical argument, even the IMF say:

> Our work built on the tentative[102] consensus in the literature that inequality can undermine progress in health and education, cause investment-reducing political and eco-

---

99 The sources rely on the earlier version of the Guidelines: C. Chatterjee, 'The OECD Guidelines for Multinational Enterprises: An Analysis' (2002) Amicus Curiae 18; J Karl, 'The OECD Guidelines for Multinational Enterprises' in M Addo (ed), *Human Rights Standards and the Responsibility of Transnational Corporations* (Kluwer, 1999).

100 Dine and Koutsias, *Nature of Corporate Governance* (Edward Elgar, 2013).

101 P Muchlinski, 'The Changing Face of Transnational Business Governance: Private Corporate Law Liability and Accountability of Transnational Groups in a Post-Crisis World' (2011) 18 Indiana Journal of Global Studies 666, A Ogus, *Regulation: Legal Form and Economic Theory* (Clarendon Press, 1994) 24.

102 In fact there is a growing and strong consensus that is significantly getting worst: Thomas Picketty, *Capital in the Twenty-first Century* (Harvard University Press, 2014); UNDP, *Beyond Scarcity; Power, Poverty and the global water crisis* (Human Development Report, 2006); U Beck, *Power in the Global Age* (Polity Press, 2005) 24–25, D Green, *From Poverty to Power* (Oxfam, 2008/9); J Stiglitz, *The Price of Inequality* (Allan Lane, Penguin, 2012); R Wilkinson and K Pickett, *The Spirit Level* (Penguin, 2009 and 2010); WorldHunger, '2015 World Hunger and Poverty Facts and Statistics' <http://www.worldhunger.org/articles/Learn/world%20hunger%20facts%202002.htm> accessed 28 July 2012; United Nations Development Programme, *Report* (2010) <http://hdr.undp.org/en/content/human-development-report-201> accessed 10 July 2015; G Nwaobi, 'Inequality. Poverty and Hunger in Developing Countries: Sustainability Implications' (2014) <http://mpra.ub.uni-muenchen.de/53962/1/MPRA_paper_53962.pdf> accessed 10 July 2015.

nomic instability, and undercut the social consensus required to adjust in the face of shocks, and thus that it tends to reduce the pace and durability of growth.

However they also say:

That equality seems to drive higher and more sustainable growth does not in itself support efforts to redistribute. In particular, inequality may impede growth at least in part because it calls forth efforts to redistribute that themselves undercut growth. In such a situation, even if inequality is bad for growth, taxes and transfers may be precisely the wrong remedy.[103]

Indeed a *very* tentative argument. In a 2014 IMF seminar there was not a focus on re-engineering the neo-liberal paradigm, rather the participants suggested stopping tax avoidance by tax havens[104] and other mechanisms, which are used by MNEs and wealthy individuals. It is a very small step[105] but at least the IMF recognises the problem, not because it is ethically right but because inequality harms growth. This is problematic because there is a rising consensus that further growth seriously harms the planet.[106] It is clear that since IMF policies have been strongly neo-liberal promoting the Washington Consensus orthodoxy, realising that their policies are harming their own economic model is hard. Picketty's seminal book focuses on inequality, choosing the word 'Capital' for the title, but an early book by Michael Hardt and Antonio Negri chose 'Empire' referring to capitalism.[107] Both of them are right but the pernicious hold of fundamental capitalism has been augmented by neo-liberal doctrines implemented by the IMF, World Bank and the World Trade Organization to strangle poorer countries.[108] Most of all the Structural Adjustment Policies make individuals and countries poor while MNEs cream the profits from forced privatisations.

The IMF–World Bank reforms brutally dismantle the social sectors of developing countries, undoing the efforts and struggles of the post-colonial period and reversing 'with the stroke of the pen' the fulfilment of past progress. Throughout the world, there is a consistent and coherent pattern: the IMF–World Bank reform package constitutes a coherent programme of economic and social collapse.[109]

---

103 J Ostry, A Berg and C Tsangarides, *Redistribution, Inequality and Growth* (IMF Staff Discussion Noye, 2014) 4. See also, IMF, 'Inequality Seriously Damages Growth' (*IMF Survey Magazine*, 12 April 2014) <http://www.imf.org/external/pubs/ft/survey/so/2014/res041214a.htm> accessed 13 October 2013

104 Which could devastate the Caribbean economy; Bahamas derives 35% of its GDP from financial services, The World Fact Book, 'Central America and Caribbean: Bahamas' <https://www.cia.gov/library/publications/the-world-factbook/geos/bf.html>, accessed 9 November 2014.

105 Although it is unlikely that the IMF will suggest policies which must involve government legislations since their policies suggest liberalization of markets and a small state. The OECD is tasked to draft a code on tax havens but this is a soft law instrument likely to be sidelined by powerful governments, their elites and their MNEs (Multinational Enterprises).

106 Naomi Klein, *This Changes Every Thing* (Allan Lane, 2014).

107 T Picketty, *Capital in the Twenty-First Century* (Harvard University Press, 2014) and M Hardt and A Negri, *Empire* (Harvard University Press, 2001).

108 John Pilger, *The New Rulers of the World* (Verso, 2002).

109 M Chossudovsky, *The Globalisation of Poverty* (Zed Books, 1998) 68–69.

Cahn argues that the World Bank is a governance institution, it is exercising its power:

> through its financial leverage to legislate entire legal regimens and even . . . [altering] the constitutional structure of borrowing nations. Bank-approved consultants often rewrite a country's trade policy, fiscal policies, civil service requirements, labor laws, health care arrangements, environmental regulations, energy policy, resettlement requirements, procurement rules, and budgetary policy.[110]

It is well documented that the consequent 'austerities' have in the past caused cuts in all social and, in particular, health programmes, a move of the population away from rural areas into cities, the vicious-circle effects of poor health and lack of proper food and education, and a consequent willingness of a population to work at any task however ill-paid and poorly regulated.[111] The structural adjustment policies imposed by the lending institutions now have a 'softer' face as each of the Least Developed Countries (LDCs) must prepare a Poverty Reduction Strategy Plan (PRSP) as a condition of increased or continued finance or to bid for forgiveness or rescheduling of debt. However, although these plans are often carefully prepared and considered there is still considerable emphasis on free trade solutions, including open markets and growth as creating the answer to the nation's poverty.[112] Although Haiti is not in the Commonwealth Caribbean, it is an example of neo-liberal economics. In Haiti the World Bank's documents show that Haiti has regressed between 2009 and 2012, despite a soup of acronyms including Heavily Indebted Poor Countries (HIPIC) (which should eventually give some debt relief), the National Growth Poverty Reduction Strategy (NGPRS), Millennium Development Goals (MDG) and Poverty Reductions Growth Facility (PRGF). Haiti is getting poorer, the GDP-debt ratio is 195% (2012). The figure of people in extreme poverty is 37.9%, those in poverty is 69.3%. The National Strategy seems to be a desperate bid to leave the country as it is, promoting agriculture, tourism and infrastructure, but the burden of debt weighs heavily on the society and undoubtedly lives are being lost. Chang believes that proper development can only happen when there is industrialisation. He cites the way that all developed countries use protectional strategies, including protecting infant industries. This would be anathema to the IMF and therefore it will not be in the National Strategy for Haiti or any other indebted country. Similarly, Jamaica has a lack of industry; its economy revolves around tourism and remittances (80%).[113]

110 J Cahn, 'Challenging the New Imperial Authority: The World Bank and the Democratization of Development' (1993) 6 Harvard Human Rights Journal 160.

111 David Korten, *When Corporations Rule the World* (2nd edn, Berrett-Koehler, 2001); Chossudovsky, *The Globalisation of Poverty and the New World Order* (2nd edn, Global Research, 2003); Paul Harrison, *Inside the Third World* (3rd edn, Revised edn, Penguin, 1993); I Wilder, 'Local Futures: From Denunciation to Revalorisation of the Indigenous Other' in G Teubner (ed), *Global Law Without a State* (Dartmouth, 1996); H Heerings and I Zeldenrust, *Elusive Saviours* (International Books, 1995).

112 For an oversight of PRSPs see the World Bank website.

113 The World Fact Book, 'Central America and Caribbean: Jamaica' <https://www.cia.gov/library/publications/the-world-factbook/geos/jm.html> accessed 9 November 2014.

The inequality between states is starkly exposed by the desperate situation in Haiti and Jamaica. However, it seems that the IMF does not suggest radical redistribution. Why not? The answer is that to redesign all of their policies and simultaneously help the other Washington Consensus institutions to dismantle their neo-liberal policies is at the moment too radical. 'Judging by the Ms Lagarde and the World Bank's Jim Yong Kim, the assumptions might now be that the Washington consensus is dead, killed off the deepest slump since the 1930s and a weak recovery unaccompanied by rising living standards'[114] and a significant rise of inequality, but the World Bank's Doing Business Report instead suggests cutting corporate takes, minimising labour protections and cutting minimum wages.[115] Elliot argues that development cannot happen during the reign of neo-liberal economics historically:

> There were four things that ensured shared prosperity in the 1950s and the 1960s: strong trade unions; redistribution through the tax system; higher public spending; and curbs on the financial system. Apart from suggesting that some countries, such as Germany might care to spend a bit more on infrastructure, the fund is not really in favour of any of them.[116]

Inequality is part of the neo-liberal equation, as the early section of the chapter argues. Theoretically rich entrepreneurs and companies trickle down to poor people and countries.[117] It will need an enormous paradigm shift to change this model.

THE CARIBBEAN SITUATION: POST-COLONISATION OR A NEW FINANCIAL COLONISATION?

In my 2005 *Companies, International Trade and Human Rights* I charted the despicable cruelty involved in the Caribbean slave trade. I can hardly reread the text, it makes me violently angry because the trade was excused and promoted as a faux-free-trade policy. Faux because English laws, and England, protected the slave-traders and amassed huge wealth on the back of the trade. Eric Williams famously showed how the capital amassed by the slave traders financed the Industrial Revolution, tracing the huge fortunes made by slaving into the banking, heavy industry and insurance sectors of the eighteenth century: 'The industrial expansion required finance. What man in the first three-quarters of the eighteenth century was better able to afford ready capital than a West Indian sugar planter or a West Indian slave trader?'[118] Family by family he traces the fortunes of the planters and traders into

114 'Global financial institutions; The IMF's new concern over inequality now needs to be matched with actions' (*Guardian*, 14 October 2014) 34.

115 DoingBusiness, *Smarter Regulations for Small and Medium Size Enterprises* (10th edn, The World Bank and International Finance Corporation 2013) <http://www.doingbusiness.org/~/media/GIAWB/Doing%20Business/Documents/Annual-Reports/English/DB13-full-report.pdf> accessed 20 October 2014.

116 Larry Elliot, 'Financial Peace in our time? That's a bit rich' (*Guardian*, 13 October, 2014).

117 Ha-Joon Chang, *23 Things They Don't Tell about Capitalism* (Penguin, 2011) 137.

118 Eric Williams, *Capitalism and Slavery* (1st edn, The University of North Carolina Press, 1994) 98.

more 'respectable' occupations. Notable among the banking families that owed its foundation to slaving was the Barclay family, which combined with other Quaker families of Gurney and Freame gave rise to Barclays Bank.[119] Williams traces the financing of some of the great inventions of the age to capital accumulated via the triangular trade. Boulton and Watt received advances from Lowe, Vere, Williams and Jennings – later the Williams Deacons Bank. Watt had some anxious moments when the West Indian fleet was threatened with capture by the French. 'Even in this emergency', wrote Boulton to him hopefully, 'Lowe, Vere and Company may yet be saved, if ye West Indian fleet arrives safe from ye French fleet . . . as many of their securities depend on it'.[120] Nor were the benefits confined to England: Rolston shows how Belfast also prospered:

> There were many benefits for towns such as Belfast from involvement in provisioning the Caribbean, and these were not confined to agriculture. The importation of sugar encouraged the development of a sugar-refining industry. Such industries as rope-making, meat packing, flour milling and the salting of beef and fish were highly dependent on West Indian trade. And, of course, linen production benefited; cheap Belfast linen was exported to clothe the slaves.[121]

One of the slave traders, Waddell Cunningham, made enormous wealth from the slave trade, returning to Belfast in 1765 to run a diverse and powerful trading empire with 'business contacts from Antigua to Jordan, and from St Petersburg and Danzig to Holland and Spain'.[122] He also set up a bank and became involved in the insurance business.[123] Unfortunately the same protectoral devices are rife now, although the neo-liberal doctrines and actors pretend that they are all free-market policies. This is a financial empire, where the rich countries promote and enforce policies, which leave poor countries with raw materials and poor wages from services.

MULTILATERAL AND BILATERAL TREATIES

Ostensibly both multinational and bilateral treaties seek to make the regulatory framework for FDI more transparent, stable, predictable and secure, and thus more attractive for foreign investors. If frameworks liberalise FDI entry and operations, they

119 ibid 43, 101.

120 ibid 103.

121 B Rolston, 'A Lying Old Scoundrel' (2003) 1(1) Ireland's History Magazine <http://www.historyireland.com/18th-19th-century-history/a-lying-old-scoundrel> accessed 10 July 2015. 'Waddell Cunningham and Belfast's Role in the Slave Trade' Dublin, <http://www.culturenorthernireland.org/article/101/hidden-connections-slavery-and-belfast>, accessed 10 July 2015 and see B Rolston and M Shannon, *Encounters – How Racism Came to Ireland* (Colour Books Ltd, 2002).

122 ibid 3.

123 Extracted from J Dine, *Companies, International Trade and Human Rights* (Cambridge University Press, 2005) 142.

reduce obstacles to FDI. This may be achieved by reducing barriers to entry, eliminating protectionist measures such as state aids and setting

> . . . up a system of self-imposed disciplines on States to counter the natural tendencies of governments to be captured by protectionist and narrow ideological special interest groups with an influence that is stronger in the domestic political process than the non-voting and politically and emotionally always easily exploitable 'foreign' companies.[124]

This theory has fuelled the enormous proliferation of both multilateral and bilateral investment treaties with the number of bilateral treaties alone growing from 385 in 1989 to 2,676[125] by 2010. The system is now universal, nearly every country has signed a BIT and many have a number of them.[126] Much of the proliferation of bilateral treaties occurred as a result of the breakdown of the multilateral negotiations at Cancun. There is good reason to believe that the most powerful trading nations and blocks are bypassing the multilateral process and picking off the poorer countries one by one. In July 2004 three of the 'Singapore' issues, which were unpopular with developing countries but very much part of the agenda of the rich trading blocks, were dropped from the Doha round. These were Investment, Competition and Transparency in Government Procurement.

> Although this could be seen as some evidence of Least Developed Countries (LDCs) and Developing Countries (DCs) being able to influence the Doha negotiating agenda, in reality the Quad countries, and in particular the United States, has circumvented the difficulties of negotiating in a multilateral forum by pursuing exactly the same issues of investment, transparency and competition in bilateral trade agreements and Free Trade Agreements.[127]

The same procedure has led to a 'Global Intellectual Property Racket'[128] by including provisions protecting intellectual property which are more stringent than those required by TRIPS. Normally included in both multilateral and bilateral agreements are national agreements or most favoured nation treatment clauses as well as non-discrimination standards. These clauses, applied within a network of overlapping agreements lead to a continuously tightening noose on the ability of countries to use their sovereign 'policy space' to regulate incoming multinational companies and afford any type of protection to their domestic industries, enforce any provisions as to technology transfer or local training and restrain capital flight. Their development potential is therefore questionable at best. Further, the interpretation of these treaties is

124 T Waelde and A Kolo, 'Environmental Regulation, Investment Protection and "Regulatory Taking" in International Law' (2001) ICLQ 811, 814.

125 UNCTAD, *Recent Development in International Investments Agreements*, United National, UNCTAD/WEB/DIAE/IA/2009/8 (New York, 2009).

126 UNCTAD, *Development Implications of International Investment Agreements*, United Nations, UNCAD/WEB/ITE/IIA\2007/2 (New York, 2007).

127 S Anderman and R Kariyawasam, 'Intellectual Property Rights and BITs' in J Dine and A Fagan (eds), *Human Rights and Capitalism* (Edward Elgar, 2005).

128 P Drahos, *Bilateralism in Intellectual Property* (Oxfam Report, 2001) 13.

in the hands of international arbitrators who are trained in the rich world and who appear to have little sympathy for the development goals of poor countries. Without this the poor nations are going to be squeezed more. A new international jurisprudence is needed, particularly a constitutional settlement allowing states policy space regulating their public interest. Without this there are indications that the arbitrators are set to expand their jurisdiction without consideration having been given to the democratic legitimacy of this process of law making.

An important component of the World Bank's governance structure is the dispute mechanism for BITs. The International Centre for Investment Disputes (ICSID) is linked to the World Bank. The jurisprudence of ICSID is evolving and it seems that arbitrations are predicated on contractual principles rather than an understanding that governments have many stakeholders, including environmental issues, public interests and democratic principles.[129] There is a tension between commercial contracts and constitutional principles. ICSID cannot easily resolve this tension.

Sweet[130] believes that the system must either go back to contractual arrangements or change into a constitutional system. The former would mean some chaos, since commercial contracts should be certain, and if each arbitrator adjudicated only their cases with no knowledge of precedence the economy would be severely damaged. Commercial trade needs certainty. On the other hand judicialisations or constitutionalising has significant dangers. The most obvious one is the flexibility of the arbitration system. Sweet uses a theory of delegation to highlight how judicial systems are understood. In essence principals and agents are always in tension, since the interests of principal and agent always clash. In a judicial system each court has more or less discretion.[131] For example, the lower courts have less discretion than any Constitutional Court or Supreme Court who have wide discretion; in a parliamentary system the parliament is the principal, the courts are the agents. Sweet puts a lens on this delegation theory in international investment treaties and realises that the principals in our modern system of international investment treaties are the contracting parties, and the agents are the arbitrators. However, the principal in this theory is not clearly delineated. Any judicial system has a parliament, in modern BITs there is nothing similar, there is only a loose complex set of treaty obligations which are nothing as clear cut as a sovereign parliament. Something needs to become solidified if the system is to be changed into a judicial structure involving governmental stakeholders in arbitration. The jurisprudence of arbitration is of enormous moment in bilateral treaties and the dispute mechanism in the Caribbean area.

---

129 M Sornarajah, *The International Law on Foreign Investment* (2nd edn, Cambridge University Press, 2004) 344; J Dine, *Multinational Companies and the Allocation of Environmental Risk in International Investment Treaties* (September/October 2014) Business Law Review.

130 Alec Sweet, 'Investor-State Arbitration: Proportionality's New Frontier' (2010) 4(1) Law and Ethics of Human Rights 47.

131 ibid.

THE COTONOU AGREEMENT, ECONOMIC AGREEMENTS AND CARIBBEAN BILATERAL TREATIES

The Cotonou Agreement[132] sets out the framework for future African, Caribbean and Pacific States (ACP) and EU trade cooperation. Part III of the agreement sets out 'Co-Operation Strategies' together with 'Development Strategies' and emphasises that development strategies and economic and trade co-operation are 'interlinked and complementary and that the efforts undertaken in both areas must be mutually reinforcing'.[133] Article 34.4 specifies that economic and trade cooperation must be 'in full conformity with the provisions of the WTO, including special and differential treatment'. Special deals may only be obtained in defence of the countries' special interests. Adjustments in favour of the weakest trading nations are provided for in GATT rules but 'ACP countries judge them insufficient, poorly defined and not rigorous enough, particularly in their application, and believe that they pay only lip service to development needs'.[134] Although the official EU line is that development needs are a primary concern, the negotiations are viewed with all the suspicions inherent in trade negotiations between the rich countries and impoverished nations, ranging from the belief that the motive behind liberalisation is to open up ACP countries to EU companies to real anger at the protectionist measures adopted by the EU in agriculture.[135]

IMPLICATIONS FOR BARBADOS: A CASE STUDY

In 2002 the Country Strategy Paper for Barbados for the period 2002–2007 set out an agreement between the government of Barbados and the European Commission.[136] At this point, sugar exports accounted for around 3% of GDP. The response to the threat to these exports is to attempt to diversify into other food crops including 'onions, hot peppers, tomatoes, paw paws and mangoes'.[137] Development aid of €17 million

---

132 (EC) 483/2000. See Europa, 'Cotonou Agreement' (2000) <http://europa.eu/legislation_summaries/development/african_caribbean_pacific_states/r12101_en.htm> accessed 20 October 2014.

133 ibid.

134 K Karl, 'Economic Partnership Agreements: Hopes, Fears and Challenges' (November–December 2002) 195 *The Coufier* ACP–EU, 22 <https://www.google.co.uk/search?client=safari&rls=en&q=K+Karl,+%E2%80%98Economic+Partnership+Agreements:+Hopes,+Fears+and+Challenges%E2%80%99+(November%E2%80%93December+2002)+195+the+Coufier+ACP%E2%80%93EU,+22&ie=UTF-8&oe=UTF-8&gfe_rd=cr&ei=_jSeVbe0EOmq8weq0IHgAg> accessed 10 July 2015.

135 ibid.

136 European Commission DG Development, 'Barbados – European Community' (Country Strategy Paper and National Indicative Programme for the period 2002–2007) <http://www.unicef.org/lac/spbarbados/Planning/national/Barbados/EU_bb_csp_en.pdf>.

137 ibid 14.

was spent supporting the Caribbean rum sector to limit the damage caused by liberalisation of the spirits market.

> Barbados being the location of some important distilleries, is likely to benefit substantially from this programme. Bearing in mind the decline of cane sugar, this programme may play an important role in diversifying into higher value added products.[138]

The paper drew a picture of a hitherto robustly developing country with excellent life expectancy rates (79 for women, 74 for men), good social security, health and education provision but 14% of the population falling below the poverty line of Bds $5,502 per annum and 9.9% unemployment (2001). However the prescient report said:

> The Caribbean region is currently facing huge challenges on the external front as it grapples with the effects of globalisation and international trade commitments under the World Trade Organisation (WTO) alongside pressures arising from economic groupings such as the Free Trade Area of the Americas (FTAA) . . . The EPA,[139] as envisaged under the Cotonou Agreement will progressively eliminate barriers to trade between the parties and enhance cooperation in all areas relevant to trade. By virtue of deeper trade liberalisation imperatives and being signatories to hemispheric and multilateral trade-related disciplines in particular, trade strategies and policy governing trade relations with countries outside the Caribbean must now evolve.[140]

Heron argues that the EPAs are evolving as part of the EU's bilateral strategies to liberalise trade, the EPA were meant to have a package of societal advantages for the affected countries, these are being diluted.[141] The text is vague and inevitably in negotiations the weaker party is likely to be disadvantaged.

There are a number of assessments of the possible benefits or disadvantages of the EPA programme. The EU Commission says that EPAs will be beneficial for the ECP countries and for EU consumers and producers 'by creating employment, giving access to a wider range of good quality products, reducing average prices and generating income'.[142] However, a number of NGOs are extremely critical: Action Aid believes

---

138 ibid 21.

139 Economic Partnership Agreement [2000] L 289/I/3.

140 European Commission DG Development (n 136) 19.

141 T Heron and G Siles-Brügge, 'Competitive Liberalization and the "Global Europe" Services and Investment Agenda: Locating the Commercial Drivers of the EU–ACP Economic Partnership Agreements' (2012) 50(2) JCMS 250 <http://core.ac.uk/download/pdf/13505077.pdf> accessed 10 July 2015.

142 EPAs help create the right conditions for trade and investment. Together with development aid, they can deliver a number of benefits for ACP countries:

- *more markets, more sales* – by opening the EU market fully to imports from ACP countries, strengthening and boosting trade between ACP countries themselves
- *better infrastructure, administration and public services* – to increase and improve productive capacity, training opportunities and knowledge transfer
- *more transparency/political and economic stability* – political dialogue has become an integral part of the ACP–EU relationship, aiming to uphold democratic standards, good governance and human rights.

Economic Partnership Agreements <http://trade.ec.europa.eu/doclib/docs/2013/april/tradoc_151010.pdf> accessed 27 October 2014. I put this extract in footnotes because I thought it was highly patronising and likely to damage the Caribbean countries.

that they will be disastrous for the APC countries, Traidcraft agrees.[143] Trade Justice has given a detailed assessment of the agreements and believes that the EU is bullying the APC countries to sign the treaties:

> Developing countries have long argued that there is insufficient focus on development and have resisted a number of Commission proposals, such as the inclusion of the 'Singapore issues' of investment, services, procurement and competition. The Commission's approach is also in direct contradiction to the spirit of the Cotonou Agreement which commits the EU to leave ACP countries no worse off under new arrangements than under previous regimes, and to provide alternatives to EPAs. Whatever they decide to do, it is clear that this proposal would lead to countries within African and Pacific regions having widely varying arrangements with the EU. This has potential grave implications for work towards regional integration.[144]

Although the EPAs have clauses detailing human rights obligations (including labour obligations), sustainability obligations and poverty eradications obligations it is unlikely that obligations can be enforced;

Despite certain infelicities in wording, the human rights clause is sufficiently robust and flexible to enable the EU to ensure that it can withdraw from any commitment that would imperil its obligation to respect human rights and democratic principles in its external relations. It is more difficult to answer this question in the context of the EU's commitment to sustainable development and the eradication of poverty. What would happen if the agreement turned out to have negative effects on sustainable development or poverty? In this case, the EU would have little power to withdraw from commitments that contribute to this situation, nor could it take coercive steps with a view to enforcing the other country's own obligations in this regard. But this comparative weakness does not matter, because the EU is required merely to pursue the objectives of sustainable development and the eradication of poverty. So long as the EU does not act in a manner that has a high likelihood of contradicting these objectives, it is unlikely to fall foul of this obligation.[145] Caribbean commentators are critical: Norman Girvan was a fierce critic of the EPAs, believing that precisely what Chang chronicles will happen when these agreements are implemented. The parties of these treaties are the EU and Cariforum (CF) and it seems that they are highly unequal. CF would have EU access for goods, services phased during a 15-year liberalisation process without any certainty of development support, no more funding than the Cotonou provided. The agreement is very wide and CF will be bound by commitments stopping new policy arrangements, leaving

143 Traidcraft, 'Policy and Campaigns' <http://www.traidcraft.co.uk/international_development/policy_work/trade_policy/epas> <http://www.actionaid.org.uk/trade/epas> accessed 27 October 2014.

144 Trade Justice Movement, 'European Partnership Agreement' <http://www.tjm.org.uk/trade-issues/related-campaign-issues/european-partnership-agreements.html> accessed 10 July 2015.

145 Lorand Bartels, 'Human Rights and Sustainable Development Obligations in EU Free Trade Agreements' (2012) University of Cambridge Faculty of Law Research Paper No 24/2012 <http://ssrn.com/abstract=2140033> accessed 27 October 2014.

the governments less 'policy space' to develop as other issues arise. This is anti-democratic and is particularly damaging for development:[146]

> Despite its over-riding policy on emphasis on poverty eradication and sustainable development . . . the negotiations are primarily about one thing, namely achieving the progressive and reciprocal liberalisation of trade in goods and services . . . not taking into account the level of development of the ACP countries and the economic, social and environmental constraints they are facing.[147]

An assessment of the EPAs is less critical, a report from Sussex University states: 'The claim that EPAs will necessarily result in ACP markets being thrown open to EU imports appears to be overstated, but evidence suggests that they may well cause serious problems for regional integration and for government revenue.'[148] This report was written during the negotiations (2005) and points out that the governments will be able to exclude some products and services but because of the variety of the products and services in the particular country it will be difficult to have a coherent plan. Since negotiations will have a powerful imbalance between the EU and a set of very poor states there is the danger of divide and rule between the ACP countries.

CF will be bound by intellectual property treaties but it is not clear whether the EU obligations of sustainability and poverty eradication which are embedded in the EPAs are real obligations or have teeth.[149] Chang argues that the way South Korea made huge economic progress was to use clever reverse engineering, ignoring patents and protecting particular industries. Korea is highly prosperous.[150] It is therefore very dangerous to be bound by IP stringent commitments in the way that the EU is trapping the Caribbean into a free-market system which will be good for the EU but disastrous for the ACP countries. However, Henning argues that the sustainability clauses are more than vague promises and they could be 'interesting'. The EC–CARIFORUM EPA has been called a 'Trade Partnership for Sustainable Development' where 'sustainable development is the presiding principle governing the whole agreement'.[151] Henning argues that this means that the objective could be judicialising the process:

> Giving effect to sustainable development *as a treaty objective* means that its core principle of integration guides the interpretation of individual treaty provisions. Based on the

146 Norman Girvan, 'The CARIFORUM-EC EPA: A Critical Evaluation' (27 April) *Caribbean Political Economy* <http://www.normangirvan.info/the-epa-a-critical-evaluation-norman-girvan-powerpoint-presentation-270408/> accessed 27 October 2014.

147 Clive Thomas, 'The Design and Architecture of the EPA' (*Stabroek News*, 24 February 2008).

148 Christopher Stevens and Jane Kennan, 'EU–ACP Economic Partnership Agreements: The Effects of Reciprocity' (2005) Institute of Development Studies, <http://www.ids.ac.uk/files/CSEPARECBP2.pdf> accessed 27 October 2014.

149 Economic Partnership Agreement [2000] L 289/I/3, Art 143.1.

150 Chang, *Bad Samaritans* (Random House Business, 2007) 15–18.

151 Henning Ruse-Khan, 'The Concept of Sustainable Development in International Intellectual Property Law – New Approaches from EU Economic Partnership Agreements?' (2010) Max Planck Institute for Intellectual Property, Competition and Tax Law Research Paper No. 10–04 <http://ssrn.com/abstract=1542486> <http://dx.doi.org/10.2139/ssrn.1542486> accessed 27 October 2014, 26.

> notion of *pacta sunt servanda*, this balancing must primarily be performed in the process of treaty implementation by states as the main addressees of a sustainable development treaty objective. Here, the ambiguous nature of the integration principle secures policy space when states implement treaty provisions in light of the sustainable development objective . . . International Courts and Tribunals have to recognise this domestic policy space to balance economic, social and environmental concerns. Hence they must exercise deference when assessing a disputed implementation of provisions originating from treaties with a sustainable development objective.[152]

As well as the EPAs there are a network of treaties between Caribbean countries and other states.

BILATERAL TREATIES (BITS)

The complexity of the trade pattern for the Caribbean is illustrated by the fact that there is a large number of bilateral treaties (BITs) between Jamaica, in fact 15; Argentina, China, Egypt, France, Germany, Indonesia, Italy, Netherlands, Nigeria, Spain, Switzerland, the UK, the US, Zimbabwe and recently Kuwait (2014).[153] International Investment Agreements are concluded by MNEs to reduce the risk of investment in host states. They are used by poor countries to attempt to attract foreign direct investment (FDI) and by rich countries to minimise risks to their multinational companies. As we saw from the EPA debate BITs pose the same dangers for the Caribbean countries, BITs are dangerous because of the disparate bargaining power which underlies the signing of such treaties. The role of law in a market economy is the proper allocation of risk, in international investment treaties should balance the risk for investors (nearly always MNEs) and risk for the state of the freedom to regulate. A proper balance would be more likely to result from understanding that the balance is being struck between the risk that the profits of large companies might be reduced, a risk which can only be removed by putting poorer communities in danger by removing or preventing regulations that seek to protect them, sometimes from risks of injury to health and the environment. The misrepresentation is compounded by making exaggerated claims as to the degree to which property rights should be protected; especially intellectual property.

CORPORATE GOVERNANCE IN THE CARIBBEAN

We have seen that corporate governance is bounded by international economic and legal restrictions. Any reform involving corporate governance should be looked at from a prism, which recognises the danger of the neo-liberal model. Chang has shown us that free-market fundamentalism is very bad for any developing country. To develop,

152 ibid 25.

153 Foreign Trade Information System, 'Information on Jamaica: Bilateral Trade Agreements' <http://www.sice.oas.org/ctyindex/JAM/JAMBits_e.asp> accessed 20 October 2014.

the rich states used significant protections for developing manufacturing, including tariffs, loose IP regulations, wars, slavery, public ownership of companies (socially owned enterprise (SOEs)) and governmental initiatives. It was only when they were powerful and secure that they opened their markets.[154] It is sensible to resist any more liberalisation. For corporate governance this means resisting neo-liberal pressure to conform to the shareholder primacy model. In *The Nature of Corporate Governance: The Significance of National Cultural Identity*[155] the authors argue that the reason that national diversity in corporate governance is still widespread is because of the history, philosophy and economy of each country as shown in its cultural heritage, and which gives its identity. It is very cheering that the forces pushing the converging of corporate governance have been withstood:

> Most of the Commonwealth Caribbean territories have by now adopted the Canadian model of corporate legislation which amongst other things shifted the focus from the old UK agency (shareholder primacy) model of company law to a stakeholder model of company law. The corporate governance provisions of the company's legislation include a focus on considerations, which include a wide group of stakeholders. The duties and responsibilities of directors and officers must take into account shareholders, employees and even the community in which the company operates. Various stakeholders are also permitted to sue on behalf of the company for wrongs done to the company through the derivative action and to apply to the court for remedies for oppressive conduct meted out by directors, officers or the company.[156]

The reason that inclusive models of companies are crucial is that the shareholder primacy ignores public interests and promotes private power whether on environmental, social issues or labour issues. This is very important for the neo-liberal agenda.[157] Fiduciary duties are a key part of understanding a company model. Although there are small differences between the legislation in the Commonwealth Caribbean jurisdictions they are clearly stakeholder driven. Perhaps the strongest expression of this doctrine is to be found in Jamaica: section 174(4) of the Jamaica Company Act provides 'in determining what are the best interests of the company, a director or officer may have regard to the interests of the company's shareholders and employees and the community in which the company operates'.[158] The UK Companies Act 2006 has a wider set of 'stakeholders' but section 172(2) narrows the stakeholder credibility to provide:

> Where or to the extent that the purposes of the company consist of or include purposes other than the benefit of its members, subsection (1) has effect as if the reference to

154 Chang, *Kicking Away the Ladder: Development Strategy in Historical Perspective* (1st edn, Anthem Press, 2003) and *Bad Samaritans* (Random House Business, 2007).

155 Dine and Koutsias, *Corporate Governance* (Edward Elgar, 2013).

156 Suzanne Ffolkes-Goldson, 'The Use and Misuse of the Corporate Oppressive Remedy in the Commonwealth Caribbean' (Paper presented at UWI Mona Law Series (MLS) 2 (13) 7 February 2013).

157 Loraine Talbot, *Progressive Corporate Governance for the 21st Century* (Routledge, 2013); Ulrich Beck, *Power in the Global Age* (Polity Press, 2005); Andrew Keay, *The Corporate Objective* (Edward Elgar, 2011).

158 Jamaica Company Law 2004; Goldson (n 156) 6–7.

promoting the success of the company for the benefit of its members were to achieving those purposes.

It seems that the directors have only a duty to 'regard' other stakeholder's interests, many commentators have suggested that this is a not very successful whitewash of the shareholder primacy model, partly because only shareholders can sue via a derivative action.[159] The shareholders *might* sue the company if the directors do not have regard to other stakeholders, but it seems that it is very unlikely, given the costs of such action. As for the UK unfair prejudice action, this is confined to shareholders.[160] Of course the enforcement of the remedy is vital. Many scholars have grappled with the difficulty of whether a stakeholder model can be implemented; the more inclusive the model is the more difficult it is to prioritise the interests of the stakeholders.[161] In the Commonwealth Caribbean there is some confusion about the enforcement remedies, the focus on the Oppressive Remedy, first copied from Canadian legislation, specifically sections 238–241 of the Canada Business Corporation (CBCA) 1985. Most of the Commonwealth Caribbean jurisdictions have adopted the provisions with small variations on the definition of the complainants and/or the stakeholders. Barbados Company Law, Section 225 provides:

> If upon an application under subsection (1), the Court is satisfied that in respect of a company or any of its affiliates
>
> (a) any act or omission of the company or any of its affiliates effects a result,
> (b) the business or affairs of the company or any of its affiliates are or have been carried on or conducted in a manner, or
> (c) the powers of the directors of the company or any of its affiliates are or have been exercised in a manner that is oppressive or unfairly prejudicial to, or that unfairly disregards, the interest of, any shareholder or debenture holder, creditor, director or officer of the company, the Court may make an order to rectify the matter complained of.

One difficulty is that the stakeholders in the company are not precisely mirrored with the complainants. Leaving the same problem that the UK has, why would the complainants pursue an act for someone else?

Under Section 225 of the Barbados Companies Act, a complainant is:

i) A shareholder or debentureholder, or a former holder of a share or debenture of a company or any of its affiliates;
ii) A director or an officer or former director or officer of a company or any of its affiliates;
iii) The Registrar
iv) Any other person who, in the discretion of the Court, is a proper person to make an application under that part of the Act.

---

159 UK Company Act 2006, ss 260–266, only the shareholders have a right to sue the company (the derivative action).

160 UK Company Act 2006, s 994.

161 Andrew Keay, *The Corporate Objective* (Edward Elgar, 2011), Dine and Koutsias, *Corporate Governance* (Edward Elgar, 2013).

The wide discretion of the Court to allow a 'proper person' to complain is missing in the Jamaican company law and the Report of the Review Committee on the Reform of Company Law (Committee Report) also suggested excluding this discretion.[162] The substance is the action is conduct that is 'oppressive or unfairly prejudicial to . . .' and the contested class of the victims and complainants. Goldson rightly argues that the contested words on the classes who can sue and be a victim are a 'recipe for confusion'.[163] This confusing situation was not helped by Lord Hoffman's judgment in *O'Neill v Phillips*, an unfair prejudice action in the UK[164] on which scholarship has been extended but which is not pellucid.[165] It seems that the Review Committee on the Reform of Company Law 1991 was hesitant about 'permitting actions for conduct that "unfairly disregards" the complainant' and the Jamaican law excludes this phrase.[166] It seems that the action is diluted if the stakeholders are disregarded. In the UK including the derivative or the unfair prejudice actions could be very powerful. The Canadian Supreme Court ruled that the test for oppression, unfair prejudice or unfair disregard under the relevant legislation was:

> whether the complainant is required to establish (i) that he had a reasonable expectation and (ii) that the reasonable expectation was disregarded . . . having regard to the facts of the specific case, the relationship at issue, and the entire context, including the fact that there may be conflicting claims and expectations.[167]

It is always dangerous to pronounce on other's laws but it seems that, if the oppressive action could be tidied up, Commonwealth Caribbean jurisdictions could have a significant contribution to stakeholder corporate governance which is a small way to deter rampant neo-liberalism. In these actions the Court has a very wide discretion to act including the power to amend the company's articles, appointing directors, compensating 'an aggrieved person, and liquidating the company'.[168] In other ways, as well, the remedy is very wide; it includes 'affiliates' of the company as a complainant and as defendants. This is very a wide definition because it seems to include a wide power to lift the company veil, which is also a way to protect small jurisdictions against large corporations which use 'jurisdictional arbitrage'.[169]

---

162 Goldson (n 156) 9 and Report of the Review Committee on the Reform of Company Law 1991, 89.

163 Goldson (n 156) 10.

164 [1999] WLR 1092.

165 Dine and Koutsias, *Corporate Governance* (Edward Elgar, 2013) 155.

166 S Ffolkes-Goldson 'The Use and Misuse of the Corporate Oppression Remedy in the Commonwealth Caribbean' (2014) 35(7) Company Lawyer 195 and Report of the Review Committee on the Reform of Company Law 1991.

167 *BCE Inc v 1976 Debentureholders* [2008] 3 SCR 560–562.

168 Jamaica Company Act 2004, s 213A.

169 Janet Dine, 'Jurisdictional Arbitrage by Multinational companies' (2012) 3(1) Journal of Human Rights and the Environment 44–69.

CONCLUSION

To consider 'Corporate Governance' is also to consider competing models of capitalism and competing global economic models. For poor countries and emerging markets liberalisation of markets are anathema. Chang shows convincingly that all of the developed states used a set of strategies to boost growth whether the schemes were ethical or legal. Only when their economies became strong did they open trade barriers. At the moment developing countries are hamstrung by legal, institutional power relations not allowing them to develop. The western economic orthodoxy is based on contract without regulation, which could soften power relations between individuals, countries, governments and multinational companies. A free-market contractual economic model, inevitably increases inequality for individuals and countries. Although capitalism has created wealth, market fundamentalism is dangerous for society, as the IMF has recently acknowledged although their policies have been part of the problem rather than the solution. This paper charts some of the philosophers who have argued about economic matters from ethical, theological, rational and utilitarian perspectives. The overall conclusion is that all philosophy and economic thought is likely to be subverted by special interests whether by institutions or individuals. Pogge is relentless:

> . . . moral norms, designed to protect the livelihood and dignity of the vulnerable, place burdens on the strong. If such norms are compelling enough, the strong make an effort to comply. But they also, consciously or unconsciously, try to get around the norms by arranging their social world so as to minimise their burdens of compliance.[170]

It seems clear that capitalism can have ethical principles embedded in its philosophy. However the temptations are also very clear, only significant principles can limit capitalism, the neo-liberal paradigm allows the worst enticement by the promotion of selfishness and the credence that selfishness is good for society. Free market economists, while claiming moral neutrality for their theories,[171] use a discourse, which has the effect of disguising power differences causing a sliding slope of perception from actual equality to formal equality. Formal equality is not real; economic theories positing equality rest on the concept of equal bargaining power (including equality of information) and the resultant 'efficiency'. The result of assuming equality of bargaining power means that there is no justification in intervening in the resultant property distribution. Such an intervention is an interference in the 'freedom to choose' to carry out a particular transaction. The defence of freedom may thus be prayed in aid of a market system, which is then free to create enormous inequalities. This concept of freedom of choice has considerable resonance both at national and international levels, applying

170 T Pogge, *World Poverty and Human Rights* (Polity Press, 2002 and 2008) 5.

171 According to D Campbell, 'Reflexivity and Welfarism in the Modern Law of Contract' (2000) Oxford Journal of Legal Studies 477, a claim most powerfully made by F Hayek in *The Road to Serfdom* (Routledge, 1986).

to individuals, corporations and states. Assertions of freedom and equality disguise the real power relations.

The cultural heritage in each state is identifiable in the Company Law and Corporate Governance Codes. The neo-liberal agenda that predicates deregulation, privatisation and the liberalisation of markets is moulding many jurisdictions into an Anglo-American model of corporate governance, which is dangerous for a number of reasons:[172]

- It is an extreme sort of utilitarianism without significant ethical principles.
- It allows the growth of mega companies backed by powerful international institutions including the International Monetary Fund (IMF), the World Bank (WB), the Organisation for Economic Cooperation and Development (OECD) and the World Trade Organization (WTO).
- It changes the balance of power between states, individuals and countries and the mega companies including the financial sector ('the markets') and the international institutions.
- It is disastrous because of the burgeoning inequality between nations and individuals.
- It is profoundly anti-democratic because of the powerful actors.
- It is disastrous for the environment.

How uplifting it is to see that the Caribbean Commonwealth has chosen a corporate governance model which has the possibility to reach stakeholders other than shareholders. It is clear that corporate governance cannot change all of the devastation that the neo-liberal paradigm has wrecked but by diverging from the Anglo-American corporate governance, but the Caribbean countries have set a precedent for a more equal society.

BIBLIOGRAPHY

'Global financial institutions; The IMF's new concern over inequality now needs to be matched with actions' (October 2014) *Guardian*

Ainger, K, 'A Financial Coup d'Etat: The Spanish government may be happy to sacrifice sovereignty for a bailout. But not the Indignos' (September 2012) *Guardian*

Anderman, S and Kariyawasam, R, 'Intellectual Property Rights and BITs' in J Dine and A Fagan (eds), *Human Rights and Capitalism*, 2005, London: Edward Elgar

Antoine, R, *Commonwealth Caribbean Law and Legal Systems*, 2nd edn, 2008, Routledge-Cavendish

Attenborough, D, 'Giving Purpose to the Corporate Purpose Debate: An Equitable Maximisation and Viability Principle' (2012) 32(1) Legal Studies 4

Bakan, J, *The Corporation: the Pathological Pursuit of Profit and Power*, 2004, Free Press

Barbier, E, *A Global Green New Deal*, 2010, United Nations Environment Programme (UNEP)

Bartels, L, 'Human Rights and Sustainable Development Obligations in EU Free Trade Agreements' (2012) University of Cambridge Faculty of Law Research Paper No 24/2012 <http://ssrn.com/abstract=2140033>

Beck, U, *Power in the Global Age*, 1st edn, 2005, Polity Press

172 Loraine Talbot, *Progressive Corporate Governance for the 21st Century* (Routledge, 2013).

Bible, 2014, New King James Version

Birch, K and Mykhnenko, V, 'Introduction – A World Turned Right Way Up' in K Birch and V Mykhnenko (eds), *The Rise and Fall of Neo-liberalism: The Collapse of an Economic Order?*, 2010, Zed Books

Boeger, N and others (eds), *Perspectives on Corporate Social Responsibility*, 2008, Edward Elgar Publishing

Bottomley, S, *The Constitutional Corporation*, 2007, Ashgate

Brennan, F and Packer, J (eds), *Colonisation, Slavery, Reparations and Trade; Remedying the 'Past'*, 2013, Routledge

Brennan, F, *Race Rights, Reparations, Institutional Racism and the Law*, 2015, Ashgate

Burke, J, 'Rana Plaza: one year on from the Bangladesh factory disaster' (April 2014) *Guardian* <http://www.theguardian.com/world/2014/apr/19/rana-plaza-bangladesh-one- year-on>

Cahn, J, 'Challenging the New Imperial Authority: The World Bank and the Democratization of Development' (1993) 6 Harvard Human Rights Journal 160.

Campbell, D, 'Reflexivity and Welfarism in the Modern Law of Contract' (2000) Oxford Journal of Legal Studies 477

Chang, H, *23 Things They Don't Tell You about Capitalism*, 2010, Penguin

Chang, H, *Bad Samaritans*, 2007, Random House Business

Chang, H, *Economics; The User's Guide*, 2014, Pelican

Chang, H, *Kicking Away the Ladder: Development Strategy in Historical Perspective*, 1st edn, 2003, Anthem Press

Chatterjee, C, 'The OECD Guidelines for Multinational Enterprises: an analysis' (2002) *Amicus Curiae* 18.

Cheffins, B, *Company Law: Theory, Structure and Operation*, 1997, Clarendon Press

Chossudovsky, M, *The Globalisation of Poverty*, 1998, Zed Books

Chossudovsky, M, *The Globalisation of Poverty and the New World Order*, 2nd edn, 2003, Global Research

Clapham, A, 'The Question of Jurisdiction under International Criminal Law over Legal Persons' in M Kamminga, and S Zia-Zarifi (eds), *Liability of Multinational Corporations under International Law*, 2000, Kluwer Law International

Collins, H, *The Law of Contract*, 1986, Butterworths

Committee on the Financial Aspect of Corporate Governance, Report on the Financial Aspect of Corporate Governance, 1992, Burgess Science Press and Gee and Co Ltd

Cornes, R and others, *The Judicial System of the Virgin Islands; Options for Reform*, 2006, Essex University

Dignam, A and Galanis, M, *The Globalization of Corporate Governance*, 2009, Ashgate Publishing

Dignam, A and Galanis, M, 'Corporate Governance and the Importance of Macroeconomic Context' (2008) 28 *Oxford Journal of Legal Studies* 201

Dine, J, *Governance of Company Groups*, 2009, CUP

Dine, J, *Companies, International Trade and Human Rights*, 2005, CUP

Dine, J, 'Jurisdictional Arbitrage by Multinational companies' (2012) 3(1) *Journal of Human Rights and the Environment* 44–69

Dine, J and Kousias, M, *The Nature of Corporate Governance; The Significance of National Cultural Identity*, 2013, Edward Elgar

Doing Business, Smarter Regulations for Small and Medium Size Enterprises, 10th edn, 2013, The World Bank and International Finance Corporation 2013 <http://www.doingbusiness.org/~/media/GIAWB/Doing%20Business/Documents/Annual-Reports/English/DB13-full-report.pdf>

Drahos, P, *Bilateralism in Intellectual Property*, 2001, Oxfam Report

Eagleman, D, *Incognito: The Secret Lives of the Brain*, 2011, Cannongate

Economic Partnership Agreement (2000) L 289/I/3, Art 143.1

Elliot, L, 'Financial Peace in our time? That's a bit rich' (October 2014) *Guardian*

European Commission DG Development, 'Barbados – European Community' (Country Strategy Paper and National Indicative Programme for the period 2002–2007) <http://www.unicef.org/easterncaribbean/spmapping/Planning/national/Barbados/EU_bb_csp_en.pdf>

Ffolkes-Goldson, S, 'The Use and Misuse of the Corporate Oppression Remedy in the Commonwealth Caribbean' (2014) 35(7) *Company Lawyer* 195

Foreign Trade Information System, 'Information on Jamaica: Bilateral Trade Agreements' <http://www.sice.oas.org/ctyindex/JAM/JAMBits_e.asp>

Foxley, A, *Groundwork for Inclusive Development, Responses to Emergent Challenges for Latin American and Caribbean Economies*, 2004, Center for Latin American and Latino Studies, American University, Washington, DC

Giddens, A, *Introduction of Weber, Protestant Ethics and Capitalism*, 1992, Routledge

Girvan, N, 'The CARIFORUM-EC EPA: A Critical Evaluation' (April 2008) Caribbean Political Economy <http://www.normangirvan.info/the-epa-a-critical-evaluation-norman-girvan-power point-presentation-270408/>

GlobalPost, 'Greek unemployment soars with one fifth out of work' <www.globalpost.com/dispatch/news/business-tech/debt-crisis/120412/greek-unemployment-soars-over-one-five-out-work>

Green, D, *From Poverty to Power*, 2008, Practical Action Publishing in association with Oxfam GB for Oxfam International, 2008/9

Grim, CE, 'The Possible Relationship between the Transatlantic Slave and Hypertension in Blacks Today' in JE Inikori and L Engerman (eds), *The Atlantic Slave Trade*, 1992, Duke University Press

Hansmann, H and Kraakman, R, 'The End of History for Corporate Law' (2000) Harvard Law School John M Olin Center for Law, Economics and Business Discussion Paper Series

Hardt, M and Negri, A, *Empire*, 2011, Harvard University Press

Harrison, P, *Inside the Third World*, 3rd edn, 1993, Penguin

Hayek, F, *The Road to Serfdom*, 1986, Routledge

Heerings, H and Zeldenrust, I, *Elusive Saviours*, 1995, International Books

Helm, D and Hepburn, C (eds), *The Economics and Politics of Climate Change*, 2009, OUP

Heron, T and Siles-Brügge, G, 'Competitive Liberalization and the "Global Europe" Services and Investment Agenda: Locating the Commercial Drivers of the EU–ACP Economic Partnership Agreements' (2012) 50 (2) JCMS 250 <http://core.ac.uk/download/pdf/13505077.pdf>

Hertsgaard, M, *Earth Odyssey*, 1999, Abacus

Hill, J, 'Visions and Revisions of the Shareholder' (2000) *American Journal of Comparative Law* 39

Hulme, M, *Why We Disagree about Climate Change*, 2009, CUP

IMF, 'Inequality Seriously Damages Growth' (2014) (IMF Survey Magazine) <http://www.imf.org/external/pubs/ft/survey/so/2014/res041214a.htm>

Inikori, JE and Engerman, SL (eds), *The Atlantic Slave Trade; Effects on Economics, Societies, and Peoples in Africa, the Americas, and Europe*, 1992, Duke University Press

Ireland, R, 'Company Law and the Myth of Shareholder Ownership' (1999) MLR 62

Karl, J, 'The OECD Guidelines for Multinational Enterprises' in M Addo (ed), *Human Rights Standards and the Responsibility of Transnational Corporations*, 1999, Kluwer

Karl, K, 'Economic Partnership Agreements: Hopes, Fears and Challenges' (November-December 2002) 195 the Coufier ACP-EU

Karliner, J, *The Corporate Planet*, 1997, Sierra Club

Keay, A, *The Corporate Objective*, 2011, Edward Elgar

Keynes, JM, *Essays in Persuasion: The Collected Writings of John Maynard Keynes*, Vol 9, 1972, CUP

Klein, N, *The Shock Doctrine: The Rise of Disaster Capitalism*, 2007, Allen Lane

Klein, N, *This Changes Everything*, 2014, Allen Lane

Korten, D, *When Corporations Rule the World*, 2nd edn, 2001, Berrett-Koehler

Kwa, A, *Power Politics in the WTO*, 2003, Focus on the Global South

Kwarteng, K and others, *Britain Unchained*, 2012, Palgrave Macmillan

Machiavelli, N, *The Florentine History*, Vol 2, 2010, Nabu Press

Macneil, IR, 'Bureaucracy and Contracts of Adhesion' (1984) 22 *Osgoode Hall Law Journal* 5

Marlowe, C, *The Tragical, History of the Life and Death of Doctor Faustus*, 2014, CreateSpace Independent Publishing Platform

Monastiriotis, V, 'The Greek Crisis in focus, Austerity, Recession and the path to Recovery' (2011) Hellenic Observatory, LSE <www2.lse.ac.uk/europeanInstitute/research/hellenicObservatory/pdf/GreeSE/GreeSE%20Special%20Issue.pdf>

Monbiot, G, *Heat: How can we stop the planet burning*, 2006, Allen Lane, Penguin

Muchlinski, P, 'The Changing Face of Transnational Business Governance: Private Corporate Law liability and Accountability of Transnational Groups in a Post-Crisis World' (2011) 18 *Indiana Journal of Global Studies* 666

Muzaffer, E, *Multinational Enterprises and Tort Liabilities*, 2008, Edward Elgar

Novak, M, *The Spirit of Democratic Capitalism*, 1993, Free Press

Nwaobi, G, 'Inequality, Poverty and Hunger in Developing Countries: Sustainability Implications' (2014) <http://mpra.ub.uni-muenchen.de/53962/1/MPRA_paper_53962.pdf>
Ogus, A, *Regulation: Legal Form and Economic Theory*, 1994, Clarendon Press
Ostry, J, Berg, A and Tsangarides, C, *Redistribution, Inequality and Growth*, 2014, IMF Staff Discussion Noye
Oxfam America Oil Gas and Mining: Poor Communities Pay the Price, 2001, Oxfam
Oxfam Global Finance, Tax Havens: Releasing the Hidden Billions for Poverty Eradication <http://policy-practice.oxfam.org.uk/our-work/aid-development-finance>
Parkinson, J, 'The Socially Responsible Company' in M Addo (ed), *Human Rights Standards and the Responsibility of Transnational Corporations*, 1999, Kluwer
Parkinson, JE, *Corporate Power and Responsibility: Issues in the Theory of Company Law*, 1993 Clarendon Press
Percival, Y, 'DPhil thesis', 2014, Queen Mary, University of London
Picketty, T, *Capital in the Twenty-First Century*, 2014, Harvard University Press
Picketty, T, *Capital in the Twenty-First Century*, 2014, Harvard University Press
Pilger, J, *The New Rulers of the World*, 2002, Verso
Pogge, T, *World Poverty and Human Rights*, 2nd edn, 2008, Polity Press
Quintyn, M, Ramirez, S and Taylor, M, 'The Fear of Freedom: Politicians and the Independence and Accountability of Financial Supervisors in Practice' in D Masciandaro and M Quintyn (eds), *Designing Financial Supervision Institutions: Independence, Accountability and Governance*, 2007, Edward Elgar, 61
Redclift, M and Benton, T (eds), *Social Theory and the Global Environment*, 1994, Routledge
Report of the Review Committee on the Reform of Company Law, 1991
Reports on the Observance of Standards and Codes (ROSC) <http://www.worldbank.org/ifa/rosc_cg.html>
Reynold, C, 'The Political Economy of Caribbean Regionalism in the Twenty-First Century: Rebirth or Resuscitation?'(2012) <http://ssrn.com/abstract=2297556>
Riley, A, 'Understanding and Regulating the Corporation' (1995) 58(4) *Modern Law Review* 595
Rolston, B, 'A Lying Old Scoundrel' (2003) *Ireland's History Magazine* <www.historyireland.com/magazine/features/11.1Feat.html>
Rothbard, MN, 'Biography of Ludwig Von Mises (1881–1973)' (Ludwig Von Mises Institute) <http://mises.org/about/3248>
Ruse-Khan, H, 'The Concept of Sustainable Development in International Intellectual Property Law – New Approaches from EU Economic Partnership Agreements?' (2010) Max Planck Institute for Intellectual Property, Competition and Tax Law Research Paper No 10–04 <http://ssrn.com/abstract=1542486 or http://dx.doi.org/10.2139/ssrn.1542486>
Schous, PA, *Reasoned Freedom*, 1992, Cornell University Press
Sedgwick, PH, *Christian Ethics*, 1999, CUP
Sedlacek, T, *Economics of Good and Evil: The Quest for Economic Meaning from Gilgamesh to Wall Street*, 2011, OUP
Sen, A, *The Idea of Justice*, 2009, Penguin
Skidelsky, R, *Keynes; The Return of the Master*, 2009, Penguin
Skidelsky, R and Skidelsky, E, *How Much is Enough? Money and the Good Life*, 2012, Allen Lane
Smith, A, *The Theory of Moral Sentiments*, 1853, HG Bonn
Smith, A, *The Wealth of Nations*, 1991, Prometheus Books
Stern, N, *The Economics of Climate Change*, 2008, CUP
Stevens, C and Kennan, J, 'EU-ACP Economic Partnership Agreements: The Effects of Reciprocity' (2005) Institute of Development Studies <http://www.ids.ac.uk/files/CSEPARECBP2.pdf>
Stiglitz, J, 'There is no invisible hand' (December 2002) *Guardian*
Stiglitz, J, *The Price of Inequality*, 2012, Allen Lane, Penguin
Stiglitz, JE, 'Multinational Corporations: Balancing Rights and Responsibilities' (2007) 101 Proceedings of the Annual Meeting (American Society of International Law)
Talbot, L, *Progressive Corporate Governance for the 21st Century*, 2013, Routledge
The Commonwealth, 'Member Countries' and 'Members of the Commonwealth Federation' <http://thecommonwealth.org/member-countries>
The World Fact Book, 'Central America and Caribbean: Bahamas' <https://www.cia.gov/library/publications/the-world-factbook/geos/bf.html>

The World Fact Book, 'Central America and Caribbean: Jamaica' <https://www.cia.gov/library/publications/the-world-factbook/geos/jm.html>

Thomas, C, 'The Design and Architecture of the EPA' (February 2008) *Stabroek News*

Thomas, H, *The Slave Trade: History of the Atlantic*, 2006, W&N

UN Human Rights Council (HRC), 'Report of the Special Representative of the Secretary-General on the issue of human rights and transnational corporations and other enterprises' (2011) UN Doc A/HRC/17/31

UNCTAD, Recent Development in International Investments Agreements, United National, UNCTAD/WEB/DIAE/IA/2009/8 (2009) New York

UNCTAD, Development Implications of International Investment Agreements, United Nations, UNCAD/WEB/ITE/IIA\2007/2 (2007) New York

United Nations Development Programme (UNDP), *Beyond Scarcity; Power, Poverty and the global water crisis*, 2006, Human Development Report

United Nations Development Programme (UNDP), *Human Development Report 2010: The Real Wealth of Nations: Pathways to Human Development*, 2010, Palgrave Macmillan <http://hdr.undp.org/sites/default/files/reports/270/hdr_2010_en_complete_reprint.pdf>

United Nations Development Programme (UNDP), Report (2010) <http://hdr.undp.org/en/content/human-development-report-201>

Waelde, T and Kolo, A, 'Environmental Regulation, Investment Protection and "Regulatory Taking" in International Law' (2001) ICLQ 811

Weber, M 'The Meaning of "Ethical Neutrality" in Sociology and Economics' (1917) in E Shils and H Finch (eds), *Max Weber on the Methodology of the Social Sciences*, 1949, Glencoe

Weber, M, *The Protestant Ethic and the Spirit of Capitalism*, 1992, Routledge

Wilder, I, 'Local Futures: From Denunciation to Revalorisation of the Indigenous Other' in G Teubner (ed), *Global Law Without a State*, 1996, Dartmouth

Wilkinson, R and Pickett, K, *The Spirit Level*, 2010, Penguin

Williams, E, *Capitalism and Slavery*, 1st edn, 1994, The University of North Carolina Press

World Hunger Education Service, '2015 World Hunger and Poverty Facts and Statistics' (Updated March 2015) <http://www.worldhunger.org/articles/Learn/world%20hunger%20facts%202002.htm>

Worldatlas, 'Caribbean' <http://www.worldatlas.com/webimage/countrys/carib.htm>

Zerk, J, *Multinational and Corporate Social Responsibilities: Limitations and Opportunities in International Law*, 2006, CUP

CHAPTER 2

EMERGENCE OF CORPORATE GOVERNANCE IN THE COMMONWEALTH CARIBBEAN

SANDRA GLASGOW

INTRODUCTION: WHAT IS CORPORATE GOVERNANCE?

> Corporate governance comprises a country's private and public institutions, both formal and informal, which together govern the relationship between the people who manage corporations ('corporate insiders') and all others who invest resources in corporations in the country. These institutions notably include the country's corporate laws, securities laws, accounting rules, generally accepted business practices and prevailing business ethics.[1]

The Organization for Economic Co-operation and Development (OECD) defines corporate governance as involving 'a set of relationships between a company's management, its board, its shareholders and other stakeholders. Corporate governance also provides the structure through which the objectives of a company are set and the means of attaining those objectives and monitoring performance are determined. Good corporate governance should provide proper incentives for the board and management to pursue objectives that are in the interests of the company and shareholders and should facilitate effective monitoring.'

THE ORIGINS OF CORPORATE GOVERNANCE

A review of the voluminous literature on corporate governance provides interesting contexts for the factors that have influenced and shaped the emergence of existing corporate governance systems across the globe. What is clear is that these systems have developed in countries and regions in direct response to socio-economic and political events, including scandals and corporate failures, changes in market characteristics and shareholder activism.

The origin of the modern corporation dates back to events in England as early as the 17th century. Until the beginning of this century, partnerships were the dominant means of organising businesses that were jointly owned and partners bore unlimited personal liability for the contractual obligations of the firm. One of the first corporations that came into existence was the British East India Company, a joint-stock company, which was granted an English Royal Charter by Queen Elizabeth I on 31 December 1600 for the purpose of trading into the East Indies. The company began with 218 members and was governed by a General Court of Proprietors, comprised of those with voting rights and a Court of Directors, which was the executive body

---

1 C Oman, Steven Fries and Willem Buiter, 'Corporate Governance in Developing, Transition and Emerging–Market Economies' (OECD Centre Policy Brief No 23, 2003) <http://www.oecd.org/social/poverty/28658158.pdf>.

responsible for the running of the company. The governance structure of the Company bore great similarity to that of a modern company: the Court of Proprietors was comprised of shareholders who met in annual general meetings; the Court of Directors was the board which was assisted by subcommittees, and the Royal Charter laid down the boundaries within which the Company could work. Over the next 200 years, corporations were generally small institutions chartered for specific purposes, such as banking. Corporations could only exist for a limited time, were not allowed to make any political contributions, and could not own stocks in other companies.

The beginning of the era of industrialisation changed this scenario significantly. Industrialisation saw the emergence of new large firms, especially in the railroad industry, with huge requirements for capital. Concurrently corporations were allowed to write broader and less restrictive charters, which saw owners and managers avoiding responsibility for harm and losses caused by the corporation, and led to the concept of limited liability. Between 1895 and 1904, the first great merger wave in the US consolidated companies into mega corporations with limited responsibility and limited accountability. In response, markets for the exchange of shares opened in New York and some European capital cities. But by the end of the 19th century and the beginning of the 20th century, control of corporations had essentially shifted into the hands of managers and ownership and control separated, creating what is known as the 'agency problem'. In the 18th century, Adam Smith drew attention in *The Wealth of Nations* to this governance issue in his commentary on joint stock companies:

> The directors of such companies however being the managers rather of other people's money than of their own, it cannot well be expected that they should watch over it with the same anxious vigilance which the partners in private copartnery frequently watch over their own . . . Negligence and profusion, therefore, must always prevail, more or less, in the management of the affairs of such a company.[2]

In the 20th century, discussions about corporate governance on both sides of the Atlantic largely focused on the consequences of the separation of ownership and management. Sir Adrian Cadbury, in his book *Corporate Governance and Chairmanship: A Personal View*[3] provides a telling treatise on the collapse of Penn Central in 1970, related by board member Louis Cabot, a Harvard professor, who had served on the board for 'one fateful year'. Penn Central was the United States' largest railway company and was the sixth largest company in the country. Cabot painted a picture of poor board practices: meetings that were poorly led by the Chairman, sketchy financial reports that were rarely discussed in detail, requests for capital expenditure without proper justification, oral reports by the Chief Executive Officer always promising better results in the next month but which never came true. By the time he wrote to the chairman to express his concerns, Penn Central had already collapsed and Cabot was being sued along with the other directors. The Securities and Exchange Commission

2 Adam Smith, *An Inquiry into the Nature and Causes of the Wealth of Nations* (Edwin Cannan, ed. 1904 edn) <http://www.econlib.org/library/Smith/smWN.html> accessed 18 December 2014, 439.

3 A Cadbury, *Corporate Governance and Chairmanship: A Personal View* (Oxford University Press 2002) 10–03.

(SEC) instituted an enquiry into the misrepresentation of earnings and the subsequent collapse of the company. Its official report was severely critical of the shortcomings of the board and pointed to the need for board independence and for vigilant outside directors. The SEC's response primarily to the Penn Central collapse was to approve, in 1977, a rule by the New York Stock Exchange that all US listed companies should establish audit committees composed solely of outside, independent directors. This reaction underscored the principle that governance was a basic responsibility of the board and that independent outside directors were critical for the structure of boards, in order for them to hold management properly accountable.

The regulatory ruling of the SEC influenced the way in which the UK responded to similar governance concerns, including a concern about the reliability of the reports and accounts of some UK companies. The Committee on the Financial Aspects of Corporate Governance was established in May 1991 by the Financial Reporting Council, a body responsible for accounting standards, the London Stock Exchange and the accountancy profession with terms of reference to consider issues in relation to financial reporting and accountability and to make recommendations on good practice. The recommendations would relate to:

1. the responsibilities of executive and non-executive directors for reviewing and reporting on performance to shareholders and other financially interested parties, and the frequency, clarity and form in which information should be provided;
2. the case for audit committees of the board, including their composition and role;
3. the principal responsibilities of auditors and the extent and value of the audit;
4. the links between shareholders, boards and auditors;
5. any other relevant matters.

The work of the Committee was underway when there were other corporate failures, including the demise of the Bank of Credit and Commerce International. The Committee published a draft Report and Code of Best Practice in May 1992 and circulated it widely with the objective of seeking comments. The recommendations were widely accepted and helped to stimulate similar approaches worldwide, so much so, that many countries subsequently developed their own codes of corporate governance. The development of international governance codes, such as the report to the OECD by the Business Sector Advisory Group on Corporate Governance led to the publication of the *OECD Principles of Corporate Governance* and organisations such as the World Bank, the IMF and the Commonwealth Association for Corporate Governance also issued their own guidelines. Major institutional investors also took the lead by publishing their own codes of best practice setting out the standards that boards of the companies in which they invest were expected to follow.

Becht et al[4] summed up the reasons why corporate governance had gained such prominence over the decades of the 1980s and 1990s: (i) the worldwide wave of

4 M Becht, P Bolton and Ailsa Röell, 'Corporate Governance and Control' (2005), European Corporate Governance Institute Finance Working Paper No 02/2002 (Updated August 2005) <http://unpan1.un.org/intradoc/groups/public/documents/apcity/unpan033582.pdf> accessed 18 December 2014.

privatisation of the 1980s and 1990s, (ii) pension fund reform and the growth of private savings; (iii) the takeover wave of the 1980s; (iv) deregulation and the integration of capital markets; (v) the 1998 East Asia crisis, which put the spotlight on corporate governance in emerging markets and (vi) a series of USA scandals and corporate failures in the 1990s. Kirpatrick[5] attributes the burst of the high tech bubble in the late 1990s to severe conflicts of interest by brokers and analysts and the Enron/Worldcom failures to issues relating to auditor and audit committee independence and deficiencies in accounting standards.

Many analysts trace the origins of the credit crisis of 2008 to the 9 August 2007 acknowledgement by BNP Paribas, a French financial group, that it had been impacted by the subprime crisis in America by closing two funds exposed to it. The debacle had come about because of irresponsible mortgage lending in the US in which loans were doled out to 'subprime' borrowers with poor credit histories who then were unable to repay them. These risky mortgages had been passed on to financial engineers at the big banks, who packaged them into supposedly low-risk securities by putting large numbers of them together in pools. While BNP Paribas escaped the crisis, other large European and American financial institutions, most notably, Lehman Brothers, a global bank, collapsed and triggered what is acknowledged as the most serious global financial crisis since the Great Depression of 1929.

Kirpatrick[6] lays the blame for the crisis squarely on

> the significant failures of risk management systems in some major financial institutions made worse by incentive systems that encouraged and rewarded high levels of risk taking. Since reviewing and guiding risk policy is a key function of the board, these deficiencies point to ineffective board oversight. In addition, disclosure and accounting standards and the credit rating process have also contributed to poor corporate governance outcomes in the financial services sector.
>
> Undoubtedly, through all these crises, the underperformance of boards of directors and excessive risk taking have cost investors billions of dollars and shaken investor confidence and highlighted the critical role that corporate governance plays across the globe.[7]

FINANCIAL FAILURES AND SCANDALS IN THE CARIBBEAN

Jackson[8] makes the point that poor regulatory systems, inexpertness of directors and sheer negligence on the part of directors in exercising due care and diligence in discharging their responsibilities have led to serious consequences in the Caribbean. In Jamaica in the 1990s, six locally owned commercial banks which accounted for 60% of all deposits in a total of nine banks, five life insurance companies which accounted

5 G Kirkpatrick, 'The Corporate Governance Lessons from the Financial Crisis' (2009) OECD Financial Market Trends Pre-publication version 2009 (1).

6 ibid.

7 ibid 3.

8 M K Jackson, 'Ownership, Corporate Governance and Liquidity in Caribbean Firms' (MPhil thesis, Queensland University of Technology 2013) <http://eprints.qut.edu.au/63853/>.

for 90% of the premium income, and a third of all merchant banks along with several building societies were deemed insolvent and subsequently closed. As a result, the Bank of Jamaica had to provide J$18 billion of special support to the banks and insurance companies to meet the demands from depositors.

In Barbados, Trade Confirmers Limited, a finance company that had been offering higher than market interest rates on deposits collapsed in 1987, leaving depositors out of pocket to the sum of US$1.2 million. The failure of Colonial Life Financial Group, based in Trinidad & Tobago, in December 2007 was the most serious in the region. It was the largest conglomerate in the Caribbean, encompassing over 65 companies in 32 countries with consolidated assets amounting to US$16 billion. William Layne, retired Permanent Secretary in the Ministry of Finance in Barbados, in a paper entitled, 'Recent Financial Failures in the Caribbean – What were the Causes and What Lessons Can be Learnt?',[9] gives a detailed account of these crises and corporate governance failures between 1986 and 2009.

CORPORATE GOVERNANCE DEVELOPMENTS IN THE COMMONWEALTH CARIBBEAN

The countries of the Commonwealth Caribbean are characterised by a set of corporate governance, market characteristics and actors that include government and para-statal organisations, conglomerates operating across major industries and a preponderance of family-owned and controlled companies, including a significant number of small and medium enterprises. Additionally, domestic capital markets are still in the relatively nascent stages of development. All of these characteristics pose challenges for creating a climate that can attract and retain local and foreign direct investment and escalate the need for robust corporate governance practices. An improved investment climate is viewed as a key component of fostering economic growth and reducing poverty in the region and studies have demonstrated the positive correlation between good governance and economic growth.

Jackson[10] chronicles a number of steps that were taken in the Caribbean since 1999 to improve corporate governance in the Caribbean, beginning with an initiative emanating from the Commonwealth Heads of Government Edinburgh Economic Declaration in October 1997. The mandate was for the region to 'establish and strengthen a national corporate governance code relevant to Caribbean Countries'.[11] In 1999 a workshop, 'Towards a Caribbean Governance Program', was held in Trinidad & Tobago with the objectives to create national/regional codes of conduct, propose

9 William Layne, 'Recent Financial Failures in the Caribbean – What were the Causes What Lessons Can Be Learnt?' (*Barbados Underground*, 6 March 2012) <http://da-academy.org/Financial_Crisis_in_the_Caribbean.pdf>.

10 William Layne 'Recent Financial Failures in the Caribbean – What were the Causes What Lessons Can Be Learnt?' (*Barbados Underground*, 6 March 2012) <http://da-academy.org/Financial_Crisis_in_the_Caribbean.pdf>.

11 ibid 13.

national strategies to develop best practices and debate on corporate governance and to train directors in best practices. This initiative, however, failed to engender any unified approach to creating governance standards that were appropriate for the Caribbean. There were, however, some attempts by countries, notably Jamaica and Barbados, to train directors, but the lack of agreed standards and guidelines for boards stymied the achievement of the objectives of the 1999 workshop.

Four years later, in 2003, the Caribbean Corporate Governance Forum was held, under the leadership of the Eastern Caribbean Central Bank along with the Eastern Caribbean Securities Exchange (ECSE), the Commonwealth Secretariat, the Global Corporate Governance Forum (a programme of the World Bank) and the Caribbean Development Bank. A number of international and regional private sector entities also participated as Associate Sponsors, and included the Center for International Private Enterprise, the National Commercial Bank of Dominica Limited, the Royal Bank of Trinidad & Tobago, the Bank of Nova Scotia (St Kitts) and St Kitts Nevis Anguilla Bank Limited. The Forum re-energised the fledgling movement and created, for the first time, a platform for stakeholders across the region to discuss and explore ways to enhance corporate governance in all countries in the region. Sixteen of the 24 countries that were invited from the region attended the Forum, with a total of 120 participants.

In a presentation to the Forum,[12] Trevor E Blake, General Manager of the ECSE, noted that the CCGF would be a pan Caribbean forum committed to promote good corporate governance standards in the region to bringing the Caribbean into the global corporate governance debate and facilitating a regional consensus on the way forward. According to Blake, the objectives of the CCGF were to:

- raise the profile of corporate governance in the region;
- identify the key issues of corporate governance which are relevant to the investment and development needs of the region;
- provide a platform to assess current levels of activity of corporate governance in all countries of the region;
- provide the opportunity to form a regional network to exchange information and experiences; and
- establish a consensus position on the Caribbean's concept of corporate governance.

The Forum provided an opportunity for participants to assess developments in corporate governance worldwide and launch a unified corporate governance movement in the Caribbean. In an effort to raise the profile of corporate governance in the region, identify the key issues that are relevant to the region's investment and development needs and place it on the policy agenda, participants discussed a number of topics, including:

- global trends in corporate governance and their implications for emerging economies;
- corporate governance challenges for the Caribbean;

12 Trevor Blake, 'Corporate Governance in the Caribbean Environment. The Caribbean Corporate Governance Forum' (Power Point) <http://www.caricom.org/caribbean_corporate_governance_forum>.

- corporate governance from the institutional investors' perspective;
- the role of governments and corporations in promoting governance;
- the role of banks;
- corporate governance issues for non-bank financial institutions;
- governance practices in statutory corporations and small and medium-size enterprises; and
- the role of securities markets in promoting healthy corporate governance practices.

DEVELOPMENT OF CORPORATE GOVERNANCE PRINCIPLES AND CODES IN CARIBBEAN COUNTRIES

Out of the Forum came a Caribbean Technical Working Group on corporate governance (CTWG) with membership from the task forces constituted at the Forum, representing participating countries and sectors. The CTWG was set up as a working committee that would promote and assist in the implementation of corporate governance initiatives in the region. The CTWG met several times and identified priority initiatives for roll out across the region, however its most significant output was a set of draft Principles of Corporate Governance for the Caribbean. The Principles focused on six broad areas:

I. *Overall Objective*. The development of transparent and efficient markets, based in the rule of law and high ethical standards.
II. *Shareholder rights*. The framework should protect and facilitate the exercise of shareholders rights.
III. *Equal Treatment*: Ensure the equitable treatment of all shareholders, including minority and foreign shareholders.
IV. *Rights of other Stakeholders*. Recognition of the legal or other rights of other stakeholders. Addresses family-owned businesses and state-owned/controlled enterprises.
V. *Disclosure and Transparency*. Timely and accurate disclosure of all material issues
VI. *Board Responsibilities*. Strategic guidance of the entity and in effectively monitoring management as well as the Board's accountability to the entity and to stakeholders.

The CTWG agreed that the Principles should also:

- be consistent with International Standards;
- focus on publicly held companies, but relevant to privately held, family-owned and state-owned enterprises as well as overall public sector;
- encourage the protection of stakeholder rights;
- be cognisant of unique economic, social, legal and cultural circumstances of region
- suited to region's state of development;
- support integration movement;
- be non-binding and non-prescriptive so that they retain relevance in varying legal, economic and social contexts; and
- be intended to serve as a reference tool in the development of national and/or sector specific codes and in the further development of national legal and regulatory frameworks.

In support of the objectives of the Forum in June 2005, in collaboration with the Commonwealth Association for Corporate Governance (CACG) and the Commonwealth Secretariat, courses for Directors and Chairpersons were held in St Kitts and St Lucia. The Directors' courses aimed at introducing participants to international best practice; foster acceptance of the need for ethical, transparent practice; promote commitment to formal training; and facilitate the production of Personal Action Plans. The Chairpersons' seminars dealt with guidelines for discharging chairpersons' duties and responsibilities.

CARICOM also played a role in supporting the establishment of a strong Corporate Governance Framework, building on the initiatives made by regional stakeholders. CARICOM's position was that a strong framework would 'facilitate economic development by strengthening market discipline, improving business transparency, enhancing disclosure, facilitating effective regulation and encouraging Corporate Social Responsibility'.[13]

Regional Stock Exchanges have also played a role in promoting corporate governance reforms. In the Caribbean, there are more than a dozen national Stock Exchanges but only one formalised regional securities market known as the Eastern Caribbean Securities Exchange (ECSE). Among the largest are the Jamaica Stock Exchange (JSE), the Trinidad & Tobago Stock Exchange (TTSE) and the Barbados Stock Exchange (BSE). The JSE, which is the oldest Exchange in the region, was incorporated as a private limited company in August 1968. The TTSE was formally opened in 1981 under the auspices of the Ministry of Finance and the BSE, formerly known as the Securities Exchange of Barbados (SEB), was established in 1987. These Exchanges offer the market a range of investment opportunities comprising equities, mutual funds and government bonds. In addition to the main markets, the JSE, TTSE and BSE have a junior or a secondary market for attracting SMEs.

The four main regional securities exchanges – the JSE, TTSE, BSE and the ECSE – promote good governance among listed companies, through the issuance of standards for listing, disclosure and de-listing, as well as their ongoing monitoring of companies' compliance with their rules. The regulatory and enforcement functions performed by these exchanges are of course limited by the authority of the legislation and market regulation in each country and are in essence delegated by the securities regulators. All of the region's stock exchanges, some more recently than others, have broadened their regulatory role to collaborate with other entities to address corporate governance concerns and have contributed to the development of corporate governance codes and principles and encouraged their adoption by companies listed on their exchanges.

In February 2002, in an address to delegates of the Council of Securities Regulators of the Americas (COSRA), the Minister of Finance of Trinidad & Tobago, the Hon Conrad Enill, noted his Government's view that:

> . . . good corporate governance influences all stages of the investment process and by extension the ability of the private sector to contribute to socio-economic progress

13 N Girvan, 'Towards a Single Economy and a Single Development Vision' (University of the West Indies In Collaboration with the CARICOM Secretariat and the Special Task Force on the Single Economy 2006) 136.

> and in that regard, encouraged the Trinidad and Tobago Stock Exchange to 'establish immediately for all its listed companies a code of good corporate governance, which is consistent with international best practices.'[14]

Yet it was Jamaica, through the Private Sector Organisation of Jamaica (PSOJ), the most important advocate for private sector interests in the country that took the lead in publishing a Code on Corporate Governance. The PSOJ published its Code, modelled on the 2003 Combined Code on Corporate Governance issued by the Financial Reporting Council (FRC) of the United Kingdom (UK), in October 2006. The PSOJ's Corporate Governance Committee led the development of the Code which outlined some core Principles contained in Part 1 of the document and became effective for all publicly listed companies in Jamaica and non-listed companies operating in the financial services sector, for annual reporting periods commencing on or after 1 January 2007. Part 2 of the Code contained 'Best Practices', which the PSOJ hoped companies would adopt 'as soon as practicable'. The Code required companies to confirm that they complied with the Code's Principles or – where they did not – to provide a reasoned explanation.[15]

In 2008, the PSOJ's Corporate Governance Committee embarked on a revision of its 2006 Code and with grant support from the Canadian International Development Agency (CIDA), published a second edition of the Code (Volume 1) in 2009 with an accompanying Volume 2, the *Handbook and Tool Kit – Best Practices in Good Governance. The Handbook and Tool Kit* is a compilation of guidelines, models and templates that are particularly useful for SMEs as they introduce or improve corporate governance practices in their companies. Through the CIDA-funded project, The PSOJ aimed to 'develop awareness and acceptance of good corporate governance (CG) and corporate social responsibility (CSR) practices within the Jamaican private sector; increase the number of female business owners and senior managers trained in leadership, CG and CSR matters and increase the number of women serving on corporate boards'. The attempt in this second edition was not to depend as heavily on the UK's Combined Code (which had by then been revised in 2008), but to include provisions contained in Codes published in other jurisdictions.[16]

The 2006 Code had been written specifically for 'all publicly listed companies in Jamaica and non-listed companies operating in the financial services sector'.[17] The 2009 Code, on the other hand, is written for a broader range of listed and unlisted companies, including small, medium, family-owned and large companies. PSOJ

---

14 Conrad Hill (Address, Senator, Minister, Ministry of Finance), 'Statement of the council of securities Regulators of the Americas' (Trinidad Hilton and Conference Centre, 19 February 2001) <http://www.ttsec.org.tt/content/sp020219.pdf>.

15 The Private Sector Organisation of Jamaica (2006) *Corporate Governance, The Way Forward.* http://psoj.org/files/Code_on_Corporate_Governance__Vol__1_0.pdf

16 The author was the Chief Executive Officer of the PSOJ from 2007 to 2013 and did much of the work to revise the Code and compile the *Handbook and Tool Kit: Best Practices in Good Governance*, along with Consultant Georgia Simpson as well as typeset and edit both Volumes 1 and 2. Many of the models and templates included in Volume 2 were adaptations of material contained in the Global Corporate Governance Forum's International Finance Corporation, *Learn Before you Lead: Corporate Governance Board Leadership Training Resources Kit* (IFCSmartLessons January 2010), with the expressed permission of the Forum.

17 PSOJ Code 2006, Preamble 1.

submits that the recommendations in the 2009 Code are not mandatory and while it expects companies to 'comply wholly or substantially with the recommendations, it is accepted that companies may elect not to comply in particular circumstances if good governance can achieved by other means'.[18] For companies listed on the Jamaica Stock Exchange, the PSOJ recommends that companies describe in the annual reports, their general adherence to the Code's main principles as well as explain their non-compliance with any of the Code's provisions.

The PSOJ sees the Code as a key part of Jamaica's corporate governance framework and it embodies the six Principles of Corporate Governance developed by the Organisation of Economic Cooperation and Development (OECD):[19]

I. Ensuring the Basis for an Effective Corporate Governance Framework

'The corporate governance framework should promote transparent and efficient markets, be consistent with the rule of law and clearly articulate the division of responsibilities among different supervisory, regulatory, and enforcement authorities.'

II. The Rights of Shareholders and Key Ownership Functions

'The corporate governance framework should protect and facilitate the exercise of shareholders' rights.'

III. The Equitable Treatment of Shareholders

'The corporate governance framework should ensure the equitable treatment of all shareholders, including minority and foreign shareholders. All shareholders should have the opportunity to obtain effective redress for violation of their rights.'

IV. The Role of Stakeholders in Corporate Governance

'The corporate governance framework should recognise the rights of stakeholders established by law or through mutual agreements and encourage active cooperation between corporations and stakeholders in creating wealth, jobs, and the sustainability of financially sound enterprises.'

V. Disclosure and Transparency

'The corporate governance framework should ensure that timely and accurate disclosure is made on all material matters regarding the corporation, including the financial situation, performance, ownership, and governance of the company.'

VI. The Responsibilities of the Board

'The corporate governance framework should ensure the strategic guidance of the company, the effective monitoring of management by the board, and the board's accountability to the company and the shareholders.

These principles are intended to assist governments in their efforts to evaluate and improve the legal, institutional, and regulatory framework for corporate governance in their countries and to provide guidance and suggestions for stock exchanges, investors, corporations, and other parties that have a role in the process of developing good corporate governance.'

The Code itself contains two sections dealing with Companies and Institutional Shareholders. Each of the sections contains principles, supporting principles and a number of Code Provisions. The layout is as follows:

18 PSOJ, Code on Corporate Governance, 2nd edn (2009) 1, 8.

19 OECD, *Principles of Corporate Governance* (OECD, Paris 2004), <http://www.oecd.org/corporate/oecdprinciplesofcorporategovernance.htm>

Section 1 Companies

A. Directors

A.1 The Board
A.2 Decision-making
A.3 Chairperson and Chief Executive
A.4 Board balance and independence
A.5 Appointments to the Board
A.6 Information and professional development
A.7 Performance evaluation
A.8 Re-election

B. Remuneration

B.1 The level and make-up of remuneration
B.2 Procedure

C. Accountability and Audit

C.1 Financial reporting
C.2 Internal controls
C.3 Audit committee and auditors

D. Relations with shareholders

D.1 Dialogue with Institutional Shareholders
D.2 Constructive use of the AGM

E. Timely and balanced disclosures

Section 2 Institutional shareholders

F. Institutional Shareholders

F.1 Dialogue with companies
F.2 Evaluation of governance disclosures
F.3 Shareholder voting

An Appendix provides specific requirements for disclosure in the Annual Report.

Although there were early attempts to draft a Corporate Governance Code for Trinidad and Tobago,[20] it was not until 2013 that a Code was finally published under a project led by the Caribbean Corporate Governance Institute (CCGI) in partnership with the Trinidad and Tobago Chamber of Commerce and Industry and the Trinidad and Tobago Stock Exchange. A team of industry stakeholders as a working group supervised the drafting and development of the Code, with CCGI acting as the Secretariat. The Code follows globally accepted best practices in corporate governance

20 'The draft report for Trinidad and Tobago was informed by the review of the Securities Industry Act 1995, its by-laws and associated legislation. Among the recommendations coming out of the review were new provisions on management discussion and analysis, publication of interim (quarterly) financial statements, certification of annual financial statements by the CEO and CFO, and development of corporate governance requirements, including the functioning, responsibility and composition of boards of directors and the development of audit committee responsibilities.' Caribbean Community Secretariat- Economic Intelligence and Policy Unit, *Caribbean Trade and Investment Report: Strategies for Recovery, Renewal and Reform* (Ian Randle Publishers, Jamaica 2010) 348.

but has been customised to suit the local economy and business dynamics of Trinidad and Tobago.

The format of the Code includes five high-level concepts of 'Principles' that 'encapsulate the foundation of good corporate governance'. Each Principle includes a number of Recommendations and Guidance in better understanding the practical application and benefits of adopting each recommendation. The Principles are:

1. Establish a Framework for Effective Governance: *Every company should be headed by an Effective Board which is collectively responsible for the long-term success of the company.*
2. Strengthen the Composition and performance of Board and Committees: *There should be a balance of independence and diversity of skills, knowledge, experience, perspectives and gender among Directors so that the Board works effectively.*
3. Reinforce Loyalty and Independence: *All Directors should act honestly and in good faith, in the best interest of the company, ahead of other interests.*
4. Foster Accountability: *The Board should present accurate, timely, balanced and understandable assessment of the company's performance, position and prospects.*
5. Strengthen Relationships with Shareholders: *The Board should promote constructive relationships with all shareholders that facilitate the exercise of their ownership rights and encourage their engagement with the company.*

Both the PSOJ, for Jamaica, and CCGI, for Trinidad and Tobago, have already begun working on revisions of their codes with the input of regulators and the business community.

The Barbados Stock Exchange (BSE) released its C*orporate Governance Recommendations for the Listed Companies on the Barbados Stock Exchange Inc.* in 2013 and the recommendations came into effect on 1 January 2014. This publication represents the first set of corporate governance guidelines for listed companies and complements, and in some cases supplements, statutory guidelines contained existing legislation and regulations. The 64 recommendations are organised into ten sections as follows:

1. Introduction
2. The General Meeting
3. The Board of Directors
4. Committees of the Board
5. Managing Director/Chief Executive Officer
6. Other Management
7. Disclosure of Director and Executive Compensation
8. Internal Controls, Risk Management and Internal Audit
9. Insider Administration
10. Communication and Disclosure

The publication stresses that recommendations are not meant to be prescriptive and requires companies to comply with or explain their deviation from particular recommendations.

In terms of other national codes on corporate governance, the central banks of Barbados, Jamaica and Trinidad and Tobago, have all issued guidelines specifically for the Banks' licensees. The Central Bank of Barbados issued its revised *Corporate Governance Guideline* to its licensees in February 2013, updating guidelines first issued in October 2006. The Central Bank of Trinidad and Tobago published guidelines on Corporate Governance in May 2007 and is applicable to (i) institutions licensed under the Financial Institutions Act, 1993 (FIA) (ii) institutions registered under the Insurance Act, Chap 84:01 (IA). The Bank of Jamaica published its *Standard of Best Practices for Effective Corporate Governance of Deposit-Taking Entities* in July 2008.

Underpinning all the country corporate governance codes and guidelines are the OECD Principles of Corporate Governance which were first published in 1999, focusing on publicly traded companies with the aim of helping governments in member countries improve the legal, institutional and regulatory framework that reinforces corporate governance. The Principles, which are neither prescriptive nor binding, have been the benchmark of good governance used by stock exchanges, investors, corporations and other parties, concerned with promoting good corporate governance, particularly in emerging economies. In April 2004, a revised version of the Principles was approved by OECD members in the wake of corporate scandals and crises at the turn of the century and a series of new and modified recommendations were included. The revised Principles give shareholders an increased role in a number of areas, including executive remuneration and the appointment of board members, and companies are now urged to ensure that mechanisms to address possible conflicts of interest, to recognise and safeguard the rights of stakeholders and to protect individual whistle-blowers are in place. Additionally, the Principles call on company boards to be truly accountable to shareholders and to take ultimate responsibility for their firm's adherence to a high standard of corporate behaviour and ethics.

Undoubtedly, though somewhat late in the game, countries in the Caribbean are taking the steps necessary to improve the region's productivity and competitiveness and its ability to attract investment in order to drive economic growth and prosperity for the citizens of the region. The factors driving competitiveness and growth are many and varied, but undoubtedly, along with issues such as education and training, technological progress, macroeconomic stability, firm sophistication and market efficiency, good governance is a key contributor.

The 2014–2015 Global Competitiveness Report published by the World Economic Forum, gives a snapshot of the standings of Jamaica, Trinidad and Tobago and Barbados on several indicators that impinge on good governance. Comparing the results of the 2013–2014 report indicates that while there were significant improvements in the scores for Jamaica in all but one indicator (strength of auditing and reporting standards, which slipped by one point), Barbados saw an improvement in only one indicator, 'strength of investor protection', and declines in all others. While Trinidad and Tobago's ranking on the indicator 'strength of investor protection' was the best in the region and improved year over year, the country scored poorly on all of the other selected indicators.

Table 1 Comparison of selected global competitiveness indicators for Barbados, Jamaica and Trinidad and Tobago

Indicator	*Barbados*		*Jamaica*		*Trinidad & Tobago*	
	2014–2015 out of 144	*2013–2014 out of 148*	*2014–2015 out of 144*	*2013–2014 out of 148*	*2014–2015 out of 144*	*2013–2014 out of 148*
Efficacy of corporate boards	42	32	50	61	110	116
Ethical behaviour of firms	28	25	74	97	125	118
Strength of investor protection	130	134	68	69	22	25
Protection of minority shareholders' interests	51	39	41	51	116	111
Regulation of securities exchanges	33	25	28	28	95	79
Strength of auditing and reporting standards	22	18	35	34	87	95

THE ROLE OF INFLUENCERS IN PROMOTING BEST PRACTICES IN DISCLOSURE

In a 2002 Global Investor Opinion Survey by McKinsey & Company,[21] institutional investors indicated that they put corporate governance on a par with financial indicators when evaluating investment decisions, with strengthening the quality of accounting disclosure as the top priority. Corporate governance is at the heart of investment decisions – an overwhelming majority of investors are prepared to pay a premium, between 20% and 25% in Latin America for companies adhering to high standards of governance. Governance reforms implemented by countries have been welcomed by investors with more than 60% of the respondents in the study indicating that governance considerations might lead them to avoid individual companies with poor governance. In addition to strengthening corporate transparency, investors want companies to create more independent boards and achieve greater boardroom effectiveness through such steps as better director selection, more disciplined board evaluation processes and greater time commitment from directors.

The Intergovernmental Working Group of Experts on International Standards of Accounting and Reporting (ISAR) is the only intergovernmental expert body focused on corporate transparency and accounting issues. Hosted by the United Nations Conference on Trade and Development (UNCTAD), ISAR's work covers a range of financial and non-financial corporate reporting issues and assists developing countries and

21 McKinsey & Company's Global Investor Opinion Survey was undertaken between April and May 2002, in cooperation with the Global Corporate Governance Forum. The survey is based on responses from over 200 institutional investors, collectively responsible for some US$2 trillion of assets under management (their organisations manage an estimated US$9 trillion AuM (or assets under management)).

economies in transition to implement best practices in corporate transparency and accounting in order to facilitate investment flows and economic development.

A study on corporate governance disclosure undertaken by Syntegra Change Architects in Trinidad and Tobago in 2011[22] found that the average enterprise in Trinidad and Tobago was disclosing less than half of the items in the benchmark of good practices in corporate governance disclosure developed by ISAR. The study further found that while 12 of the items in the ISAR benchmark of 51 items were disclosed by more than two-thirds of the enterprises studies, 37 items were disclosed by less than half of these enterprises. The absolute number of disclosure items found for each company ranged from three to 45, indicating a high level of variability between 'best practice' companies and companies with minimal disclosure practices. The study concluded that:

> . . . while the sample has relatively high rates of disclosure for a few topics, with most companies exceeding the disclosure requirements of Trinidad and Tobago, the overall level of disclosure remains low compared to other emerging markets.

The study examined a sample of 31 large enterprises listed on the TTSE.

A similar study to evaluate the level of implementation of good practices in corporate governance disclosures using the ISAR benchmark, was undertaken in the following year in Jamaica, in collaboration with the PSOJ and the Institute of Chartered Accountants of Jamaica (ICAJ). The sample comprised 26 of the 38 firms listed on the main market of the JSE that make up the JSE's Composite Index. Like the Trinidad and Tobago study, the study did not attempt to measure the quality of the disclosure of the individual items on the benchmark list, but rather to determine whether the company disclosed at all. The results showed that there were 31 of the 51 items on the ISAR benchmark that are required to be disclosed under Jamaican laws and regulations and that 77% of the companies in the sample had disclosed less than the 31 items.[23]

TRAINING FOR DIRECTORS

There have been various initiatives over the past decade to train directors in the essentials of corporate governance. In the early 2000s there were a few isolated initiatives undertaken by some institutions to organise conferences and Central Banks and institutes of chartered secretaries hosted workshops to sensitise their members to corporate governance.

---

22 Dr Axel Kravatzky (ed), *Corporate Governance Disclosure in Trinidad and Tobago A case study by Syntegra Change Architects of Trinidad and Tobago* (Paper Presented to UNCTAD Working Group of Experts on International Standards of Accounting and Reporting (ISAR), Session, 12–14 October 2011, Palais des Nations, Geneva, Syntegra Change Architects Ltd, 14 October 2011).

23 Dennis Brown and Axel Kravatzky (Presenters), 'Review of the Implementation Status of Corporate Governance Disclosures: Case Study Jamaica' (Report by Syntegra Change Architects Ltd of Trinidad and Tobago in collaboration with the PSOJ, UNCTAD ISAR 2012).

One international body that has been active in the region throughout the period is the Global Corporate Governance Forum, a programme of the World Bank/International Finance Corporation based in Washington, DC. From 31 March 31 to 5 April 2008, the Forum hosted a six-day International Faculty Workshop financed through a multi-donor trust fund that was co-founded by the World Bank Group and the OECD. The Forum promotes global, regional, and local initiatives that aim to improve the institutional framework and practices of corporate governance and developed a Corporate Governance Board Leadership Training Resource Kit that was designed to serve the growing need for curriculum and training methodologies for CG training provided by Institutes of Directors, Corporate Governance Associations, professional bodies, universities and other educational institutions. The 2008 workshop hosted 18 participants from 17 countries in Latin America, Europe, Africa, Middle East/North Africa and South East Asia. Jamaica was the only Caribbean country represented.

In March 2009, the PSOJ and the Forum organised and hosted a 3 ½ day regional 'train-the-trainer' programme in Kingston, Jamaica for 18 trainers. The goal of this highly interactive workshop was to enhance director-training capacity in the region and help participants become familiar with and learn how to use the Corporate Governance Board Leadership Training Resources Kit produced by the Forum. The workshops were led by international faculty – Anne Molyneux, a consultant in financial market regulation, corporate governance, financial reporting, accounting, audit regulation and practice, Dr Mary Jo Larson, Principal of FlexAbility International and Santiago Chaher, consultant to the IFC – and the PSOJ's CEO Sandra Glasgow, who was trained by the Forum as a Trainer in the use of the Resources Kit at the international workshop held in 2008. Twelve Jamaicans representing public sector agencies, including the Ministry of Finance and the Public Service and the Financial Services Commission, private sector companies and the University of the West Indies participated in the workshop. Six of the participants hailed from Trinidad and Tobago and Barbados representing private sector companies and the UWI's Cave Hill and St Augustine campuses.

Since 2008, train-the-trainer workshops, using the Resources Tool Kit, have been held in Jamaica, Trinidad and Tobago and the Bahamas. Workshops for directors have also been delivered in Jamaica, Trinidad and Tobago, St Lucia and the Bahamas, using the Tool Kit.[24]

Between 2009 and 2013, the PSOJ implemented a project, supported by the Multilateral Investment Fund (MIF) of the Inter-American Development Bank to raise awareness among family businesses (FBs) in Jamaica about the importance of corporate governance and to provide training and technical assistance in family business governance and strategies. Over 1,000 persons were directly or indirectly sensitised about the value of corporate governance and related management practices for FBs, across the island, 30 firms received training and technical assistance and ten FBs received in-depth technical assistance and access to external resources to address their

24 Under an agreement with the IFC, the author was the 'master trainer' for the Caribbean in the use of the Resources Tool Kit.

specific needs. Seven case studies were published, as well as a video case, to share the lessons learned and for use in training and sensitising other FBs.

Other institutions in the Caribbean have also provided training in corporate governance. One of the better known institutions is GovStrat Limited,[25] a Jamaican Management Consulting and Learning Facilitation firm founded in 2003 by Vindel Kerr, CEO and Chief Corporate Governance & Strategic Planning Consultant. GovStrat has been a key player in training regional Boards of Directors and Senior Executives in courses covering *Effective Corporate Governance, Strategic Planning, Enterprise Risk Management & Internal Control, Managing Corporate Reputation and Brands* and *Performance Management*. The Caribbean Governance Training Institute,[26] based in St Lucia, offers courses for Board Members, Key Committee Chairs and Board Chairs of Caribbean Organisations, Executive Directors and senior Caribbean Organisation staff. More recently, the Caribbean Corporate Governance Institute, the only non-profit professional membership organisation in the Caribbean was formed in September 2013.[27] CCGI serves directors, investors, and corporate governance stakeholders through its work in developing and shaping best practice Corporate Governance Standards across the Caribbean, providing access to accredited educational programmes and helping directors improve their access to peer and international networks of corporate governance leaders.

WOMEN ON BOARDS

While many countries and businesses have made strides toward narrowing the gender gap, the vast potential of women to contribute to business and economic growth has yet to be realised. Enlightened people around the world see this gap as an opportunity for change – to realise and harness the powerful and positive effect that women's empowerment and leadership can have on local economies and on the wider global economy. As a director who has sat on the boards of private and publicly listed companies, public sector agencies and not-for-profit entities, and as a female, I am particularly passionate about this topic.

The International Labour Organisation (ILO) in its January 2015 report, *Women in Business and Management: Gaining Momentum*, has compiled data[28] which ranks Jamaica number one as having the largest share of women in management (59.3%) among 108 countries in the world. Barbados ranks 13th with 43.4% and Trinidad and Tobago 14th with 43.1%.

Research undertaken in a Canadian International Development Agency-sponsored study in 2007 by the Women's Resource Outreach Centre (WROC) in Jamaica, revealed that while women have made significant strides in educational and

25 GovStrat: Governance, Development and Competitiveness Consultants and Learning Facilitators, 'Who We Are' <http://www.govstratltd.com/who-we-are/>.

26 Caribbean Governance Training Institute <http://caribbeangovernancetraining.com/>.

27 ibid.

28 International Labour Office, *Women in business and management gaining momentum* (International Labour Organisation 2015).

professional development, their participation on corporate boards had only moved by 2% from 14% to 16% over the ten-year period, 1998–2007, notably worse than the data for public sector boards where women's participation moved by 4% from 29% to 33% over the same period.

A survey in 2013 conducted by the not-for-profit organisation, Catalyst Inc. on the percentage of board seats held by women in 44 countries revealed that in just four countries – Finland, Sweden, Norway and the United Kingdom – women represent over 20% of board members; in 13 countries, between 10% and 20%; in four countries between 5% and 10% and in 13 countries less than 5%.

An examination of the Annual Reports of 46 companies listed on the Main and Junior Markets of the Jamaica Stock Exchange revealed that 17% of the board seats in these companies were held by women and that on only two of these Boards were women the Chairpersons. A similar exercise with the Barbados Stock Exchange showed that of the ten companies listed, 19% of the board members were women; on the Eastern Caribbean Securities Exchange, of nine companies listed, 23% of board members were women.

There is no disputing the fact that women in the Caribbean have attained high levels of education, expertise and track records that more than qualify them for board membership; but like other women around the world, they remain at a competitive disadvantage with men because it is generally men who make board appointments and they tend to look for new candidates to be appointed to boards within their own personal and professional networks.

In 2011, an alliance of women's organisations and individuals, the 51% Coalition, was formed to advocate for quotas as a way of achieving equity and empowering more than half of the Jamaican population: women. Their goal is for legislation to be enacted that will see to it that no gender should have more than 60% or less than 40% of seats in the Senate (Upper House of Parliament), or on boards in the private or public sectors.

Proponents of the argument for gender diversity on boards and indeed on quotas as a means of accelerating women's participation in the governance process often cite a number of competences that women bring to board deliberations and make the claim that companies having more women on their boards perform better than male-dominated boards. As reported by the 2015 ILO study, in 2011 a report published by Catalyst Inc. found that:

> Fortune 500 companies with the most women board directors outperformed those with the least by 16 per cent on return on sales. Companies with the most women on their boards outperformed those with the least by 26 per cent on return on invested capital. Companies with high representation of women – three or more – on their boards for at least four to five years, significantly outperformed those with low representation by 84 per cent on return on sales, by 60 per cent on return invested capital and by 46 per cent on return on equity.[29]

29 International Labour Office, *Women in business and management gaining momentum* (International Labour Organisation 2015) 9.

The significant presence of women at all management levels in Caribbean societies increases the pool of talented and qualified people to be appointed to boards. Improved corporate performance is therefore a logical outcome. Women are running more businesses and consumer spending decisions are increasingly being made by them and, since women constitute the majority of consumers in Jamaica and Barbados (50.75% of the Jamaican population; 50.1% in Barbados), it would seem wise for companies to see the value of having women on their boards in order for them to be better attuned to the needs of their stakeholders.

A basic tenet of good corporate governance is that boards should have an appropriate mix of skills, experience and independence to enable their members to discharge their duties and responsibilities effectively. It is now generally accepted and included in the Corporate Governance Codes for the three countries in the Caribbean that have been discussed. The PSOJ Code, however, goes the furthest in defining the notion of diversity (A1.1):

> The composition of the Board should enable this important decision-making body to properly exercise its role and add value to the company and all shareholders. The number of directors, diversity and experience, skills and knowledge, and the directors' ability to independently challenge the management and provide strategic advice on the direction of the company are all elements that shape the board's effectiveness. Diversity relates to academic qualifications, technical expertise, relevant industry knowledge, gender, age and ethnicity.

The Barbados Recommendation (#13) on the qualification of directors states:

> The effectiveness of the Board will require an appropriate level of knowledge by the individuals comprising the Board of the company's strategy and operations and an understanding of the industry in which the company operates. It is imperative that the Board be composed of Directors with versatile and mutually complementing capabilities and competencies. The age mix and gender proportion should also be taken into account in shaping the composition of the Board to ensure that the necessary balance is achieved.

The Trinidad & Tobago Code (Recommendation 2.2) states:

> Directors should be selected and appointed through rigorous and formal processes designed to give the Board a balance of independence and diversity of skills, knowledge, experience, perspectives and gender among Directors so that the Board works effectively.

The Guidance further states that: 'The Board should formalise its position and approach toward boardroom diversity. These policies and targets should be disclosed in the annual report along with measures taken to meet those targets.'

Despite the forward thinking of the framers of these Codes, the continued inequity in appointing women as directors appears to reflect a myopic view of women's capabilities and the justification of the retention of all-male boards may hinge on the perception by men that it is easier to achieve board solidarity and collegiality by excluding women. There is also a lingering view that women are not as well equipped with the 'hard' business or financial skills as are their male counterparts. And yet the empirical research does not support either viewpoint. In fact, there is plenty of evidence that suggests that encouraging frank debate among board members who have diverse views and experiences can and does enhance the leadership and stewardship of companies.[30] Moreover, a major study conducted by the Conference Board of Canada in 2002[31] on women and corporate boards suggested a strong link between female numbers on boards and good-governance credentials. The researchers found that:

- 94% of boards with three or more women (compared to 58% of all-male boards) insist on conflict-of-interest guidelines;
- more female than male directors pay attention to audit and risk oversight and control;
- women, more than men, tend to consider the needs of more categories of stakeholders; and
- women, more than men, tend to examine a wider range of management and organisational performance.
- 72% of boards with two or more women conduct formal board performance evaluations, while only 49% of all-male boards do;
- companies that provide boards of directors with formal, written limits to authority have a greater percentage of women directors than do organisations with no formal limits to authority; and
- organisations that provide boards of directors with formal orientation programmes have a greater percentage of women directors than do organisations with no such programme.

According to the same report:

> . . . strategic thinking and a strong ability to foresee and manage risk are enhanced by ensuring a varied set of perspectives around the boardroom table. Not only will the board more accurately mirror the diverse owners and stakeholders of the organisation, it will lead to better strategic decision-making and planning.

So having established the basis for women's participation on boards and dispelling the myth that women are not as well qualified to serve on boards we must now turn our minds to 'how' we can change the existing paradigms and break the proverbial glass ceilings that keep many women out of the boardroom. Or, if companies have been visionary enough to ensure that women are represented on their boards, how to ensure that there is greater equity in their participation.

---

30 Much of the discussion presented in this section has been adapted from a speech given by the author at the launch of the Women's Resource Outreach Centre's publication, 'Gender & Governance: Implications for the Participation of Women on Boards & Commissions in Jamaica' and the launch of Training Programme, *Strengthening Women's Leadership in Jamaica* at the Jamaica Pegasus Hotel on 25 March 2009. Parts of the speech were also used in the PSOJ's publication, *Handbook and Tool Kit: Best Practices in Good Governance* (2009) 2, Section 3.1: The Case for Gender Diversity on Boards.

31 The Conference Board of Canada, 'Women on Boards . . . Not just the Right Thing . . . But the "Bright" Thing' (2002).

So what are some of the strategies that advocates for women on boards can employ to overcome these hurdles?

1. Identify those with the power to award or influence a directorship and help them to identify good candidates who could be considered for board membership. Unfortunately, women with education, expertise and the necessary qualifications for board membership are not often on the radar screens of the people, usually men, who make board appointments and this is, in part, because these professional women tend not to be part of their personal and professional networks. So those that make these appointments need our support.
2. Actively seek out women who could be future directors and encourage them to prepare themselves through training.
3. Proactively develop and maintain databases of qualified female candidates who desire to sit on boards.
4. Encourage and support women who are potential future directors, by inviting them to events and activities that will assist them in breaking into the networks that matter (e.g. service clubs, corporate boxes at entertainment and sporting events, and so on) and mentoring them, preferably by an existing director.
5. Ensure a transparent selection process, particularly for boards in the public sector.
6. Mobilise investor and minority shareholders, who can be very effective lobbies for gender equity on boards. (Here let me acknowledge Mrs Clark-Allwood who has been an ardent advocate for greater female participation on boards, at annual general meetings of listed companies in Jamaica.)
7. Advocate for Central Government and Regulators (including Stock Exchanges, Central Banks and Industry Associations) to develop their own strategies. These bodies should modify their Corporate Governance Principles and Standards to qualify what is meant by 'appropriate range of skills and experience' with examples that include diversity in board membership, as the PSOJ has done in its 2009 Code. Publicly listed companies and public bodies should be required to report annually on the diversity of their boards and committees.
8. Civil society groups should host round table events, institute programmes and make representation to the Government on the need for more women on the boards of public bodies.

Undoubtedly, advocates for more women on boards (men and women) must continue to press for these changes, for as Kouzes and Posner in their book *The Leadership Challenge*[32] assert:

> Leaders are at their best when they challenge the process, inspire a shared vision, enable others to act, model the way, and encourage the heart.

32 James Kouzes and Barry Posner, *The Leadership Challenge* (3rd edn, Jossey Bass 2002).

CONCLUSION

It is now generally accepted that good corporate governance plays a pivotal role in improving investor confidence and creating long-term value for companies – public and private – and stimulating competitive and efficient markets that support economic growth, poverty alleviation and income distribution in the Commonwealth Caribbean.

The Caribbean region has had its fair share of corporate failures and scandals, and though the impact of these events had not been as deleterious as those in the US and UK or other parts of the world, efforts to bolster corporate governance frameworks at the regional and country level and in-firm practices have nevertheless been crucial to broadening the investor base and attracting equity capital for development. The countries of the Commonwealth Caribbean have made significant strides, over the last decade, in improving their policy and regulatory frameworks and introducing world class standards in governance. Regrettably, efforts to forge a regional strategy and to develop a regional Code on Corporate Governance have largely failed. However, three countries, Jamaica, Trinidad and Tobago and Barbados, have formalised and published their own Codes on Corporate Governance as Guidelines and Recommendations to publicly listed and unlisted companies – small, medium and large – to help company directors adopt world-class practices as a normal part of doing business. The rationale for these codes is that not only will the firms themselves benefit, but so too will the economies of each country, and indeed the region. Actors in the region's economies have clearly accepted the 'business case' for good corporate governance, that adopting best practices brings about:

- better access to external finance;
- lower cost of capital;
- improved performance;
- reduced risk of corporate crises and scandals;
- increased company values; and
- higher firm valuations and share performance.

Accepting that these benefits exist is, however, not enough. The region as a whole must continue on the path to harmonising its regulatory frameworks and must build on the work done in Barbados, Jamaica and Trinidad and Tobago to create a solid platform that will demonstrate the region's seriousness and commitment to limiting the risks of failures and scandals that could threaten the stability of the region's economies and tarnish the reputation of corporate leaders and directors. Addressing issues of diversity and, in particular, utilising the skills and experiences of the region's women, as well as deepening the knowledge base of existing and potential directors must be at the forefront of development efforts as the region strives to accelerate its development as an attractive and competitive market for investment.

BIBLIOGRAPHY

'Gender & Governance: Implications for the Participation of Women on Boards & Commissions in Jamaica' (2009) Presented at the Training Programme: Strengthening Women's Leadership in Jamaica, Women's Resource Outreach Centre

Axel Kravatzky, Dr A (ed), 'Corporate Governance Disclosure in Trinidad and Tobago: A case study by Syntegra Change Architects of Trinidad and Tobago' (2011) UNCTAD Working Group of Experts on International Standards of Accounting and Reporting (ISAR), Session, 12–14 October 2011, Palais des Nations, Geneva, Syntegra Change Architects Ltd

Becht, M, Bolton, P and Röell, A, 'Corporate Governance and Control' (2005) European Corporate Governance Institute Finance Working Paper No 02/2002 <http://unpan1.un.org/intradoc/groups/public/documents/apcity/unpan033582.pdf> accessed December 2014

Blake, T, 'Corporate Governance in the Caribbean Environment. The Caribbean Corporate Governance Forum' (Power Point) <www.caricom.org/caribbean_corporate_governance_forum>

Brown, D, and Kravatzky, A (Presenters), 'Review of the Implementation Status of Corporate Governance Disclosures: Case Study Jamaica' (2012) Report by Syntegra Change Architects Ltd of Trinidad & Tobago in collaboration with The PSOJ, UNCTAD ISAR

Cadbury, A, *Corporate Governance and Chairmanship: A Personal View*, 2004, OUP

Caribbean Community Secretariat, Economic Intelligence and Policy Unit, Caribbean Trade and Investment Report: Strategies for Recovery, Renewal and Reform, 2010, Jamaica: Ian Randle Publishers

Caribbean Governance Training Institute <http://caribbeangovernancetraining.com/>

Conference Board of Canada, *Women on Boards . . . Not just the Right Thing . . . But the 'Bright' Thing*, 2002

Girvan, N, 'Towards a Single Economy and a Single Development Vision' (2006) University of the West Indies in Collaboration with the CARICOM Secretariat and the Special Task Force on the Single Economy

GovStrat: Governance, Development and Competitiveness Consultants and Learning Facilitators, 'Who We Are' <http://www.govstratltd.com/who-we-are/>

Hill, C (Address, Senator, Minister, Ministry of Finance), 'Statement of the council of securities Regulators of the Americas' (2001) Trinidad Hilton and Conference Centre <http://www.ttsec.org.tt/content/sp020219.pdf>

International Labour Office, *Women in Business and Management Gaining Momentum*, 2015, International Labour Organisation

Jackson, MK, 'Ownership, Corporate Governance and Liquidity in Caribbean Firms' (2013) MPhil thesis, Queensland University of Technology <http://eprints.qut.edu.au/63853/>

Kirkpatrick, G, 'The Corporate Governance Lessons from the Financial Crisis' (2009) OECD Financial Market Trends Pre-publication

Kouzes, J and Posner, B, *The Leadership Challenge*, 3rd edn, 2002, Jossey Bass

OECD, *Principles of Corporate Governance*, 2004, Paris: OECD <http://www.oecd.org/dataoecd/32/18/31557724.pdf>

Oman, C, Steven, F and Willem, B, 'Corporate Governance in Developing, Transition and Emerging-Market Economies' (2003) OECD Centre Policy Brief No 23 <http://www.oecd.org/social/poverty/28658158.pdf>

PSOJ, *Code on Corporate Governance*, 2nd edn, 2009

PSOJ, *Corporate Governance, The Way Forward*, 2006

PSOJ, *Handbook and Tool Kit: Best Practices in Good Governance*, 2009

Smith, A, 'An Inquiry into the Nature and Causes of the Wealth of Nations' (1904) Edwin Cannan (ed) <http://www.econlib.org/library/Smith/smWN.html> accessed 18 December 2014

William, L, 'Recent Financial Failures in the Caribbean – What were the Causes What Lessons Can Be Learnt?' (2012) *Barbados Underground* <http://da- academy.org/Financial_Crisis_in_the_Caribbean.pdf>

CHAPTER 3

DUTIES AND RESPONSIBILITIES OF DIRECTORS AND OFFICERS

Suzanne Ffolkes-Goldson

INTRODUCTION

Much of the emphasis on increased corporate governance standards in the Commonwealth Caribbean region has focussed on the role and responsibilities of directors and officers of the company. This is no doubt due to the fact that there is general consensus that many of the corporate failings worldwide have been due, in some part, to poor management and accountability. This is true of the corporate collapses in the Commonwealth Caribbean, in particular, the financial crisis in Jamaica in the early 1990s[1] and financial debacles in Trinidad and Tobago in the early 2000s.[2] Where much of the Commonwealth Caribbean has adopted the Canadian style company law model, they have also incorporated a greater degree of director and officer responsibility and liability. With the increased exposure of directors and officers in Companies Acts in the region there has also been an introduction of varying degrees of protection, including a due diligence defence, and director and officer indemnification. The legislation also permits the availability of insurance protection which was previously unavailable. The business judgment rule has also emerged through Canadian case law as a defence for directors' breach of duty and arguably could therefore form a part of the Commonwealth Caribbean corporate law jurisprudence.

The corporate governance responsibilities of directors and officers may be found in a wide range of legislation, including legislation and rules regulating financial institutions and environmental legislation. This chapter focusses on the Companies Acts and Corporate Governance Codes in the region. The duties and responsibilities of directors and officers as a part of public sector governance, are discussed elsewhere in this publication.

FIDUCIARY DUTY – COMPANIES ACTS

The Companies Acts in the Commonwealth Caribbean typically provide that:

(1) Every director and officer of a company in exercising his powers and discharging his duties must/shall;
   (a) act honestly and in good faith with a view to the best interests of the company; and

---

1 Wilberne Persaud, Jamaica Meltdown: Indigenous Financial Sector Crash 1996 (iUniverse, Inc. 2006) 25–26.

2 Hindu Credit Union Report by the Hon Sir Anthony Colman, July 2014 [K35].

(b) exercise the care, diligence and skill that a reasonably prudent person would exercise in comparable circumstances.[3]

Section 1(a) reflects the fiduciary duty of the company and, arguably, is a codification of the common law which includes the duty not to have a conflict of interest, the duty not to make a secret profit and the duty to act in the best interest of the corporation and not for an improper purpose.[4] A conflict of interest is technically a breach of fiduciary duty, however, it may be cured by appropriate disclosure.[5]

Subsection (2) widens the scope of the fiduciary duty to 'take into account' the interests of employees in general as well as the interests of shareholders and most Commonwealth Caribbean Companies Acts typically state:

> (2) In determining what are the best interests of a company, a director **must/shall** have regard to the interests of the company's employees in general as well as to the interests of its shareholder.[6]
>
> (Emphasis added)

although the fiduciary duty is to the company alone. The wording in the Jamaica statute differs and states that:

> In determining what are the best interests of the company, a director or officer may have regard to the interests of the company's shareholders and employees and the community in which the company operates.[7]

It is submitted that directors and officers of companies 'must' consider a number of stakeholders including employees and shareholders in most of the Commonwealth Caribbean territories, however in Jamaica, the directors and officers of companies 'may' take into account an even wider group including the community in which the company operates. While these provisions appear to incorporate corporate social responsibility into the duties of directors and officers, the fiduciary duty is owed to the company alone. Further, the various legislation reminds us that the fiduciary duty of directors and officers is to the company alone. Most of the Commonwealth Caribbean territories refer to subsection (2) above by stating that:

> The duty imposed by subsection(2) on the directors of a company is owed by them to the company alone; and the duty is enforceable in the same way as any other fiduciary duty owed to a company by its directors.[8]

3 Antigua and Barbuda Companies Act 1995 (A&B), s 97(1); Barbados Companies Act- Cap 308 (Bds), s 95(1); Dominica Companies Act 1994 (Dom), s 97(1); Guyana Companies Act 1994- Cap 89:01 (Guy), s 96(1); Jamaica Companies Act 2004 (Ja), s 174(1); St Christopher and Nevis (St Kitts) Companies Act 1996 (St Kitts), s 75 (1); St Lucia Companies Act 2008- Cap 13:01 (St Lucia), s 97(1); Trinidad and Tobago Companies Act 1995- Cap 81:01 (T&T), s 99(1).

4 S Ffolkes-Goldson, 'The Reform of the Law Relating to Duties of Directors in the Commonwealth Caribbean' (2002) *The Company Lawyer* 378–384.

5 A&B, ss 91–93; Bds, ss 89–91; Dom, ss 91–93; Guy, ss 90–92; Ja, ss 193–194; St Kitts, ss 75; St Lucia, ss 89–93; T&T, ss 93–95.

6 A&B, s 97(2); Bds, s 95(2); Dom, s 97(2); Guy, s 96(2); St Kitts, s 75(2); St Lucia, s 97(2); T&T, s 99(2).

7 Ja, s 174(4).

8 A&B, s 97(3); Bds, s 95(3); Dom, s 97(3); Guy, s 96(3); St Lucia, s 97(3); T&T, s 99(3).

However, Jamaica and St Kitts refer to the entire subsection (1) which includes the fiduciary duty and the duty of care, diligence and skill by stating that 'The duties imposed by subsection (1) on the directors or officers of a company is owed to the company alone'.[9]

The consequence of this is that actions brought against directors and officers for breach of their fiduciary duty should be brought as a derivative action, on behalf of the company, as the duty is to the company. It is submitted that since the fiduciary duty is owed to the company alone, where there are competing interests, the interest of the company trumps the interests of any other groups.[10]

The provision on the fiduciary duty of directors and officers in Canadian statutes, on which the provisions of many of the Commonwealth Caribbean company law statutes are based, have been interpreted in the Supreme Court of Canada, as requiring companies to be 'good corporate citizens'.

> In considering what is in the best interests of the corporation, directors may look to the interests of, **inter alia, shareholders, employees, creditors, consumers, governments and the environment** to inform their decisions.[11]
>
> (Emphasis added)

This means that companies ought to take into account the interests of a wide group of stakeholders including employees, customers, the government and the environment. The Supreme Court of Canada, however, has also emphasised that, where there are competing interests, the overriding duty is to the company.

DUTY OF CARE, DILIGENCE AND SKILL – COMPANIES ACTS

Most Commonwealth Caribbean territories include a provision on the duty of care, diligence and skill by stating, in addition to the fiduciary duty found in subsection (1)(a) of the relevant section, that:

> (1) Every director and officer of a company in exercising his powers and discharging his duties must/shall; . . .
>
> (b) exercise the care, diligence and skill that a reasonably prudent person would exercise in comparable circumstances.

This duty has seen an evolution from very little expectation of directors and officers based on a purely subjective standard, found at common law,[12] to what has been accepted as an objective/subjective test of that which 'a reasonably prudent person would exercise in comparable circumstances'.[13]

---

9 Ja, s 174(5); St Kitts, s 74(3).

10 *BCE Inc. v 1976 Debentureholders* [2008] SCC 69 [37], confirming *Peoples Department Stores Inc. (Trustee of) v Wise* [2004] SCC 68.

11 *BCE Inc. v 1976 Debentureholders* [2008] SCC 69 [40], confirming *Peoples Department Stores Inc. (Trustee of) v Wise* [2004] SCC 68.

12 *Re City Equitable Fire Insurance Company Limited* [1925] 1 Ch 407 (CA).

13 A&B, s 97(1)(b); Bds, s 95(1)(b); Dom, s 97(1)(b); Guy, s 96(1)(b); St Lucia, s 97(1)(b); St Kitts, s 74(1)(b); T&T, s 99(1)(b); Ja, s 174(1)(b) which has the additional words 'including, but not limited to the general knowledge, skill and experience of the director or officer'.

The Supreme Court of Canada in *Peoples Department Stores Inc. (Trustee of) v Wise*, stated that the duty of care, diligence and skill 'imposes a legal obligation upon directors and officers to be diligent in supervising and managing the corporation's affairs' and that the test is an objective test and that the words 'in comparable circumstances' introduces a contextual element.[14]

> The standard of care is an objective one. The decisions of directors and officers must be reasonable business decisions in light of all the circumstances, including the prevailing socio-economic conditions, about which they knew or ought to have known.[15]

It remains to be seen whether this interpretation of the provision relating to the duty of care, diligence and skill will be adopted in the Commonwealth Caribbean. It may be argued, however, that the test is objective/subjective in Jamaica, as the provision in the Jamaica Companies Act adds the wording, 'including, but not limited to the general knowledge, skill and experience of the director or officer', thereby deliberately including a subjective element.

It is important to note that the Companies Acts of the territories which include the subsection which states that 'the duty imposed by subsection (2) on the directors of a company is owed by them to the company alone; and the duty is enforceable in the same way as any other fiduciary duty owed to a company by its directors' is making reference only to the fiduciary duty imposed by subsection 1(a) and not to the duty of care, diligence and skill. It is only in Jamaica (which makes reference to the entire section 1) and St Kitts (which makes reference to sections 1 and 2), that the fiduciary duty and duty of care, diligence and skill are owed to the company alone.

This difference is significant, as realised in the *Peoples* case (confirmed in *BCE Inc. v 1976 Debentureholders*[16] (*BCE*)), where it was noted that the duty of care, diligence and skill was owed to stakeholders, including creditors.[17] It appears therefore, that creditors may bring an action for breach of care, diligence and skill, where the statute does not limit the duty to the company alone. The *Peoples* case was decided under the Canada Business Corporations Act (CBCA); however, the Ontario Business Corporations Act (OBCA), which had similar wording, was amended after the ruling in *Peoples*, to require, in addition to the fiduciary duty, that the duty of care, diligence and skill is to the corporation alone.[18]

There is no distinction made between the duties of executive and non-executive directors,[19] however, section 174(6) of the Jamaica Companies Act provides:

> Where pursuant to a contract of service with a company, a director or officer is required to perform management functions, the terms of that contract may require the director

14 *Peoples Department Stores Inc. (Trustee of) v Wise* [2004] SCC 68 [62]. See also S Ffolkes-Goldson, 'Corporate Directors' Duty of Care, Diligence and Skill: *Soper v The Queen*' (1998) *Caribbean Law Bulletin* 53–59.

15 *Peoples Department Stores Inc. (Trustee of) v Wise* [2004] SCC 68.

16 *BCE Inc. v 1976 Debentureholders* [2008] SCC 69.

17 *Peoples Department Stores Inc. (Trustee of) v Wise* [2004] SCC 68 [57].

18 Business Corporations Act RSO 1990, Chapter B.16, s 134(1): 'Every director and officer of a **corporation** in exercising his or her powers and discharging his or her duties to the **corporation** shall . . .' (emphasis added).

19 Ja, s 174(6).

or officer in the exercise of those functions, to observe a higher standard than that specified in subsection (1).

Whether directors owe a fiduciary duty to creditors in the vicinity of insolvency is yet to be decided in the Commonwealth Caribbean. At common law there appeared to be a duty to creditors where the company was in the vicinity of insolvency;[20] however, with the introduction of the oppression remedy, which lists creditors as a member of the victim class, it appears that the oppression remedy is the appropriate remedy for creditors. This is especially the case in most Commonwealth Caribbean territories, where the 'complainant' as well as the victim may be creditor. It is not so clear under the Jamaica Companies Act, in the absence of the ability of a creditor to be a 'complainant' although, as stated earlier, a creditor is a member of the victim class.[21]

DEFENCES

It is accepted in Canadian jurisprudence that a defence to a charge of breach of fiduciary duty and/or breach of the duty of care diligence and skill, is that the director or officer acted in good faith in the best interest of the corporation. In the *Peoples* case it was stated that, 'Directors and officers will not be held to be in breach of the duty of care under s 122(1) (*b*) of the CBCA if they act prudently and on a reasonably informed basis'.[22]

Directors may also invoke a defence of disclosure in accordance with the Companies Act, where the alleged breach of fiduciary duty involves a conflict of interest. The Companies Acts provide that where a director has a 'material' interest in a contract with the company of which he is a director, the director must disclose the contract in accordance with the Act, and may not vote on the contract except in stipulated circumstances.[23] 'Material' is not defined, presumably because a 'material' interest depends on the size and/or type of contract and company. The contract is not void only by reason of the director or officer having a material interest, or by the presence of the director concerned at the meeting or having been counted to determine a quorum at

20 *Kinsela v Russell Kinsela Pty. Ltd (in liquidation)* (1986) 4 NSWLR 722, 730 which was cited with approval in *West Mercier Safetywear Ltd (in liquidation) v Dodd* [1988] BCLC 250 (CA). Also, *Nicholson v Permakraft (NZ) Ltd* [1985] 1 NZLR 242 and *Walker v Wimborne* (1975–1976) 137 CLR [1985] 1 NZLR 242, 249. See also P Davies and L Gower, *Principles of Modern Company Law* (7th edn, Sweet and Maxwell London 2003) 372; Farrar, Furey, Hannigan, *Farrar's Company Law* (3rd edn, Butterworths London 1991) 386; J S Ziegel, Ronald J Daniels, J G MacIntosh and D Johnston, *Cases and Materials on Partnerships and Canadian Business Corporations* (3rd edn, Carswell Toronto 1994) 176. See also, S Ffolkes-Goldson, 'Directors' Duties to Creditors on or in the Vicinity of Insolvency in the Commonwealth Caribbean: Should the Peoples Decision of the Supreme Court of Canada be Followed?' (2006) 6(1) *Oxford University Commonwealth Law Journal* 61–75.

21 S Ffolkes-Goldson, 'The Use and Misuse of the Corporate Oppression Remedy in the Commonwealth Caribbean' (2014) 35(7) *The Company Lawyer* 195–204.

22 *Peoples Department Stores Inc. (Trustee of) v Wise* [2004] SCC 68 [67].

23 A&B, ss 91–92; Bds, ss 89–90; Dom, ss 91–92; Guy, ss 90–91; St Kitts, s 76; St Lucia, ss 91–92; T&T, ss 93–94.

the meeting at which the contract is approved.[24] The Jamaica Companies Act states, however that, subject to the exceptions in the First Schedule, the director concerned, should not be in the room where the vote takes place nor shall he be counted in the quorum present at that meeting.[25] The prohibitions, however, may 'be suspended or relaxed to any extent, and either generally or in respect of any particular contract, arrangement or transaction, by the company in general meeting'.[26]

The Jamaica Companies Act differs from its Commonwealth Caribbean counterparts by the introduction of a due diligence defence through which directors and officers can find safe-haven. The provision was inspired by the due diligence provisions of the CBCA and states:

> A director or officer of a company shall not be in breach of his duty under this section if the director or officer exercised due care, diligence and skill in the performance of that duty or believed in the existence of facts that, if true, would render the director's or officer's conduct reasonably prudent.
>
> For the purposes of this section, a director or officer shall be deemed to have acted with due care, diligence and skill where, in the absence of fraud or bad faith, the director or officer reasonably relied in good faith on documents relating to the company's affairs, including financial statements, reports of experts or on information presented by other directors or, where appropriate, other officers and professionals.[27]

Directors and officers may also invoke the 'business judgment rule' which had its genesis in US law but has now been accepted as part of the Canadian Corporate Law jurisprudence. The 'business judgment rule' has been defined in *Maple Leaf Foods Inc. v Schneider Corp.* in the following terms:

> The law as it has evolved in Ontario and Delaware has the common requirements that the court must be satisfied that the directors have acted reasonably and fairly. **The court looks to see that the directors made a *reasonable* decision *not a perfect* decision. Provided the decision taken is within a range of reasonableness, the court ought not to substitute its opinion for that of the board even though subsequent events may have cast doubt on the board's determination.** As long as the directors have selected one of several reasonable alternatives, deference is accorded to the board's decision. This formulation of deference to the decision of the Board is known as the 'business judgment rule'.[28]
>
> (Emphasis added)

The Supreme Court of Canada more recently confirmed the 'business judgment rule' as a defence in the *BCE* case where it was stated:

> Courts should give appropriate deference to the business judgment of directors who take into account these ancillary interests, as reflected by the business judgment rule. The 'business judgment rule' accords deference to a business decision, so long as it lies

24 A&B, s 93; Bds, s 91; Dom, s 93; Guy, s 92; St Lucia, s 93; T&T, s 95.
25 Ja, s 193(2) and First Schedule [90].
26 Ja, First Schedule [90].
27 Ja, s 174(2) and (3).
28 (1998) 42 OR (3d) 177 at 192.

> within a range of reasonable alternatives . . . this applies to decisions on stakeholders' interests, as much as other directorial decisions.[29]

The adoption of the American style 'business judgment rule' in Canada is based on the 2004 amendments to the CBCA, through a 'due diligence' defence, and therefore, may not apply to many of the Commonwealth Caribbean territories, which did not adopt those amendments. On the other hand, under what is considered a 'Commonwealth Business Judgment Doctrine' (where a businessman's foresight is not to be substituted for his hindsight), it may be argued that the doctrine forms a part of the corporate law jurisprudence of the Commonwealth Caribbean.[30]

It appears that the 'business judgment rule' was contemplated, albeit it is submitted wrongly in the context of the fiduciary duty, in the case of *Eagle Merchant Bank of Jamaica Ltd and Crown Eagle Life Insurance Co. Ltd v Paul Chen-Young and Ajax Investments Limited and Domville Limited.*[31] This case was decided before the 2004 Companies Act and rested its decision on the common law duty of directors. However, since Jamaica introduced a due diligence defence along the lines of the amendment to the CBCA, it may be argued that the 'business judgment rule', now forms a part of Jamaica company law. Hopefully the courts in the region will address this one day in the near future.

PENALTIES – COMPANIES ACTS

Directors and officers are exposed to a wide range of criminal and civil penalties for offences under companies legislation. These include disqualification, joint and several liability, fines and imprisonment.

Disqualification by the Court may occur, on an application by the Registrar, where the director is considered unfit to be concerned in the management of the company.[32]

> In determining whether or not to make an order . . . the court shall have regard to all the circumstances that it considers relevant, including any previous convictions of the individual in [the island] or elsewhere for an offence involving fraud or dishonesty or in connection with the promotion, formation or management of any body corporate.[33]

In Jamaica, 'unfit' includes a breach of any duty in relation to the company; any misapplications or retention by the director or any conduct giving rise to account for any money or property of the company; fraudulent trading on a winding up (whether he has been convicted or not); such other circumstances as may be prescribed.[34] In

29 *BCE Inc. v 1976 Debentureholders* [2008] 3 SCC 69 [40].

30 See discussion in S Ffolkes-Goldson, 'Corporate Governance: A One Size Fits All?' in Berry and Robinson (eds), *Transitions in Caribbean Law: Lawmaking, Constitutionalism and the Confluence of International and Domestic Law* (Caribbean Law Publishing 2013) 33 at 40.

31 (19 May 2003) JM 2003 SC 26.

32 A&B, s 67; Bds, s 69; Dom, s 67; Guy, s 65; St Kitts, s 79; St Lucia, s 67; T&T, s 69; Ja, s 180.

33 A&B, s 67; Bds, s 69; Dom, s 67; Guy, s 65; St Lucia, s 67; T&T, s 69.

34 Ja, s 180(7).

Jamaica, shareholders, directors, creditors, the liquidator or the trustee may have a right to make an application to the court after a complaint is made to the Registrar and the Registrar has investigated the complaint. The Registrar may also apply to the court. A director may be disqualified for up to five years.

In Jamaica, a director may also be disqualified for persistent breaches of the Act[35] for seemingly minor offences as failing to fulfil the requirements for the filing, delivering or sending of any return, account or other document or the giving of notice of any matter to be given to the Registrar. The Jamaica Companies Act does not specify who may bring an action in the case of persistent breaches of the Act; however, it is assumed that it would be the same persons who are entitled under the section relating to the fitness of a director.

The concept of a 'shadow director' is found in the Jamaica Companies Act, and is defined as a person in accordance with whose directions or instructions the directors of the company are accustomed to act. A person will not be deemed to be a 'shadow director' if the directions or instructions they give are given in a professional capacity. The concept of 'shadow director' is derived from UK legislation,[36] and the Explanatory Notes to the UK Companies Act 2006 suggest that 'shadow directors' may be held to the same standard as directors under the UK Companies Act, where the common law rule or equitable principle is replaced by the statute.[37] It is unclear whether the fiduciary duty and duty of care, diligence and skill apply to 'shadow directors' given conflicting UK case law.[38] It is arguable, that despite the reference to 'shadow director' in specific sections of the Jamaica Companies Act, wherever the Act refers to 'director' the responsibilities and exposure of 'shadow directors' are the same. It is also arguable that a parent company could be deemed a 'shadow director' in the absence of a clear provision excluding parent companies.[39]

DIRECTOR AND OFFICER INDEMNITY AND INSURANCE

Directors and officers may seek shelter from actions against them through indemnification and insurance.[40]

Indemnity may be against all costs, charges and expenses reasonably incurred by the party in respect of any civil, criminal or administrative action or proceeding to which he is made a party by reason of being or having been a director or officer. The

35 Ja, s 182.

36 UK Companies Act 1985, s 741.

37 B Hannigan, *Company Law* (2nd edn, Oxford University Press 2009) 146 [6–28].

38 *Ultraframe (UK) v Fielding* [2005] All ER (D) 397 and *Re Mea Corporation Ltd, Secretary of State for Trade and Industry v Aviss* [2007] 1 BCLC 618.

39 *Re Hydrodam (Corby) Ltd* [1994] 2 BCLC 180 at 184; B Hannigan, *Company Law* (2nd edn, Oxford University Press 2009) 146 [6–27].

40 A&B, ss 99–101,103; Bds, ss 97–99; Dom, ss 99–101, 103; Guy, ss 99–101, 103; Ja, ss 201–203, 205; St Lucia, ss 99–101, 103; T&T, ss 101–103, 105. St Kitts permits companies to indemnify any person against certain liabilities, s 78(2).

CBCA was amended to expand the indemnity to provisions to apply to investigations, save in the instances of fraud or other illegal activity.[41]

The director or officer must have:

i) acted in good faith with a view to the best interests of the company; and
ii) had reasonable grounds for believing that the conduct was lawful in the case of a criminal or administrative action or proceeding enforced by a monetary penalty.

A right to indemnity arises where the person a) has been substantially successful on the merits in his defence of the action or proceeding; and b) has acted in good faith with a view to the best interests of the company and had reasonable grounds for believing that his conduct was lawful in the case of a criminal or administrative action or proceeding enforced by a monetary penalty; and c) is fairly and reasonably entitled to indemnity.

Companies legislation in the region also enables a company to purchase and maintain insurance for the benefit of anyone it can indemnify in his capacity as a director or officer of the company other than liability for fraud.[42] There is no provision for advancement of defence costs, when the director or officer or former director or former officer may need it most. The CBCA was amended to include advancement of defence costs, charges and expenses.[43]

CODES OF CORPORATE GOVERNANCE

Barbados – The Corporate Governance Recommendations for Listed Companies on the Barbados Stock Exchange Inc. 2014

The Corporate Governance Recommendations for Listed Companies on the Barbados Stock Exchange Inc. (Barbados Code)[44] provides guidelines for directors and officers listed on the Barbados Stock Exchange (BSE) on a 'comply or explain' basis. Matters relating to the General Meeting and Disclosures are outlined in Chapter 4, on Stakeholder Protection. The shareholders elect the directors at General Meeting in accordance with the Barbados Companies Act.[45]

Section 3.0 of the Barbados Code states:

> The Board is responsible for the supervision of senior Management and overseeing the operations of the company in their fiduciary capacity of acting with a view to the best interests of the company. The Board should adopt a written Mandate in which it explicitly acknowledges responsibility for the stewardship of the company . . .

41 CBCA, s 124.
42 A&B, s 102; Bds, s 100; Dom, s 102; Guy, 102; Ja, s 204; St Lucia, s 102; T&T, s 104.
43 CBCA, s 124(2).
44 Available at <www.bse.com.bb>.
45 Bds, s 66(3).

The written mandate should outline the 'essential duties and working principles' of the Board in order to permit shareholders to evaluate the operation of the Board.

The Barbados Code also outlines recommendations for disclosure of the number of meetings of the Board and Board committees and director attendance at meetings which gives shareholders the opportunity to evaluate the 'effectiveness and contribution' of the Board.

It is further recommended that the Board undergo an annual performance evaluation and the performance evaluation process and the results should be disclosed. The evaluation may be done by internal self-evaluation or by an external evaluator.

The Board should be composed of at least five directors for a term not exceeding three years, with one-third of the Board subject to election on an annual basis.

Recommendation 13 states, *inter alia*, that in order to achieve a balanced board, it 'is imperative that the Board be composed of Directors with versatile and mutually complementing capabilities and competencies' and that the age mix and gender proportion should also be taken into account.

Directors are also mandated to render the necessary time, attention and level and engagement in order to fulfil their roles as directors by taking into account their main occupation, secondary occupations and simultaneous board memberships. There is, however, no recommendation of a limit to the number of directorships chairpersons or directors may have. There should be orientation and continuing education for new and incumbent directors.[46]

While not specifying a number or percentage of directors who are independent, the Barbados Code requires that there should be a 'cadre' of independent directors.[47] Directors should be independent of a significant shareholding of the company and,

> . . . independent of Management and free from any material interest and any business or other relationship, which could, or could reasonably be perceived to, interfere with the director's ability to act with a view to the best interests of the company.[48]

Recommendation 18 provides a list of persons who may be considered as having a 'material interest' in the company and thereby non-independent. Disclosure of the background, biographical details, compensation and shareholdings of directors are found in Recommendation 19 and are discussed in Chapter 4 on Stakeholder Protection.

Section 4 of the Barbados Code outlines the various required Board Committees. The two principal standing Committees of the Board should include:

> i) the Audit Committee[49] to concentrate particularly on matters relating to financial reporting and control and, ii) the Governance Committee[50] to improve the effective handling of matters relating to the governance of the board and the company thereby improving the effectiveness of director nomination, appointment, election and succession planning.

46 Barbados Code Recommendation (Recommendation) 16.
47 Recommendation 17.
48 Recommendation 17.
49 Recommendations 29–32.
50 Recommendations 34–37.

There should be a written Charter for each Committee's work and the Committees should regularly report on their work to the Board. Apart from disclosure of the number of Committee Meetings and attendance of each director, there should also be an annual evaluation of the performance and working methods of each Committee. The Barbados Code also recommends that a company 'may' establish a Compensation Committee.

> The Board may establish a Compensation Committee to improve the effective handling of matters relating to the appointment and compensation of the Managing Director/CEO and other executives of the company, as well as the handling of other employee compensation systems. Where no Compensation Committee is established the duties shall be performed by the Governance Committee.[51]

If there are any other standing Committees, the company should identify them and describe their functions.

The Board is responsible for appointing the Managing Director/CEO and is required, along with the Managing Director/CEO, to clearly describe the Managing Director/CEO position including the corporate goals and objectives.[52]

Matters relating to approval of the Managing Director/CEO service contracts by the Board and disclosure of the background, biographical details and shareholdings of the Managing Director/CEO are outlined in Recommendations 45 and 46 and director and executive compensation as outlined in Section 7.0 of the Barbados Code are discussed in Chapter 4 on Stakeholder Protection.

The Barbados Code mandates that the positions of Managing Director/CEO and Chairman be separate and, where this is not appropriate, an independent director may be appointed as 'Lead Director'.[53] The separation of Managing Director/CEO and Chairman is to ensure that no one individual has unfettered powers of decision. However, the company must explain a decision to appoint the same person as Managing Director/CEO and Chairman.

Jamaica – the Private Sector Organisation of Jamaica Corporate Governance Code 2009[54]

The Private Sector Organisation of Jamaica Corporate Governance Code (PSOJ Code) 2009 makes recommendations for Directors in Sections A and B of the Code.

Section A speaks of the role of the Board and states as the main principle: 'Every company should be headed by an effective board, which is collectively responsible for the success of the company.'[55] It is recommended that a revised Code should include the 'long term' goal of the company in recognition of international standards which have included 'longtermism' as a duty of directors through statute and/or case law.

---

51 Recommendation 38.
52 Recommendation 43.
53 Recommendation 47.
54 The PSOJ Code 2009 is currently under revision.
55 PSOJ Code 2009, A.1.

The PSOJ Code recommends that the composition of the Board should enable the Board to exercise its duties to the company and all shareholders. The elements to be considered are i) the number of directors, ii) diversity, iii) experience, iv) skills and knowledge, and v) independence. Diversity relates to academic qualifications, technical expertise, relevant industry knowledge, gender, age and ethnicity.[56] The PSOJ Code contemplates a 'senior independent director' to facilitate meetings with the non-executive directors without the executives and to meet at least annually without the chairperson, to appraise the chairperson's performance.

The PSOJ Code 2009 speaks to the director's decision making, which reflects the current law, to take into account the:

> . . . reasonable expectations of their stakeholders including: shareholders, employees, customers, suppliers, creditors, consumers and the broader community in which they operate.[57]

There is a further provision for a division of the roles of chairperson and chief executive,[58] and that the chairperson should be 'independent' as described in the Code.[59] It may be argued, however, that where there is no division in the roles of chairperson and chief executive, it is only then that a senior independent director should be appointed.

The PSOJ Code states that there should be a 'balance' of executive and independent non-executive directors and that it should be of a 'sufficient size' to ensure, *inter alia*, a balance of skills and experience that are appropriate for the requirements of the business.[60] The Board is required to identify each 'independent' non-executive director in the annual report. Criteria for determining independence include:

> . . . has been an employee of the company or group within the last five years; has, or has had within the last three years, a material business relationship with the company either directly, or as a partner, shareholder, director or senior employee of a body that has such a relationship with the company; has received or receives additional remuneration from the company apart from a director's fee, participates in the company's share option or a performance-related pay scheme, or is a member of the company's pension scheme; has close family ties with any of the company's advisers, directors or senior employees; holds cross-directorships or has significant links with other directors through involvement in other companies or bodies; represents a significant shareholder; or has served on the board for more than nine years from the date of their first election.[61]

With the exception of small companies, non-executive directors, excluding the chairperson, should comprise at least half the Board.[62] Although there is a requirement in the PSOJ Code 2009 that a smaller company should have at least two independent

56 PSOJ Code 2009, A.1.1
57 PSOJ Code 2009, A.2.
58 PSOJ Code 2009, A.3.1.
59 PSOJ Code 2009, A.3.2, A.3.1.
60 PSOJ Code 2009, A.4.
61 PSOJ Code 2009, A.4.1.
62 PSOJ Code 2009, A.4.2.

non-executive directors, it may be more useful to recommend a percentage rather than a number.

The requirement for a 'formal, rigorous and transparent procedure for the appointment of new directors to the board'[63] includes induction procedures. The nomination committee should be independent, non-executive directors and should be chaired by the chair of the board or an independent non-executive director.[64] The terms and conditions of appointment of non-executive directors should be made available for inspection and non-executive directors should undertake that they would have sufficient time to meet what is expected of them, and before appointment, disclose any of their other significant commitments.[65]

Directors should receive induction on joining the Board and 'regularly update and refresh their skills and knowledge'.[66] An annual evaluation is required of its own performance, and that of its committees and individual director and a statement on how the evaluation has been conducted.[67] Election or re-election of directors should be at regular intervals, which is no more than every three years. 'Serving for more than nine years could be relevant to the determination of a non-executive director's independence.'[68] Director and executive remuneration is addressed in Chapter 4 on Stakeholder Protection.

It is recommended that the board establish an audit committee of at least three (at least two for smaller companies) who are independent, non-executive directors.[69] The main role and responsibilities of the audit committee should include:

> . . . to monitor the integrity of the financial statements of the company, and any formal announcements relating to the company's financial performance, reviewing significant financial reporting judgements contained in them; to review the company's internal financial controls and, unless expressly addressed by a separate board risk committee composed of independent directors, or by the board itself, to review the company's internal control and risk management systems; to monitor and review the effectiveness of the company's internal audit function; to make recommendations to the board, for it to put to the shareholders for their approval in general meeting, in relation to the appointment, re-appointment and removal of the external auditor and to approve the remuneration and terms of engagement of the external auditor; to review and monitor the external auditor's independence and objectivity and the effectiveness of the audit process, taking into consideration relevant UK professional and regulatory requirements; to develop and implement policy on the engagement of the external auditor to supply non-audit services, taking into account relevant ethical guidance regarding the provision of non-audit services by the external audit firm; and to report to the board, identifying any matters in respect of which it considers that action or improvement is needed and making recommendations as to the steps to be taken.[70]

63 PSOJ Code 2009, A.5.
64 PSOJ Code 2009, A.5.1.
65 PSOJ Code 2009, A.5.4.
66 PSOJ Code 2009, A.6.
67 PSOJ Code 2009, A.7.
68 PSOJ Code 2009, A.8.2.
69 PSOJ Code 2009, C.3.1.
70 PSOJ Code 2009, C.3.2.

It is recommended, however, that risk management and internal control should be enhanced, in addition to financial reporting under the section on Accountability and Audit. Section D.2 makes specific reference to the Jamaica Stock Exchange Rules, Appendix 13, on Management Discussion and Analysis.[71]

Trinidad and Tobago – Trinidad and Tobago Corporate Governance Code 2013

The Trinidad and Tobago Corporate Governance Code 2013 (Trinidad Code) is not a 'comply or explain' Code but rather relies on suasion through voluntary 'apply or explain'.[72]

In stating recommendations for the Board, the main principle states: 'Every company should be headed by an effective Board, which is collectively responsible for the long-term success of the company.'[73] The recommendations for the Board include a clear outline of the roles and responsibilities of directors which should be made publicly available; that the chairperson be a non-executive and preferably independent director; that it is supplied with information in a timely manner and that the Board take into account the legitimate interests and expectations of all stakeholders.[74]

The Trinidad Code recommends in Principle Two, that there be a balance of independence, diversity of skills, knowledge, experience, perspectives and gender on Boards. The Board should have a majority of independent, non-executive directors and all directors should undergo induction training and updating and refreshing of their skills and knowledge. The Board, Board Committees and individual directors should have a 'rigorous, transparent and formal annual evaluation'[75] of their performance and that the remuneration of Directors and Senior Management is 'transparent, fair and reasonable'.[76]

Principle Three of the Trinidad Code reflects the law by stating that the directors 'should act honestly and in good faith, in the best interest of the company, ahead of

71 'The Jamaica Stock Exchange (JSE) will now require all listed companies to include a Management Discussion and Analysis Disclosure as part of their annual report and Prospectus/Offer document to the market. This disclosure is a standard report internationally and is also a requirement of the Securities Act 1999 and The Companies Act 2004. The purpose of an MD&A is to provide an objective and easily readable analysis of the company's operation within a given period and management's assessment of the company based on past activities, future plans and other internal & external factors that can impact on its operations. MD&A's are beneficial in that they provide more transparency and disclosure, evidence that management is serving shareholders' interest and a better basis for analysis and assessment. This rule is in keeping with international best practices and has been amended to JSE Rule 404 (E) – Annual Reports and Accounts and Appendix 3 – Listing Agreement (8).' Available at <www.jamstockex.com>.

72 Trinidad and Tobago Corporate Governance Code 2013 (Trinidad Code), Implementation, 8.

73 Trinidad Code, Principle One.

74 Trinidad Code, Principle One.

75 Trinidad Code, 2.5.

76 Trinidad Code, 2.6.

other interests'. The Board should annually assess its independence and disclose in each which non-executive director it considers to be independent in its annual report and there should be re-election of all directors at intervals of no more than three years. Members of the Board and Senior Management should disclose to the Board any material interest in any transaction or matter, which they may have, which directly affects the company.[77] There is also a recommendation that directors 'demonstrate the capacity to commit the time needed to be fully effective in their roles'.[78]

CONCLUSION

Companies legislation in the Commonwealth Caribbean legislates some aspects of corporate governance by mandating that directors and officers of companies act honestly and in good faith with a view to the best interest of the company, and exercise the care, diligence and skill reflecting the common law that a reasonably prudent person would exercise in comparable circumstances. Although most of the legislation reflects the common law fiduciary duty (which has always been a very high standard), the standard of care, diligence and skill has been raised to varying degrees. Directors and officers are therefore generally highly exposed; however, safe-harbour is found through, *inter alia*, disclosure (where there is a conflict of interest), the due diligence defence (where it exists in some statutes) and the 'business judgment rule'.

The Corporate Governance Codes found in the Commonwealth Caribbean relating to the duty of directors tend to reflect the companies legislation in the region by recommending that the Boards make decisions in the best interest of the company and taking into account the interests of stakeholders. The Codes are similar in their recommendations and, generally speaking, the Codes go further than legislation by persuading Boards to introduce mechanisms to ensure adequate transparency and accountability. Common themes for Boards include diversity, independence, disclosure and corporate social responsibility.

BIBLIOGRAPHY

Davies, P and Gower, L, *Principles of Modern Company Law*, 7th edn, 2003, Sweet and Maxwell London

Farrar, JH, Furey, N and Hannigan, B, *Farrar's Company Law*, 3rd edn, 1991, Butterworths London

Ffolkes-Goldson, S, 'Corporate Directors' Duty of Care, Diligence and Skill: Soper v The Queen' (1998) *Caribbean Law Bulletin* 53–59

Ffolkes-Goldson, S, 'Corporate Governance: A One Size Fits All?' in Berry and Robinson (eds), *Transitions in Caribbean Law: Lawmaking, Constitutionalism and the Confluence of International and Domestic Law*, 2013, Caribbean Law Publishing, 33 at 40

Ffolkes-Goldson, S, 'Directors' Duties to Creditors on or in the Vicinity of Insolvency in the Commonwealth Caribbean: Should the Peoples Decision of the Supreme Court of Canada be Followed?' (2006) 6(1) *Oxford University Commonwealth Law Journal* 61–75

77 Trinidad Code, 3.1–3.3.

78 Trinidad Code, 3.4.

Ffolkes-Goldson, S, 'The Reform of the Law Relating to Duties of Directors in the Commonwealth Caribbean' (2002) *The Company Lawyer* 378–384

Ffolkes-Goldson, S, 'The Use and Misuse of the Corporate Oppression Remedy in the Commonwealth Caribbean' (2014) 35(7) *The Company Lawyer* 195–204

Hannigan, B, *Company Law*, 2nd edn, 2009, Oxford University Press

Wilberne, P, 'Jamaica Meltdown: Indigenous Financial Sector Crash 1996', 2006, iUniverse, Inc.

Ziegel, JS, Daniels, RJ, MacIntosh, JG and Johnston, D, *Cases and Materials on Partnerships and Canadian Business Corporations*, 3rd edn, 1994, Carswell Toronto

CHAPTER 4

THE PROTECTION AND EMPOWERMENT OF SHAREHOLDERS AND OTHER STAKEHOLDERS

SUZANNE FFOLKES-GOLDSON

INTRODUCTION

The corporate laws of the region have had their genesis in the now archaic UK shareholder primacy model, but in the last 20 years the Commonwealth Caribbean company law statutes have replaced the shareholder primacy model of company law in favour of the modern stakeholder theory, which recognises the importance of stakeholders other than shareholders in the success of companies. The empowerment of shareholders and other stakeholders is evident through the increased legal responsibility and accountability found in the various companies legislation and the exposure of directors and officers to direct legal actions. The codes of corporate governance in Jamaica, Barbados and Trinidad and Tobago emphasise the empowerment of shareholders and other stakeholders, reflecting the legal position as it relates to the availability of direct access to the courts and encouragement of institutional shareholder involvement.

A more recent development in Jamaica is the introduction of whistleblower protection, which, although limited to employment situations, adds another layer of stakeholder protection. The recognition of corporate social responsibility (CSR), though not legislated in the region, is arguably also introduced through the wide provisions relating to the duties of directors and officers in the companies legislation and further in the more recent introduction of CSR in the corporate governance codes.

This chapter will focus on the developments in the Commonwealth Caribbean region, which empower stakeholders under the Companies Acts, and the Protected Disclosures Act (Jamaica), as well as the Codes of Corporate Governance.

STAKEHOLDER PROTECTION AND EMPOWERMENT: PROVISIONS OF COMPANIES ACTS AND CASE LAW

Duties of directors and officers and corporate social responsibility

Provisions relating to the duties of directors and officers under most companies legislation in the Commonwealth Caribbean include a duty to take into account the interests of a wide group of stakeholders, other than shareholders, including employees and, in some cases, the community in which the company operates[1] when determining what is in the best interest of the company. The statutes typically state:

> In determining what are the best interests of a company, a director shall/must have regard to the interests of **the company's employees in general as well as to the interests of its shareholders**.[2]
>
> (Emphasis added)

Recently, the Supreme Court of Canada held that directors may take into account, *inter alia*, shareholders, employees, creditors, consumers, governments and the environment in considering what is in the best interests of the corporation.

> In considering what is in the best interests of the corporation, directors may look to the interests of**, inter alia, shareholders, employees, creditors, consumers, governments and the environment** to inform their decisions.[3]
>
> (Emphasis added)

Although the provisions of the relevant Companies Acts in the Commonwealth Caribbean do not go as far as the UK Companies Act,[4] which now includes a duty to consider the interests of an extraordinary large number of stakeholders, including the interest of employees and the impact on the community and the environment, the stakeholder theory is now entrenched in the majority of Commonwealth Caribbean company law.

(ii) The derivative action

The introduction of the Canadian style derivative action has successfully put to bed the old UK restrictions on minority shareholders and the ability to bring an action on behalf of the company for a wrong done to the company has gone further to include

1 Antigua and Barbuda Companies Act 1995 (A&B), s 97(2); Barbados Companies Act 2002- Cap 308 (Bds), s 95(2) where the word 'must' is used instead of 'shall'; Dominica Companies Act 1994 (Dom), s 97(2); Guyana Companies Act 1994- Cap 89:01 (Guy), s 96(2) where the word 'must' is used instead of 'shall'; Jamaica Companies Act 2004 (Ja), s 174(4) where the word 'may' is used instead of 'shall' and refers to shareholders, employees and the community in which the company operates; St Lucia Companies Act 2008- Cap 13:01 (St Lucia), s 97(2); Trinidad and Tobago Companies Act 1995- Cap 81:01 (T&T), s 99(2); St Kitts does not have this provision.

2 A&B, s 97(2); Bds, s 95(2) where the word 'must' is used instead of 'shall'; Dom, s 97(2); Guy, s 96(2) where the word 'must' is used instead of 'shall'; Ja, s 174(4); St Lucia, s 97(2); T&T, s 99(2); St Kitts does not have this provision. See also S Ffolkes-Goldson 'The Commonwealth Caribbean: The Reform of The Law Relating to the Duties of Directors' (2003) 24(12) *The Company Lawyer* 378, 380–381.

3 *BCE Inc. v 1976 Debentureholders* [2008] 3 SCR 560 [40] confirming *Peoples Department Stores Inc. (Trustee of) v Wise* [2004] 3 SCR 461.

4 UK Companies Act 2006, s 172.

other stakeholders who are described as 'complainants' which include a shareholder, former shareholder, debenture holder, former debenture holder of a company or any of its affiliates, a director or an officer or a former director or a former officer of a company or any of its affiliates; the Registrar or **any other person who, in the court's discretion, is a proper person** to make an application.[5]

The Jamaica Companies Act does not include 'any other person who, in the court's discretion is a proper person to make an application' in its definition of 'complainant' and it is therefore clear that the stakeholder theory is not only limited by the scope of directors' duties but also the ability of other stakeholders, beyond shareholder, former shareholder, debenture holder, former debenture holder, director or officer or former director or officer of a company or affiliated company to bring a derivative action on behalf of the company for a wrong done to the company.[6]

The legislation includes provisions to avoid frivolous and/or vexatious suits by requiring that 'complainants' (i) give reasonable notice to the directors (and officers) of their intention to bring the suit; (ii) bring the action in good faith; and (iii) it appears to the court, that it is in the interest of the company or its subsidiary that the action be brought, prosecuted or defended or discontinued.[7]

The oppression remedy

A 'complainant' may bring an action where actions by the directors (and officers) which are oppressive, unfairly prejudicial or unfairly disregard the interests of a specific class of victims.

As stated earlier, 'complainant' is defined in most Commonwealth Caribbean jurisdictions, save for Jamaica, as (i) a shareholder or debenture holder, or a former holder of a share or debenture of a company or any of its affiliates; (ii) a director or an officer or former director or officer of a company or any of its affiliates; (iii) the Registrar; or (iv) any other person who, in the discretion of the court, is a proper person to make an application.

The sections further provide:

> A complainant may apply to the court for an order under this section.
>
> If, upon an application under subsection (1), the court is satisfied that in respect of a company or any of its affiliates
>
> (a) any act or omission of the company or any of its affiliates effects a result,
> (b) the business or affairs of the company or any of its affiliates are or have been carried on or conducted in a manner, or
> (c) the powers of the directors of the company or any of its affiliates are or have been exercised in a manner,

5 A&B, s 238; Bds, s 225; Dom, s 238; Guy, s 221; St Lucia, s 238; T&T, s 239.
6 Ja, s 212.
7 A&B, ss 238, 239; Bds, ss 225, 226; Dom, ss 238, 239; Guy, ss 221, 222; St Lucia, ss 238, 239; T&T, ss 239, 240.

> that is **oppressive or unfairly prejudicial to, or that unfairly disregards the interests of**, any shareholder or debenture holder, creditor, director or officer of the company, the court may make an order to rectify the matters complained of.[8]
>
> (Emphasis added)

Beard J in the Canadian case of *First Edmonton*, appropriately described the remedy:

> By framing the remedy provisions in very broad terms, the reformers have sought to do away with the restrictive approach that the courts had previously taken when judging the conduct or misconduct of corporate management. The old view that the management of the company was in the total discretion of its directors and shareholders has been replaced by an expansive view of the court's role in balancing the interests of shareholders (majority and minority) creditors and the public in general. However the jurisdiction is one, which must be exercised with care. On the one hand stakeholders within the corporate structure must be protected from unfair treatment. On the other hand courts ought not to usurp the function of the board of directors in managing the company, nor should it eliminate or supplant the legitimate exercise of control by the majority: see *Bank of Montreal v. Dome Petroleum Ltd* (1987) 67 CBR 296 (Canada) at pp. 305–306.[9]

Oppression, unfair prejudice and unfair disregard have discrete meanings as stated by Jamadar J in *Lalla v Trinidad Cement Limited and TCL Holdings*, that 'each of these introduces a separate category of conduct, which may overlap in any given case, but each of which if proven, establish oppression as encoded in section 242 . . .'[10] It was held in *Lalla*, that unfair dismissal out of spite or malice could be a basis for finding oppression of the employee/director. In *Schnake v Trincann Oil Limited*,[11] the High Court of Trinidad and Tobago found that a variation of the claimant's pre-emptive rights in Articles of Continuance by the defendant was oppressive, prejudicial and unfairly disregarded.

In *Demerara Holdings Limited et al v Demerara Life Assurance Company of Trinidad and Tobago Limited et al (Demerara)*, the Court held:

> 'Oppression' carries the sense of conduct that is coercive and abusive, and it suggests bad faith. 'Unfair prejudice' may admit of a less culpable state of mind that nevertheless has unfair consequences. Finally, 'unfair disregard' of interests extends the remedy to ignoring an interest as being of no importance, contrary to the stakeholders' reasonable expectations . . . the phrases describe, in adjectival terms, ways in which corporate actors may fail to meet the reasonable expectations of stakeholders.[12]

The House of Lords defined 'oppressive' in *Scottish Co-Operative Wholesale Society Ltd v Meyer and another*[13] as 'burdensome, harsh and wrongful'. In this case, the Respondents, who were the majority shareholders of the company, set up a rival business, and

8 A&B, ss 239, 241; Bds, ss 226, 228; Dom, ss 239, 241; Guy, ss 222, 224; St Lucia, ss 239, 241; T&T, ss 240, 242.

9 *First Edmonton Place Ltd v 315888 Alberta Ltd* [1988] 40 BLR 28 (Alta QB) at 41 (*First Edmonton*).

10 *Lalla v Trinidad Cement Ltd* TT 1998 HC 172 Carilaw (Jamadar J).

11 TT 2008 HC 222 Carilaw.

12 *Demerara Holdings Limited et al v Demerara Life Assurance Company of Trinidad and Tobago Limited et al* TT 2011 HC 86 Carilaw [67].

13 *Scottish Co-Operative Wholesale Society Ltd v Meyer and another* [1959] AC 324.

along with their three nominee directors, schemed to destroy the company as they felt that the company had 'served its purpose'. The applicants, who were two of the five directors (the other three directors being nominees of the respondents), claimed that this was oppressive conduct. The House of Lords stated:

> . . . it appears to me incontrovertible that the society have behaved to the minority shareholders of the company in a manner which can justly be described as 'oppressive.' They had the majority power and they exercised their authority in a manner 'burdensome, harsh and wrongful' – I take the dictionary meaning of the word.[14]

This definition appears to have been refined in *Re Jermyn Street Turkish Baths Ltd.*

> In our judgment, oppression occurs where shareholders having a dominant power in a company, either (1) exercise that power to procure that something is done or not done in the conduct of the company's affairs, or (2) procure by an express or implicit threat of an exercise of that power that something is not done in the conduct of the company's affairs; and when such conduct is unfair or . . . 'burdensome, harsh and wrongful' to the other members of the company or some of them, and lacks that degree of probity which they are entitled to expect in the conduct of the company's affairs.[15]

This definition of oppression, has been applied in the Commonwealth Caribbean in a number of cases under the former and current provisions relating to shareholder oppression and petitions for 'just and equitable winding up' of companies based on oppression.[16] Commonwealth Caribbean cases have also used the case of *Ebrahimi v Westbourne Galleries Ltd*[17] as an example of 'oppressive' conduct. *Ebrahimi* was decided in the context of a petition for 'just and equitable winding up' of a company based on 'oppressive' conduct. The facts of the case involved a company, which was a quasi-partnership, formed on the basis that the two original shareholders would manage the company. One of the original shareholders and his son (who had later joined the company) used their majority shareholding to remove the other shareholder as director. This was considered by the court to be oppressive conduct, which, in the context of a quasi-partnership, warranted a 'just and equitable' winding up of the company.

In *Re Caribbean Paper Recycling Company Limited*,[18] the Supreme Court of Jamaica relied on *Ebrahimi v Westbourne Galleries Ltd and Others*[19] and *Radcliffe Butler v Norma Butler*[20] for examples of 'oppression'. In this case, the Plaintiff brought a successful application as a director under section 213A of the Jamaica Companies Act based on oppression, evidenced by his exclusion from the management of the operations and day-to-day running of the Company as a result of the breakdown in the relationship between the Plaintiff and the other directors and shareholders of the Company.

14 Per Viscount Simonds, 342.
15 [1971] 3 All ER 199.
16 *Aaberg et al v Pederson* JM 1975 CA 26 Carilaw; *Re: Golf Beach Inn Hotel Ltd* JM 1972 SC 8 Carilaw.
17 [1972] 2 All ER 492 (HL).
18 JM 2006 SC 83 Carilaw.
19 [1973] AC 360.
20 [1993] 30 JLR 348.

In *Devaux v Du Boulay Holdings Limited et al*,[21] the Court of Appeal (Saunders CJ (Ag)), in rejecting the appellant's petition for a remedy for oppression, stated:

> . . . as was stated by Smith J. in *Re Mason and Intercity Properties* (Unreported, December 10, 1984 Ont. H.C. as quoted in Butterworth's supra at note 3 to Para 18.21) when discussing the oppression remedy, – 'the door has not been opened wide to accommodate every disgruntled shareholder. Otherwise one form of abuse would be seen to be replaced by another form far more nefarious because of its effect of subjugating the will of the majority to the whimsical machinations of persons in minority positions with theoretically little risk'. [41] In order successfully to invoke the oppression remedy, Lord Cooper opined that the complainant should show that there has been conduct which – 'at the lowest involve[d] a visible departure from the standards of fair dealing, and a violation of the conditions of fair play on which every shareholder who entrusts his money to a company is entitled to rely' (See: *Elder v. Elder & Watson Ltd.* (1952) S.C. 49 at page 55). Lord Cooper further outlined that: 'The circumstances have always, I think, been such as to warrant the inference that there has been, at least, an unfair abuse of powers and an impairment of confidence in the probity with which the company's affairs are being conducted, as distinguished from mere resentment on the part of the minority at being outvoted on some domestic policy' (See: *Elder v. Elder & Watson Ltd.* (1952) S.C. 49 at page 55). [42] This case does not in my view demonstrate any abuse of power on the part of the majority . . . As the trial judge noted, there is nothing **abusive or harsh or wrongful** about this. Section 241 was not intended to override the fundamental corporate law principle of majority shareholder control.
>
> (Emphasis added)

'Unfairly Prejudicial' has been interpreted in the British Columbia Supreme Court as 'acts that are unjustly or inequitably detrimental'.[22] The Bahamas Companies Act, however, has no provision for 'unfair prejudice' but only includes conduct which is 'unfairly oppressive' in addition to conduct which is 'oppressive' or 'unfairly disregards' the interests of the victim class.

In *Stech v Davies*, the Alberta Queens Bench defined 'unfair disregard' as 'unjustly or without cause pay no attention to, ignore or treat as of no importance the interests of security holders, creditors, directors or officers'.[23]

The Supreme Court of Canada in *BCE Inc. v 1976 Debentureholders*, stated that 'unfair disregard' was the least serious of the three wrongs mentioned in the section and gave examples as including favouring a director by 'failing to properly prosecute claims, improperly reducing a shareholder's dividend, or failing to deliver property belonging to the claimant . . .'.[24]

The High Court of St Lucia in *Duyette et al v May et al*[25] concluded that there was 'unfair disregard' within the meaning of the provision where the complete absence of

21 JM 2006 SC 83 Carilaw.
22 *Diligent v RWMD Operations Kelowna* (1976) 1 BCLR 36 (SC).
23 (1987) 53 Alta LR (2d) 373 (QB).
24 [2008] 3 SCR 560, 2008 SCC 9 [94]; M Koehnen, *Oppression and Related Remedies* (Thomson Canada Limited 2004) 83–84.
25 LC 2009 HC 1 Carilaw.

financial controls reflected a degree of incompetence, which unfairly disregarded the interests of the claimants.

More recently, some Commonwealth Caribbean case law has incorporated the Canadian two-pronged test to determine whether conduct has been oppressive, unfairly prejudicial or unfairly disregards the interests of a specified stakeholder, namely (i) that he had a reasonable expectation and (ii) that the reasonable expectation was unfairly disregarded.[26]

> . . . the question is whether the expectation is reasonable having regard to the facts of the specific case, the relationships at issue, and the entire context, including the fact that there may be conflicting claims and expectations.[27]

In *Demerara Holdings Limited et al v Demerara Life Assurance Company of Trinidad and Tobago Limited et al*, the court relied on the two-pronged test to find that the policy-holders of Demerara Life were unfairly prejudiced and/or their interests unfairly disregarded in the case of a merger agreement.[28] More recently, the High Court of Trinidad and Tobago relied on the two-pronged approach in *Demerara* in the case of *Gift v Gift, Citi Hardware Limited and Ecociti Resort and Condominiums Limited.*[29]

In *Grenada General Insurance Company Limited et al v Grenada Insurance Services Limited*[30] the two-pronged test was also applied and the Court of Appeal of Grenada agreed with the judge at first instance that the actions of the defendant were unfairly prejudicial to, and unfairly disregarded the interests of the plaintiff as a shareholder in the company due to: (i) the fact that the applicant/respondent had a legitimate expectation to continue in the management of the company as a director and employee and (ii) that there was adequate evidence of unfair prejudice and unfair disregard of the applicant's/respondent's interests as a shareholder.

Stakeholder remedies are therefore limited under the provisions of the Jamaica and Bahamas Companies Acts by virtue of the omission of actions which 'unfairly disregard' and 'unfairly prejudice' stakeholders respectively, as a basis for a remedy.[31]

Most of the Commonwealth Caribbean territories have limited the victim class for oppression although there is a wide complainant class, save for Jamaica, which has limited its complainant class while including creditors in the victim class. The provision states:

> . . . that is oppressive or unfairly prejudicial to, or that unfairly disregards **the interests of, any shareholder or debenture holder, creditor, director or officer of the company**, the court may make an order to rectify the matters complained of.[32]
>
> (Emphasis added)

26 *BCE Inc. v 1976 Debentureholders* [2008] 3 SCR 560.
27 *BCE Inc. v 1976 Debentureholders* [2008] 3 SCR 560 [62].
28 TT 2011 HC 86 Carilaw.
29 TT 2012 HC 347 Carilaw.
30 GD 2000 CA 1 Carilaw.
31 S Ffolkes-Goldson, 'The Use and Misuse of the Corporate Oppression Remedy in the Commonwealth Caribbean' (2014) 35(7) *Company Lawyer* 195.
32 A&B, ss 239, 241; Bds, ss 226, 228; Dom, ss 239, 241; Guy, ss 222, 224; Ja, s 213; St Lucia, ss 239, 241; T&T, ss 240, 242.

It appears that this mismatch of complainant and victim class has proven challenging for judges in the region who have taken differing approaches to the interpretation of the provision, in some instances providing complainants outside the victim class with a remedy and in other instances, interpreting the provisions strictly by prohibiting complainants outside of the victim class from a remedy.

In *Canwest International Inc. et al v Atlantic TV Limited et al*[33] the Court of Appeal of Barbados upheld the first instance decision to permit a party to a pre-incorporation contract to be a complainant ('any other person who, in the court's discretion is a proper person') and as a result to obtain a remedy, although not a member of the victim class.

In *Five Star Medical and Ambulance Services Limited v Telecommunications Services of Trinidad and Tobago Limited*[34] the High Court of Trinidad and Tobago found a party to a contract, who was held not to be a creditor, to be a proper person, in the discretion of the Court, to make an application to the Court for a remedy for conduct where there was evidence of oppression, unfair prejudice and unfair disregard of the interests of the complainant. In *Demerara Holdings Limited et al v Demerara Life Assurance Company of Trinidad and Tobago Limited et al*, the Court found that an insurance policyholder was a victim of unfair prejudice and/or unfair disregard of his interests although not a member of the victim class.

In the more recent cases of *Lopez v Telecommunications Services of Trinidad and Tobago*[35] (High Court of Trinidad and Tobago) and *St George et al v Hayward et al*[36] (the Supreme Court of The Bahamas) the Courts took the view that a pensioner and beneficiary of a pension plan, and a person with an equitable interest in shares, respectively, were not persons within the victim class and therefore were not entitled to a remedy under the relevant provisions. It remains to be seen how the inconsistency in the case law will be resolved in the region.

The St Christopher and Nevis (St Kitts) Companies Act does not have a provision for protection of a wide group of stakeholders and retains the shareholder primacy position which was reflected in the older Commonwealth Caribbean and UK Companies Acts.[37] Section 142 of the St Kitts Companies Act limits actions to members and persons to whom shares in the company have been transferred or transmitted by operation of law or the Minister, for an order on the ground that the company's affairs are being or have been conducted in a manner which is unfairly prejudicial to the interests of its members generally or of some part of its members (including at least himself or herself) or that an actual proposed act or omission of the company (including an act or omission on its behalf) is or would be so prejudicial. If the Court is satisfied that an application is well founded, it may make such order as it thinks fit for giving relief in respect of the matters complained of.

33 BB 1994 CA 27 Carilaw.
34 TT 2002 HC 65 Carilaw.
35 TT 2004 HC 84 Carilaw.
36 BS 2008 SC 113 Carilaw.
37 St Christopher and Nevis (St Kitts) Companies Act 1996 (St Kitts), ss 142–144.

PROTECTION OF WHISTLEBLOWERS

Whistleblower protection is an important element of stakeholder protection and a key indicator of good corporate governance. High-profile whistleblowing cases such as Enron and WorldCom are good examples of the importance of whistleblowing in a corporate setting, albeit in those instances it was too late to save the companies, but at least it resulted in convictions of some of the corporate executives.[38]

Article 33 of the UN Convention Against Corruption provides that state parties '. . . **shall** consider incorporating into its domestic legal system appropriate measures to provide protection against any unjustified treatment for any person who reports in good faith and on reasonable grounds to the competent authorities any facts concerning offences established in accordance with this Convention' (emphasis added). There is therefore a duty for state parties to 'consider' incorporating whistleblowing legislation into their domestic laws. Jamaica is the only Commonwealth Caribbean territory which has to date enacted whistleblower legislation, entitled the Protected Disclosures Act 2011.

The Act is based on the UK legislation[39] and permits disclosures to an employer (section 7); a Minister of Government (section 8); a prescribed person and certain individuals appointed by the Minister (section 9);[40] the designated authority (section 10); and an attorney-at-law (section 11).[41]

The Act only applies to employment relationships (including independent contractors),[42] and there must be reasonable belief that the information revealed is true. The legislation has been criticised for limiting the protection to 'employees' when there are:

> . . . many other categories of persons who may be aware of misconduct, and who may be even affected by it, who are not employed. These include 'consumers, students, retirees, the unemployed, prisoners, and the physically and handicapped persons not in employment'.[43]

Types of 'improper conduct' by an employer include: a criminal offence; failure to comply with legal obligations; miscarriage of justice; danger to health and safety of employees; damage to the environment; hiding of information related to the above.[44]

The protection afforded by the Act is protection from 'occupational detriment'. 'Occupational detriment' could include: an act or omission resulting in disciplinary

---

38 Richard Lacayo and Amanda Ripley, 'Persons of The Year 2002: The Whistleblowers' *Time Magazine* (30 December 2002) <www.time.com/time/magazine/article/0,9171,1003998,00.html>.

39 UK Public Interest Disclosure Act 1998, c 23.

40 (Ja) Protected Disclosures Act, 2011, First Schedule.

41 (Ja) Protected Disclosures Act, 2011.

42 (Ja) Protected Disclosures Act, 2011, s 2.

43 D McKoy, 'Whistle Blowing and the Law' (2012) available at SSRN: <http://ssrn.com/abstract=2176330> or <http://dx.doi.org/10.2139/ssrn.2176330>.

44 (Ja) Protected Disclosures Act, 2011, s 2.

action; dismissal; suspension or demotion; harassment; intimidation or victimisation; transferral against one's will; refusal of a transfer or promotion; alteration of a term or condition of employment or retirement to the disadvantage of the employee; provision of an adverse reference; denial or threat of denial of appointment to any employment, profession or office; otherwise adversely affecting the employment, profession or office.[45]

Although the legal burden of proof is usually on the Plaintiff, the burden of proof shifts to the employer if alleged retaliatory action takes place at or around the same time as the disclosure.[46] Dismissal for protected disclosure is considered automatically unfair and a whistleblower may claim before the Industrial Disputes Tribunal (IDT) for compensation.[47]

It has been argued that reports to a designated authority are subject to an elaborate and demanding scheme and the scheme is cumbersome as to what is protected and what is not. This may be a disincentive for some employees to blow the whistle.[48] A further disincentive is the lack of reward[49] and the fact that there is no plea bargaining in Jamaica where a whistleblower is also a wrong-doer. Further, there can be no disclosure of information where the disclosure is itself a criminal offence,[50] or is protected by legal professional privilege.[51] McKoy argues that this is difficult to reconcile with the provision on general immunity under section 15(2) which states:

> A person who makes a protected disclosure, or receives, investigates or otherwise deals with a protected disclosure, shall not be liable in any civil or criminal proceeding or to any disciplinary proceeding by reason of having made, received, investigated or otherwise dealt with that disclosure in accordance with this Act.[52]

The operation of the Official Secrets Act is excluded only where the recipient of the information is a designated authority.[53]

> However, the exclusion in this paragraph applies only to disclosures to the designated authority and its investigations under the Act, and with the specificity of this restriction it remains a challenging question if any other recipient of a disclosure from a public official covered by the Official Secrets Act can claim a similar exemption.[54]

Despite its limitations, the Protected Disclosure Act is another mechanism to improve corporate governance in Jamaica, which could be seen as either a deterrent

45 ibid s 2.
46 ibid s 17.
47 ibid s 16.
48 D McKoy, 'Whistle Blowing and the Law' (2012) available at SSRN: <http://ssrn.com/abstract=2176330 or http://dx.doi.org/10.2139/ssrn.2176330> 7, 10.
49 ibid 10.
50 (Ja) Protected Disclosures Act, 2011, s 4(2).
51 ibid s 4(3).
52 D McKoy, 'Whistle Blowing and the Law' (2012) available at SSRN: <http://ssrn.com/abstract=2176330 or http://dx.doi.org/10.2139/ssrn.2176330> 11.
53 (Ja) Protected Disclosures Act, 2011, Third Schedule, [4].
54 D McKoy, 'Whistle Blowing and the Law' (2012) available at SSRN: <http://ssrn.com/abstract=2176330 or http://dx.doi.org/10.2139/ssrn.2176330> 11.

to corporate misdeeds or as a mechanism to arrest the wrong-doing before irreparable damage is done to a company.

STAKEHOLDER PROTECTION: PROVISIONS OF CORPORATE GOVERNANCE CODES

Barbados (Corporate Governance Recommendations for Listed Companies on the Barbados Stock Exchange 2014), Jamaica (The Private Sector Organisation of Jamaica Code on Corporate Governance 2009) and Trinidad and Tobago (Trinidad and Tobago Corporate Governance Code 2013) have corporate governance codes, which incorporate stakeholder protection and empowerment.

Barbados

The Corporate Governance Recommendations for Listed Companies on the Barbados Stock Exchange Inc. (The Barbados Code)[55] state at the outset that the Recommendations are designed to 'complement, and supplement as necessary, statutory guidelines'. The goals of the Barbados Code emphasise shareholder protection to include improving transparency; providing a basis of consistency for information provided to shareholders; improving the quality of disclosure and reinforcing appropriate accountabilities. The Barbados Code follows the 'comply or explain' principle, which is described in the following terms:

> . . . the company should comply with the entire Recommendation, and if the Board, in its business judgment, wishes to deviate from a particular Recommendation, the company should provide an explanation for doing so. The company must provide information on compliance with these Recommendations, either in its Annual Report or on its website, as directed by the Barbados Stock Exchange Inc. via the *Notices to Listed Companies*.[56]

Section 2 deals with the General Meeting and makes the following recommendations:

i) Adequate information of matters to be dealt with at the meeting should be made available to the shareholders prior to the convening of a Shareholders' Meeting;
ii) The organisation of the meeting should permit shareholders' effective exercise of their ownership rights;
iii) A majority of the directors should attend the Shareholders' Meeting;
iv) A prospective director should attend the General Meeting to give the shareholders an opportunity to meet with the prospective director.

These recommendations are designed to ensure that shareholders have every opportunity to assess information and to engage with the Board and Chief Executive and to assess the information presented to them.

---

55 See Barbados Stock Exchange Inc. <www.bse.com.bb>.

56 Corporate Governance Recommendations for Listed Companies on the Barbados Stock Exchange Inc. <www.bse.com.bb> 5.

Section 3 deals with the Board of Directors and includes in Recommendation 8 that the general meeting should elect the directors of the company in accordance with section 66(3) of the Barbados Companies Act, to enable the shareholders to provide oversight of the management and operations of the company. Recommendation 19 provides that the company should disclose the background, biographical details, compensation and shareholdings of directors to enable the shareholders to evaluate their relationships with the company. Sections 5 and 6 deals with the Managing Director/CEO and other management respectively, and Recommendations 46 and 49 require the same disclosure for the Managing Director/CEO and the five most senior members of the management team, including the most senior financial officer, as for directors under Recommendation 19.

Recommendation 33 provides for a Code of Business Conduct and Ethics and Disclosure (Code of Conduct) applicable to Directors, the Managing Director/CEO and members of the Executive Management team and other employees of the company to promote integrity and deter wrongdoing. This Code of Conduct should address: conflicts of interest; protection and proper use of corporate assets and opportunities; confidentiality of corporate information; fair dealing with the company's shareholders, customers, suppliers, competitors and employees; compliance with laws, rules and regulations (including insider trading laws); encouraging the reporting of any illegal or unethical behaviour.

The requirements for disclosure of director and executive compensation are outlined in section 7 and Recommendation 50 requires that the company describe how directors are compensated and disclose the aggregate of each element of the directors' compensation to enable shareholders to evaluate the amount of compensation (a) in relation to the contributions of the Board and (b) in comparison with the fees and benefits paid by similar companies. The fees as well as the dollar value of the benefits should be disclosed. Recommendation 53 requires that the company disclose the dollar value of shares and share-related rights granted to directors and Recommendation 54 requires that the company disclose details of director stock options.

Recommendation 55 provides that the criteria and decision-making procedure of the compensation system, each element of compensation and the present dollar value of any and all components of compensation of the Managing Director/CEO and other members of the management team, should be disclosed in the annual report of the Company.

Recommendation 60 requires that a proposal for the election of an external auditor should be disclosed in a timely manner in the invitation to the General Meeting. The audit and non-audit fees (where applicable) of the external auditor must also be disclosed during the financial year to enable shareholders to evaluate the activities of the external auditor.

Section 11.0 provides guidelines for communication and disclosure and states, *inter alia*:

> . . . The information communicated and published by the company permits Shareholders to evaluate the functioning of the corporate governance of the company and make reasoned and informed decisions concerning their holdings.

Companies are therefore required by Recommendation 64, to provide a Corporate Governance Statement on their website and in their Annual Report. The Corporate Governance Statement should include the following information: (a) information on compliance with Corporate Governance Recommendations contained in the Recommendations as well as possible deviations and their explanations; (b) Notice of General Meeting; (c) Articles and By-laws; (d) Board of Directors; (e) CEO and other executives; (f) External Auditor; (g) shares, share capital, principal shareholders (holders of 10% or more of the issued share capital of the company), shareholder agreements to which the company is party; (h) Annual Report; and (i) other circumstances to be reported in accordance with the Recommendations.

Companies are required to have a website and disclose on it 'all the information that has been published pursuant to the statutory obligation of listed companies to provide information' (Recommendations 63 and 64) to enable shareholders ease of access to information about the company and a detailed picture of the operations and financial position of the company.

The Barbados Code is strong on shareholder protection, by emphasising participation in voting in general meeting and requiring demanding disclosure requirements by the directors and officers of the company. The Barbados Code stops short of suggesting 'say on pay', but the detailed requirements for disclosure of director and executive compensation and the compensation system applied, goes a fair way to discourage excessive compensation. The Barbados Code, however, is limited in its scope for protection of a wider group of stakeholders save for the requirement for a Code of Conduct which should include a requirement for fair dealing with the company's shareholders, customers, suppliers, competitors and employees. The requirement for the Code of Conduct to include encouraging the reporting of any illegal or unethical behaviour is welcome, but will be difficult to encourage in the absence of whisteblowing legislation in Barbados. There appears to be an absence of a requirement or encouragement for companies to engage in corporate social responsibility, which is now seen as an integral part of good corporate governance, as the community in which the company operates, including the environment, are now seen as important stakeholders for long-term corporate success.

Jamaica

The Private Sector Organisation of Jamaica (PSOJ) Code 2009 embodies the Six Principles of Corporate Governance developed by the Organisation of Economic Cooperation and Development (OECD),[57] which includes, *inter alia*, the rights of shareholders and key ownership functions; the equitable treatment of shareholders, the role of stakeholders in corporate governance and disclosure and transparency.

The PSOJ Code 2009 has very limited provisions on stakeholder protection and emphasises the protection of shareholders rather than the wider constituents. The

57 OECD Principles of Corporate Governance (OECD 2004) available at <http://www.oecd.org/corporate/ca/corporategovernanceprinciples/31557724.pdf>.

PSOJ Code 2009 is not a 'comply or explain' code although the Jamaica Stock Exchange (JSE) Rules refer to the PSOJ as a code which may be consulted in order to comply with Rule 414.[58] Rule 414 of the JSE Rules mandates listed companies to adopt and disclose corporate governance guidelines which should address specified matters relating to the Board, Management and Accountability and Audit. There is no requirement that shareholder or other stakeholder interests be addressed.

Section D of the PSOJ Code sets guidelines for relations with shareholders. D.1 states that there should be dialogue with shareholders based on the mutual understanding of objectives and that the Board as a whole has the responsibility to ensure that satisfactory dialogue takes place. The Chairperson and senior independent director and other directors should maintain sufficient contact with shareholders and the senior independent director should attend sufficient meetings with a range of shareholders.[59] The Board should state in the annual report the steps they have taken to ensure dialogue with shareholders.[60]

Section D also requires that the Board should ensure constructive use of the Annual General Meeting (AGM), to communicate with investors and to encourage their participation. All directors should attend the AGM and the chairpersons of the audit, remuneration, corporate governance and nomination committees should be available to answer questions at the AGM.[61] The papers for the AGM should be sent at least 21 working days before the meeting.[62]

Section E recommends that companies promote timely and balanced disclosure of all material matters concerning the company in accordance with the Companies Act and the JSE Rules to enable investors to have equal and timely access to factual, material information incorporating both negative and positive information.

Principles relating to the responsibilities of Institutional Shareholders are outlined in Section F and include the following recommendations:

i) Institutional shareholders should enter into a dialogue with companies based on the mutual understanding of objectives.
ii) Institutional shareholders should evaluate a company's governance arrangements and compliance with the corporate governance principles.
iii) Institutional shareholders should make considered use of their votes.

It is submitted, however, that the provisions in the PSOJ Code 2009, relating to institutional shareholders, ought not to be placed in the Code, which is designed to provide guidelines for management of companies rather than investors. These recommendations may, however, be rationalised if they are intended to provide guidance to the management of a company where the company is itself an institutional shareholder. The better view, however, is that provisions relating to institutional investors are

58 Available at <www.jamstockex.com>.
59 Private Sector Organization of Jamaica (PSOJ Code) 2009, D.1.1.
60 PSOJ Code, D.1.2.
61 PSOJ Code, D.2.3.
62 PSOJ Code, D.2.4.

better placed in a Stewardship Code such as the UK Stewardship Code 2012.[63] The UK Stewardship Code 2012 states its principles in the following terms:

> So as to protect and enhance the value that accrues to the ultimate beneficiary, institutional investors should:
>
> 1. publicly disclose their policy on how they will discharge their stewardship responsibilities.
> 2. have a robust policy on managing conflicts of interest in relation to stewardship which should be publicly disclosed.
> 3. monitor their investee companies.
> 4. establish clear guidelines on when and how they will escalate their stewardship activities.
> 5. be willing to act collectively with other investors where appropriate.
> 6. have a clear policy on voting and disclosure of voting activity.
> 7. report periodically on their stewardship and voting activities.

The PSOJ Code 2009 is currently under review, and it is recommended that the PSOJ Code should include a wider range of stakeholders by introducing provisions relating to whistleblowing as introduced by the Protected Disclosures Act 2011 and corporate social responsibility, which reflects some of the growing jurisprudence relating to Company Law. Another recommendation is the introduction of a non-binding 'say-on-pay', which in effect, would allow shareholders to assert some influence on executive pay, through a non-binding vote of approval or disapproval.

Trinidad and Tobago

The Trinidad and Tobago Corporate Governance Code 2013 (the T&T Code) is not a 'comply or explain' code, but rather a voluntary code, which outlines principles and recommended practices for good corporate governance. The principles of the T&T Code, which focus on stakeholder protection, relate to accountability through disclosure (Principle Four) and strengthening of relationships with shareholders (Principle Five).

Principle Four states that the 'Board should present an accurate, timely, balanced and understandable assessment of the company's performance, position and prospects'. The T&T Code recommends that all material information should be disclosed and includes:

1. The financial and operating results of the company
2. Company objectives
3. Major share ownership and voting rights
4. Remuneration policy for members of the Board and Senior Management
5. Information about Board members, including their qualifications, the selection process, other company directorships and whether they are regarded as independent

63 Available at <www.frc.org.uk>.

6. Related party transactions
7. Foreseeable risk factors
8. Issues regarding employees and other stakeholders that may materially affect the company
9. Governance structures and policies, in particular, the content of any corporate governance code or policy and the process by which they are implemented
10. Compliance with statutory, regulatory and tax requirements.

It is recommended that directors include a statement on the integrity of the financial reports and compliance with applicable financial reporting standards and that they present a true and fair view of the financial affairs of the company (Recommendation 4.2). The board should also report annually to shareholders and stakeholders on fees to external auditors for audit and non-audit work (Recommendation 4.3). Boards should also make an annual report to shareholders on the implementation of corporate governance principles and explain any significant departure from the Recommendations supporting each Principle in the T&T Code (Recommendation 4.6).

The T&T Code recommends under Principle Five, that the Board strengthen its relationship with shareholders by facilitating the exercise of their ownership rights and encouraging their engagement with the company. 'Shareholders' include minority, foreign and institutional shareholders (Recommendation 5.1). The Board should also ensure that all shareholders have the opportunity to engage with the company and participate effectively in annual and special meetings (Recommendation 5.2). The notice for annual meetings and relevant materials should be sent to shareholders at least 21 days before the meeting for special resolutions and not less than 10 business days before other meetings.

External auditors and senior management should be available for questioning by shareholders during annual and special meetings and moderated by the chairperson. All directors and senior management should attend and chairpersons of the Audit, Remuneration and Nomination Committees should be available to answer questions.

The Trinidad and Tobago Corporate Governance Code appears to be less comprehensive than the Barbados and Jamaica Codes possibly due to the fact that the Trinidad Code operates in the form of guidelines rather than a 'comply or explain' code. It remains to be seen whether the recommendations outlined in the Trinidad Code will be as effective as those found in the other two territories.

CONCLUSION

The Companies legislation and Corporate Governance Codes in the Commonwealth Caribbean region clearly indicate that the shareholder primacy model of the past has been replaced by a stakeholder model of corporate governance which contemplates the interests of a wider group of stakeholders to include persons who may be affected by actions of the company. The empowerment of stakeholders has been effected in most of the territories, in varying degrees, by way of (i) the enlargement of the duties of directors and officers to take into consideration employees and the community in which the company operates, (ii) through the ability for complainants to bring derivative actions on behalf of the company for wrongs done to the company, and (iii) the oppression remedy, to protect some stakeholders from oppression, unfair prejudice or unfair disregard of their interests. In addition, stakeholder interests are also protected through the Protected Disclosures Act of Jamaica, which allows persons in an employment situation, who blow the whistle on 'improper conduct' by an employer, to be protected against 'occupational detriment'.

The Corporate Governance Codes in the region protect stakeholder interests principally through extensive corporate transparency and disclosure requirements, which include detailed disclosure on appointments to the Board, director and executive remuneration and financial reporting. There is emphasis on the strengthening of the relationship between the Board, management and shareholders and provisions to encourage good corporate governance practices for institutional shareholders, who have a responsibility to their own stakeholders. The quasi-legislative nature of the Barbados and Jamaica (PSOJ) Codes, through a 'comply or explain' regime, encourages compliance as a part of the rules of the stock exchanges, thereby increasing shareholder and stakeholder protection. The inclusion of a non-binding, 'say on pay', and the modern thrust for increased risk management and internal control oversight and corporate social responsibility is recommended in order to reflect the modern stakeholder emphasis found in many of the modern international corporate governance codes and legislation, which should go a long way in increasing the protection of shareholders and other stakeholders in the region.

The overall developments in stakeholder empowerment and protection augers well for the region, by providing a good precedent for Commonwealth Caribbean territories which have yet to introduce Corporate Governance Codes.

BIBLIOGRAPHY

Ffolkes-Goldson, S, 'The Use and Misuse of the Corporate Oppression Remedy in the Commonwealth Caribbean' (2014) 35(7) *Company Lawyer* 195

Koehnen, M, *Oppression and Related Remedies*, 2004, Thomson Canada Limited

Lacayo, R and Ripley, A, 'Persons of The Year 2002: The Whistleblowers', *Time Magazine* (30 December 2002) <www.time.com/time/magazine/article/0,9171,1003998,00.html>

McKoy, DV, 'Whistle Blowing and the Law' (2012) <http://ssrn.com/abstract=2176330 or http://dx.doi.org/10.2139/ssrn.2176330>

OECD Principles of Corporate Governance (OECD 2004) <www.oecd.org/corporate/ca/corporategovernanceprinciples/31557724.pdf>

CHAPTER 5

THE LEGAL MATRIX GOVERNING DIRECTORS AND OFFICERS OF FINANCIAL SUPERVISORS

Understanding their role in governance

Celia Blake

INTRODUCTION

The literature on governance in organisations is heavily concerned with commercial enterprises. Hence the term 'corporate governance', which, in the early development of the concept, and *stricto sensu*, has been taken to mean control and accountability systems for corporations[1] – business associations run largely by private capital[2] which are registered under the relevant companies enactment. Principles of corporate governance have nonetheless come to be recommended for and applied in government institutions, as efforts at restructuring and transforming the public sector[3] have been influenced significantly by private sector concepts and models.[4] An aspect of public sector transformation and modernisation has been the creation of statutory bodies[5] assigned regulatory portfolios. Particularly with this delegation of governmental power to an increasing number of statutory agencies in several jurisdictions, academic studies and commentaries on public sector governance have emerged.[6] Since the turn of the twenty-first century, there has been an emerging focus within the public sector

---

1 J Farrar, *Corporate Governance: Theories, Principles and Practice* (3rd edn, OUP 2008) 3.

2 Structural conversion by governments of public sector trading operations or services of a commercial nature traditionally delivered by public sector departments into state-owned registered companies has, increasingly, become a feature of the public sector. These companies have been referred to as 'corporatised' enterprises by J Farrar, *Corporate Governance: Theories, Principles and Practice* (3rd edn, OUP 2008) 458.

3 In the UK, public sector transformation since the 1980s has proceeded under the label 'The New Public Management'. For an overview of public sector restructuring in the Commonwealth Caribbean see, P Sutton, 'The Public Sector Reform in the Commonwealth Caribbean: A Review of Recent Experiences', Caribbean Paper No 6, Centre for International Governance Innovation 2008, available at <http://www.cigionline.org/sites/default/files/6.%20Public%20Sector%20Reform%20in%20the%20Commonwealth%20Caribbean.pdf>.

4 E Ferlie, L Ashburner, L Fitzgerald and A Pettigrew, *The New Public Management in Action* (OUP 1996). A major corporate governance study relating to the Caribbean includes what the author refers to as 'state-owned enterprises': VL Kerr, *Effective Corporate Governance* (GovStrat 2005) esp Ch 9. The term 'state-owned enterprises' does not appear to be defined in the work but it seems to be focussed on the type of firm referred to by Farrar as 'corporatised enterprises' (above n 2).

5 These are distinct from what Farrar calls 'corporatised entities' (above n 2).

6 For example, D Oliver, T Prosser and R Rawlings, *The Regulatory State* (OUP 2010); R Mulgan, *Holding Power to Account* (Palgrave Macmillan 2003); C Scott, 'Accountability and the Regulatory State' (2000) 27(1) *Journal of Law and Society* 38; E Ferlie, L Ashburner, L Fitzgerald and A Pettigrew, *The New Public Management in Action* (OUP 1996). For a Commonwealth Caribbean perspective, see, for example, S Ryan and A Bisessar (eds), *Governance in the Caribbean* (SALISES 2002); D McKoy, *Corruption: Law, Governance and Ethics in the Commonwealth Caribbean* (Hansib 2012).

governance literature on the institutions responsible for financial sector regulation and supervision.[7] This focus is perhaps understandable in view of the fact that these institutions have become governance watchdogs for the entities falling within their regulatory purview. In addition, it has been argued that regulatory governance has become a point of interest because changing business models in the delivery of financial services as well as financial sector distress have sparked debates about the most suitable structure for regulation.[8] Importantly too, there is empirical research which indicates that the quality of regulatory governance has an impact on financial system stability[9] – a critical goal of financial regulation.

In Commonwealth Caribbean jurisdictions, as elsewhere, there has been a growing tendency to establish financial regulators/supervisors as statutory organisations.[10] The Commonwealth Caribbean has not, however, featured much in the emerging literature on financial regulatory governance.[11] Additionally, despite the fact that statutory regulatory authorities are typically led by a board of directors, there appears to be few studies which examine in some detail governance issues relating specifically to

7 For example, A Page, 'Regulating the Regulator – A Lawyer's Perspective on Accountability and Control', C Goodhart, 'Regulating the Regulator – An Economist's Perspective on Accountability and Control' and R Lastra and H Sham, 'Public Accountability in the Financial Sector' all in E Ferran and C Goodhart (eds), *Regulating Financial Services and Markets in the Twenty First Century* (Hart 2001) 127, 151 and 165 respectively; D Masciandaro and M Quintyn (eds), *Designing Financial Supervision Institutions: Independence, Accountability and Governance* (Edward Elgar 2007). See especially M Quintyn, S Ramirez and M Taylor, 'The Fear of Freedom: Politicians and the Independence and Accountability of Financial Supervisors in Practice' in D Masciandaro and M Quintyn (eds), *Designing Financial Supervision Institutions: Independence, Accountability and Governance* (Edward Elgar 2007) 62–63.

8 M Quintyn, S Ramirez and M Taylor, 'The Fear of Freedom: Politicians and the Independence and Accountability of Financial Supervisors in Practice' in D Masciandaro and M Quintyn (eds), *Designing Financial Supervision Institutions: Independence, Accountability and Governance* (Edward Elgar 2007) 62–63.

9 U Das, M Quintyn and K Chenard, 'Does Regulatory Governance Matter for Financial System Stability? An Empirical Analysis' (2004) IMF WP/04/89.

10 Commonwealth Caribbean Central Banks are statutory creatures. Though monetary policy is the core function of central banks, these central banks have also been typically assigned supervisory and regulatory functions for at least part of the financial sector. In Jamaica, for example, the Central Bank's supervisory remit includes most deposit-taking financial institutions. Another statutory body, the Financial Services Commission, has oversight for the securities, insurance and private pensions sectors. The Jamaica Deposit Insurance Corporation, established under the Deposit Insurance Act 1998, as a secondary safety net regulator, completes the main structure for financial regulation in Jamaica. In Trinidad and Tobago the Central Bank has supervisory responsibility for much of the financial sector of that territory including deposit-taking financial institutions as well as the insurance and private pensions sectors. The securities sector is regulated by the Trinidad and Tobago Securities and Exchange Commission set up under the Securities Act 2012. (The Commission had previously existed by virtue of the Securities Industry Act 1995.)

11 Notably, a study on financial supervisory governance surveying 55 jurisdictions included two countries in the Commonwealth Caribbean. See D Masciandaro, M Quintyn and M Taylor, 'Financial Supervisory Independence and Accountability – Exploring the Determinants' (2008) IMF Working Paper WP/08/147, available at <https://www.imf.org/external/pubs/ft/wp/2008/wp08147.pdf> accessed May 2012.

the directors and officers of these authorities.[12] This contrasts with the overwhelming attention in the corporate governance literature devoted exclusively to directors of incorporated associations. Financial regulators, as entities established by statutes, are not automatically subject to enactments governing companies. It should not therefore be assumed that corporate governance rules emanating from companies legislation apply automatically to the directors, officers and structure of statutory boards. Though financial regulatory authorities play an important role in ensuring that the entities they regulate and supervise observe corporate governance laws and codes, the precise legal framework governing the boards and officers of these statutory bodies, particularly those in Commonwealth Caribbean jurisdictions, appears to have so far received relatively little commentary in the literature.

Against this background, this chapter examines directors and officers in the context of governance of financial regulators in the Commonwealth Caribbean. This is perhaps timely given the renewed thrust regarding governance in public sector institutions in at least one Commonwealth Caribbean jurisdiction, Jamaica. The government of this country in 2011 approved for implementation a new policy on governance in the public sector.[13] This policy, despite its currency, is necessarily general in that it is designed for all public sector entities, irrespective of their juridical nature or functional remit. Corporatised entities, for example, though subject to general public sector governance principles, may, arguably, require a nuanced governance regime when compared with other types of public sector entities. In relation to regulatory institutions in the public sector, a case has been made that financial regulators are distinctive because, unlike several other regulators, they oversee issues surrounding market failure including questions of governance. Besides, where necessary, these regulators become critical players in redressing that failure[14] by exercising considerable powers legislatively conferred on them, many of which are highly intrusive and may have a significant impact on the regulated entity and the wider financial system. Arguably then, they merit special attention in the governance literature. Besides treating with public sector bodies in a generic, undifferentiated way, Jamaica's recent public sector governance

12 The board and senior officers of financial regulators are usually discussed within the literature in the context of institutional independence which tends to be partly signalled by the bases for appointment of board members and officers, how their appointments may be revoked as well as their tenure. See, for example, the criteria for institutional independence set out in Appendix II in D Masciandaro, M Quintyn and M Taylor, 'Financial Supervisory Independence and Accountability – Exploring the Determinants' (2008) IMF Working Paper WP/08/147, available at <https://www.imf.org/external/pubs/ft/wp/2008/wp08147.pdf> accessed May 2012. See too Table 3A.2 in the Appendix in M Quintyn, S Ramirez and M Taylor, 'The Fear of Freedom: Politicians and the Independence and Accountability of Financial Supervisors in Practice' in D Masciandaro and M Quintyn (eds), *Designing Financial Supervision Institutions: Independence, Accountability and Governance* (Edward Elgar 2007) 100–101.

13 Corporate Governance Framework for Public Bodies in Jamaica, 2011, available at <http://www.mof.gov.jm/documents/documents-publications/document-centre/file/172-corporate-governance-framework-september-2011.html> accessed July 2015.

14 J Carmichael, 'Public Sector Governance and the Finance Sector' in R Litan, M Pomerleano and V Sundararajan (eds), *Financial Sector Governance: The Roles of the Public and Private Sectors* (Brookings Institution 2002) 121, 130–132.

policy document goes beyond the legal rules pertaining to governance, and deals to a large extent, with softer, less binding best practice guidelines and ethical codes. It is also aspirational in nature – recommending and seeking to promote the adoption of certain practices[15] within the public sector, which, while desirable and useful, may not necessarily be grounded in the relevant legal statutes. While this author acknowledges the importance of extra-legal principles to governance frameworks, this discussion will be confined to the legal core of the body of governance principles.[16] The mandatory nature of the legal core suggests the existence of enforceable sanctions and thus carries stronger consequential implications. In addition, despite the preference for non-legal corporate governance arrangements and codes in some jurisdictions,[17] it is arguable that, given the governmental and statutory nature of regulatory bodies, formalism via legal norms is a more appropriate means of instituting a governance framework for these bodies. Hence, a legal basis for governance rules ought, perhaps, to be viewed as indispensable for public statutory bodies like financial regulators as compared with corporate entities. This chapter thus proposes to provide an integrated statement of the laws governing the directors and officers of financial regulators in the Commonwealth Caribbean and thereby attempts to define the parameters of the legal obligations of, and the control and accountability mechanisms in the law for these persons. This, in itself, is a useful endeavour, particularly in view of the observation contained in Jamaica's policy document for governance in the public sector that '[m]ost board directors . . . do not understand the rudiments of their responsibilities'.[18] This chapter, however, will go beyond setting out this legal matrix applicable to the directors and officers of financial regulators. It offers a critique of the extent to which this matrix contributes to, and supports the contemporary notions, principles and goals of, institutional and regulatory governance.

The chapter will first discuss the main theories and elements of governance, contextualising this discussion within the framework of the public sector, and specifically financial regulatory governance. It will then, with reference to the relevant legislation and any pertinent case law, develop a matrix of the laws governing directors and senior officers of the statutory authorities responsible for financial services supervision in the Commonwealth Caribbean. Given the various legislative provisions that require examination, and the need for legal specificity, the chapter will focus on the laws of two jurisdictions, Jamaica and Trinidad and Tobago. These jurisdictions have fairly established structures for financial services regulation relative to other Commonwealth

15 For example, diversity in board composition in respect of educational background and professional experience as well as gender and age.

16 See J Farrar, *Corporate Governance: Theories, Principles and Practice* (3rd edn, OUP 2008) 4; A Young, 'Frameworks in Regulating Company Directors: Rethinking the Philosophical Foundations' (2009) *Company Lawyer* 355, 360–361.

17 This has been suggested by major corporate governance reviews, such as the Cadbury Report 1992, and stated explicitly in the Higgs Report (2003) para 1.14. See too J du Plessis, A Hargovan and M Bagaric, *Principles of Corporate Governance* (2nd edn, CUP 2011) 446–468.

18 Corporate Governance Framework for Public Bodies in Jamaica (2011, Revised 2012) 17, available at <http://www.ocg.gov.jm/ocg/sites/default/files/Revised%20Corporate%20Governance%20Framework%20%28Oct%202012%29.pdf> accessed November 2014.

Caribbean territories and these structures have also undergone some reconfiguration, particularly in response to trouble in the financial sector. In addition, Jamaica is currently revamping aspects of its banking regulations with the imminent introduction of a new Banking Services Act 2014 which will modify some of the current elements of governance in the banking regulator. Arguably then, the two jurisdictions make good candidates for an examination of the laws underpinning the organ at the helm of the respective statutory regulatory authorities. Such an examination will facilitate a comparative treatment of the nature of governance in this type of statutory authority across the two jurisdictions. This comparative perspective might indicate developing tendencies in governance as it relates to the directors and officers of financial regulators in the region. The matrix of the laws examined constitutes the data for the chapter's discussion and analysis of the degree to which the laws, as the nucleus of the structure of organisational governance, support the main elements of governance of public sector institutions, particularly of financial sector regulators.

THEORETICAL BASES AND PRINCIPLES OF FINANCIAL REGULATORY GOVERNANCE

Multiple definitions of governance have been offered both in relation to corporations[19] and to the public sector.[20] As Ryan suggests, some of these variations may be attributed to the particular sector or discipline in respect of which governance is being discussed,[21] but it may be broadly considered to be the structure and system for controlling and managing an organisation. While definitions of the term may vary, there tends to be remarkable convergence in the literature regarding the precise values or principles which are associated with the term. In *Governance in the Caribbean*, the editors identify the following factors as critical 'fundamental principles' which run across both the public and private sectors: openness or transparency, integrity and accountability.[22] These overlap with characteristics of good corporate governance outlined in the 2002 King Report on Corporate Governance for South Africa.[23] The King Report also lists independence as an important characteristic of governance which has also been highlighted in other commissioned corporate governance reports[24] as a crucial feature for checking dominance on corporate boards. These four principles of

19 See J du Plessis, A Hargovan and M Bagaric, *Principles of Contemporary Corporate Governance* (2nd edn, CUP 2011) 3–11.

20 See S Ryan, 'Good Governance: Old Wine in New Bottles?' in S Ryan and A Bissessar (eds), *Governance in the Caribbean* (SALISES 2002) 7–9; G S Cheema, 'A Governance Approach to Development: New Role for Development Co-operation' in HA Hye (ed), *Governance: South Asian Perspectives* (The University Press Limited 2000) 513, 516–517.

21 S Ryan, 'Good Governance: Old Wine in New Bottles?' in S Ryan and A Bissessar (eds), *Governance in the Caribbean* (SALISES 2002) 7.

22 S Ryan and A Bissessar, *Governance in the Caribbean* (SALISES 2002) 3.

23 Paragraph 18 of the Report. The principles are also enumerated in J du Plessis, A Hargovan and M Bagaric, *Principles of Contemporary Corporate Governance* (2nd edn, CUP 2011) 11–12.

24 For example, the Cadbury (1992), Hampel (1998) and Higgs (2003) Reports for the UK.

governance – transparency, integrity, accountability and independence – have been advanced by Das and Quintyn as necessary for 'good regulatory governance'[25] and are adopted by this chapter as the key elements of governance against which the laws will be evaluated.

Theoretical underpinnings of governance

Before elaborating on the nature and relevance of these principles to financial regulatory governance, it will be useful to explain briefly the main theoretical underpinnings of organisational governance. One theory accounting for it rests on what has been summarily described as the principal–agent problem which arises whenever tasks have been delegated by one person to another. The idea is that the interests of the principal and the agent are not neatly aligned and, consequently, conflicts inhere in the relationship, and agents may pursue their own interests in discharging their delegated tasks. This creates potential costs for the principal.[26] While this agency theory emerged within the context of the corporate and commercial environment, scholars have suggested that it is applicable as well to an analysis of a wide range of relationships[27] including relationships within the public bureaucracy.[28] In the specific context of financial regulatory agencies, their immediate principals are the political directorate, specifically the ministerial authority under whose portfolio the agency falls. The 'ultimate principals',[29] however, are the users of the regulated financial services whose interests may not coincide with those of the immediate principals. Delegation of the regulation function to an agent–regulator is rationalised on the basis of the need for technical expertise in the regulatory effort, particularly in the financial sector which is increasingly complex and sophisticated.

Enriques and Hertig have identified some of the problems which inhere in this principal–agent situation. These include the tension between technically competent supervisors versus politically motivated immediate principals who may be heavily influenced by short-term re-election goals which can frustrate the more long-term

25 U Das and M Quintyn, 'Crisis Prevention and Crisis Management: The Role of Regulatory Governance' (2002) IMF Working Paper, WP/02/163, Section II B, available at <http://www.imf.org/external/pubs/ft/wp/2002/wp02163.pdf> accessed May 2012.

26 M Jensen and W Meckling, 'Theory of the Firm: Management Behaviour, Agency Costs and Ownership Structure' (1976) *Journal of Financial Economics* 305. See too J Farrar, *Corporate Governance: Theories, Principles and Practice* (3rd edn, OUP 2008) 464–465 and J Armour, H Hansmann and R Kraakman, 'Agency Problems, Legal Strategies and Enforcement', ECGI Working Paper No 135/2009.

27 J Armour, H Hansmann and R Kraakman, 'Agency Problems, Legal Strategies and Enforcement' (2009) Oxford Legal Studies Research Paper 21/2009, part 2.1, available at <http://papers.ssrn.com/sol3/papers.cfm?abstract_id=1436555> accessed May 2012.

28 J Farrar, *Corporate Governance: Theories, Principles and Practice* (3rd edn, OUP 2008) 467 n 41 and J Carmichael, 'Public Sector Governance and the Finance Sector' in R Litan, M Pomerleano and V Sundararajan (eds), *Financial Sector Governance: The Roles of the Public and Private Sectors* (Brookings Institution 2002) 121, 128.

29 L Enriques and G Hertig, 'Improving the Governance of Financial Supervisors' (2011) *European Business Organization Law Review* 357, 364.

goals of financial regulation.[30] There is also the perceived difficulty of the regulators' notional desire for personal power and prestige which may cause misplacement in their lines of emphasis. This may not be in the interests of their ultimate or immediate principals.[31] The lack of complete alignment of the principal's and agent's interests obliges the principal to incur costs in monitoring and supervising the agent and promoting alignment of the interests of the parties in various ways such as via remuneration commensurate with performance and other rewards. McKoy argues, though, that aligning interests does not completely account for agency costs. His thesis, particularly in the context of corruption, is that agency costs are incurred where agents are not made to stand the cost of their risky or dishonest behaviour.[32]

In the regulatory environment, a locus for potential conflict also arises in the relationship between the regulator and the regulated sector. Indeed, this conflict opens the door to dishonest, corrupt behaviour and regulatory capture. The conflict here, however, exists not between the agent–regulator and the principals (immediate or ultimate) which have been identified above. This conflict introduces a third party in the form of the regulated entities who are participants in the regulatory environment. In this context, the stakeholder theory, as a basis for organisational governance, may be a more conceptually useful approach than the principal–agent problem. As in the case of the principal–agent theory, the stakeholder theory emerged in relation to the corporate firm. It presents the firm as a centre where the interests of various stakeholders[33] converge, and proposes that corporate governance structures should take these interests into account.[34] This notion is useful in this discussion of public sector, and more narrowly regulatory governance, as a descriptive model accounting for the possible tensions between regulated entities and the regulator which can affect good governance of regulatory institutions. Besides, in public sector regulatory agencies, the stakeholder model, rather than the principal–agent theory, perhaps more suitably describes the various constituencies of interests to be addressed in the governance arrangements of these agencies. This is because there is no proprietary ownership of these agencies equivalent to the nature of shareholding

30 This is related to the time inconsistency argument as summarised in M Quintyn and M Taylor, 'Robust Regulators and their Political Masters: Independence and Accountability in Theory' in D Masciandaro and M Quintyn (eds), *Designing Financial Supervision Institutions: Independence, Accountability and Governance* (Edward Elgar 2007) 8–10. Quintyn and Taylor (p 4) also argue that the politician's interest in securing rents from the financial sector for campaign contributions and other benefits makes them reluctant to delegate tasks to regulators.

31 L Enriques and G Hertig, 'Improving the Governance of Financial Supervisors' (2011) *European Business Organisation Law Review* 357, 362–364.

32 D McKoy, *Corruption: Law, Governance and Ethics in the Commonwealth Caribbean* (Hansib 2012).

33 A wide definition of the term 'stakeholder' which has application beyond the corporate sphere is 'entities or individuals that can reasonably be expected to be significantly affected by the organisation's activities . . . and whose actions can reasonably be expected to affect the ability of the organisation to successfully implement its strategies and achieve its objectives'. Global Reporting Initiative, *Sustainability Reporting Guidelines*, Version 3.1, 2000–2011, 10, available at <https://www.globalreporting.org/resourcelibrary/G3.1-Guidelines-Incl-Technical-Protocol.pdf> accessed May 2012.

34 For an overview of the stakeholder concept in corporate governance, see J du Plessis, A Hargovan and M Bagaric, *Principles of Contemporary Corporate Governance* (2nd edn, CUP 2011) 20–69.

in corporate firms. This proprietary nature of firms arguably rationalises the applicability of the concept of the owner (shareholder)–principal on whose behalf and in whose economic interest the manager–agent primarily, if not exclusively, acts in running the firm. Though the 'immediate principals' of regulators (ministers of government) may be notionally equated with shareholders as delegators of the task of managing, ministerial interest in the regulator may not be characterised as proprietary or entrepreneurial. The so-called 'ultimate principals' (users of financial services) are, too, unlike their corporate counterparts – being tenuously connected to the regulatory agency and comprising a diffused, unorganised constituency with no direct pecuniary interest in the agency. In addition, given the generic, non-commercial functions of financial regulatory agencies, managerial success for these regulators is not definable or measurable by classic bottom-line computations.[35] The dominance of the proprietary/pecuniary feature in corporate firms perhaps justifies the verticality suggested by the principal–agent relationship. Given the absence of this feature in state regulatory organisations, it may be more appropriate to refer to the various stakeholders of a financial regulatory agency in considering the various interests which can inform the governance arrangements for the agency.

Principles of good governance

In the context of the foregoing discussion on some considerations involved in theories of governance, the need for the four principles of governance alluded to above begins to become apparent. In corporate governance, the principle of independence arises in relation to balancing, indeed controlling executive power, by appointing disinterested non-executive directors to the board who can bring independent judgment to board deliberations. This type of independence acts as a countervailing force against executive corporate agents. While this does have some relevance to financial regulatory institutions, the question of independence in the context of regulators typically relates to agency autonomy from both the political directorate and the regulated sector. The idea is to guard against influence and manipulation of the agency by the political directorate, thereby insulating the operations of the agency from the kind of political interests alluded to above which may come into play.[36] Additionally, independence in financial

35 Goodhart argues that it is difficult to measure whether the aims of financial regulation, as typically outlined in legislation, have been achieved. C Goodhart, 'Regulating the Regulator – An Economist's Perspective on Accountability and Control' in E Ferran and C Goodhart (eds), *Regulating Financial Services and Markets in the Twenty-first Century* (Hart Publishing 2001) 152–153. This is unlike the case for the narrow central bank function in discharging monetary policy as shown by E Hüpkes, M Quintyn and M Taylor, 'The Accountability of Financial Sector Supervisors – Principles and Practice' (2005) *European Business Law Review* 1575, 1584–1586.

36 By way of demonstrating the risk of political influence and thereby the need for independence, reference is made to the fact that the regulator for securities in Jamaica was openly criticised in 2007 by a politician of the then ruling party for having taken enforcement action in 2006 against an entity which had been carrying on securities business without the requisite licences. The politician, in a letter to the press, described the regulator's search of the entity's business premises pursuant to a search warrant as 'a vulgar abuse of state power' and supported the apparent business model of the entity which had been paying extraordinary returns to its investors (see *Jamaica Observer*, 25 January 2007). The business was found to have been a Ponzi scheme.

regulatory agencies relates to protection from regulatory capture. It is clear that the concept of independence in financial regulatory governance contemplates a wider ambit than in corporate governance. In the latter, independence from the shareholder is not necessarily demanded and there is no notion which appears to correspond with industry capture so as to require the attendant autonomy. Autonomy for regulators is important since it encourages objectivity in decision-making and thereby enhances efficiency in the regulatory process. The nature of the independence required in regulatory agencies informs the regulator's governance arrangements, critically, the composition, power and exposure of its board and its senior officers. This has a direct bearing on the rules governing the appointment, dismissal and responsibilities of the directors and senior officers which will be examined below.

In the public sector, the independence component of governance has been traditionally criticised on the basis that it compromises another element of governance – accountability. This may be described as the duty borne by an agency to report on, and justify to the relevant stakeholders, its activities against the yardstick of its given mandate, and to bear the cost of any failing in pursuing that mandate.[37] The criticism goes further by suggesting that a diminution in accountability contributes to a lack of democratic legitimacy of independent regulatory agencies.[38] This perspective has been overtaken perhaps by the more current view that independence and accountability are not antagonistic components but are complementary and interrelated. It has been argued that appropriate accountability arrangements reinforce agency independence.[39] Unlike in corporate governance,[40] in financial regulatory governance there is a range of legitimate stakeholders to whom the duty to account is owed by the regulator. This includes the relevant minister, the legislature, the regulated financial services providers, users of these services, as well as the wider taxpaying public.[41] This range of accountees emanates from the public nature of the regulatory function in the sense that regulators perform a governmental function. This explains the primary purpose of accountability as a principle of public sector governance which is to facilitate public scrutiny of governmental activities in keeping with democratic traditions. Accountability, in this context, extends beyond the strict requirements of a principal–agent

37 R Lastra and H Shams, 'Public Accountability in the Financial Sector' in E Ferran and C Goodhart (eds), *Regulating Financial Services and Markets in the Twenty-first Century* (Hart Publishing 2001) 165, 167.

38 E Ferlie, L Ashburner, L Fitzgerald and A Pettigrew, *The New Public Management in Action* (OUP 1996) 199–200.

39 E Hüpkes, M Quintyn and M Taylor, 'The Accountability of Financial Sector Supervisors – Principles and Practice' (2005) *European Business Law Review* 1575.

40 In corporate governance and in keeping with the classic principal–agent theory of governance, the obligation to account is narrowly owed to the owners/shareholders by the board and senior managers. Though proponents of corporate social responsibility and a stakeholder theory of governance advance the view that corporate boards should also be accountable to stakeholders other than the owners, this remains a very controversial issue and appears to have very little traction in law.

41 Arguably, regulators are also accountable to the judiciary since their decisions and actions are amenable to judicial review.

relationship which suggests answerability by the agent upwards[42] to the appointing principal alone. It is argued that accountability also serves to enhance the performance and credibility of the regulating agency.[43]

Transparency, a third pillar of regulatory governance, has been defined as 'a measure of the degree to which the information about [an agency's] official activity (objectives, legal, institutional and economic framework, decisions, actions, practices, data and information over the regulatory and supervisory policies and the accountability of its senior executives) is constantly verifiable and communicated to third parties interested in the relevant information on a timely basis'.[44] Transparency is thus hinged on timely disclosure of relevant and accurate information to the various stakeholders in the regulatory environment. While the principle of transparency is recognised as being desirable or necessary for its own sake, writers have argued that it also supports the other three components of good governance.[45] Lastra and Shams explain the relationship between transparency and accountability, indicating that both principles involve the disclosure of information but they are distinguishable. Transparency demands that the disclosed information be adequate and material whereas accountability requires that the information be substantiated or justified.[46] Transparency is thus critical in the accountability process as it facilitates proper monitoring of the regulator's activities by the stakeholders. It also shores up independence since disclosure requirements reduce the propensity on the part of political actors and industry players to interfere in the decisions and activities of the regulator.

The governance component of integrity, which is concerned with probity on the part of directors and executives, is also linked to transparency. Systems of governance should be in place to insulate these persons from corruptive influences and to guard against dishonest behaviour on their part in the execution of their roles. In the corporate arena, this aspect of governance is supported by the rules relating to fiduciary duties owed by directors to their companies which have their basis in agency law principles. In public sector agencies like financial regulators, there is perhaps less reliance on the notion of directors as fiduciaries but anti-corruption mechanisms applicable to these agencies have tended to insist on, among other things, disclosure by directors as an *ex ante* means of safeguarding against conduct which compromises personal integrity. Damage to personal integrity is likely, in turn, to weaken the integrity of the regulating institution and its ability to achieve its objectives.

42 See C Scott, 'Accountability in the Regulatory State' (2000) 27(1) *Journal of Law and Society* 38, 42.

43 E Hüpkes, M Quintyn and M Taylor, 'The Accountability of Financial Sector Supervisors – Principles and Practice' (2005) *European Business Law Review* 1575, 1578–1581.

44 M Arnone, S Darbar and A Gambini, 'Governance in Banking Supervision: Theory and Practices' in D Masciandaro and M Quintyn (eds), *Designing Financial Supervision Institutions: Independence, Accountability and Governance* (Edward Elgar 2007) 150, 165.

45 M Quintyn, 'Independent Agencies: More than a Cheap Copy of Independent Central Banks?' (2009) 20 *Constitutional Political Economy* 267, 281–282.

46 R Lastra and H Shams, 'Public Accountability in the Financial Sector' in E Ferran and C Goodhart (eds), *Regulating Financial Services and Markets in the Twenty-first Century* (Hart Publishing 2001) 165, 172.

The discussion indicates that the various components of good governance, perhaps with the exception of the principle of integrity,[47] largely concern the regulator as an *institution*, that is independence, accountability and transparency are demanded of the regulatory agency as a whole in regard to its functions and operations. These principles, to some extent though, become articulated via the board of directors and the senior executives on which this chapter is focussed. An examination of the legal arrangements governing the regulator's directors and senior executives then helps in an understanding of their role in and contribution to good institutional governance.

THE LEGAL POSITION OF DIRECTORS AND SENIOR OFFICERS OF FINANCIAL REGULATORS

Directors and senior officers of regulatory agencies are governed by a network of enactments. The starting point for an examination of the rules relating to them is the various pieces of enabling legislation establishing the agencies and for which the agencies have administrative responsibility. In Jamaica, the primary financial regulators are the Financial Services Commission (FSC) established under the Financial Services Commission Act 2001 (FSC Act) and the central bank (Bank of Jamaica, BOJ) through its Department of Supervision of Banks and Financial Institutions established under the Bank of Jamaica Act 1960[48] (BOJ Act). The BOJ's supervisory remit extends to deposit-taking institutions while the FSC regulates the securities, insurance and private pensions sectors. In Trinidad and Tobago, the Central Bank (CBTT), established under the Central Bank Act 1964, is responsible for supervising the banking sector[49] as well as insurance and pensions.[50] The securities industry is regulated by the Trinidad and Tobago Securities and Exchange Commission (TTSEC) established under the Securities Act 2012, replacing its predecessor under the now repealed Securities Industry Act 1995. This chapter focusses on the directors and senior officers of the FSC and BOJ in Jamaica, and of the CBTT and TTSEC in Trinidad and Tobago. In addition to the enabling legislation for the regulatory agencies, other enactments also impinge on the roles and responsibilities of directors and senior officers of such agencies. These enactments include general public sector governance statutes,[51] legislation

47 While institutional integrity via the internal audit function is important, the majority of the dimensions of the principle of integrity in governance are personal in nature affecting individual conduct in the performance of one's duties within the regulatory institution. See U Das and M Quintyn, 'Crisis Prevention and Crisis Management: The Role of Regulatory Governance' (2002) IMF Working Paper WP/02/163, available at <http://www.imf.org/external/pubs/ft/wp/2002/wp02163.pdf> accessed May 2012.

48 Amendments to the BOJ Act which will be effected by the new Banking Services Act will cause this department of the BOJ to be renamed the *Supervisory Department.*

49 (T&T) Financial Institutions Act 2008, s 5.

50 (T&T) Insurance Act 1980, s 4. Pensions are also regulated under this Act.

51 For example, (Ja) Public Bodies Management and Accountability Act 2001.

dealing with specific areas of public administration,[52] and anti-corruption and integrity statutes.[53] The common law may also have an impact on the position of these directors and senior officers.

Board constitution and structure

Directors' appointment, termination, tenure

In Jamaica, FSC and the majority of BOJ board appointments are made by the relevant Minister.[54] The BOJ Act, however, provides for three automatic appointments to the bank's board: the Financial Secretary (the top civil servant with charge of the finance ministry),[55] the Governor and the Senior Deputy Governor,[56] but the power to appoint these latter two officers in their substantive capacities also rests with the Minister.[57] Under the impending amendments to the BOJ Act, the Governor will be appointed by the Governor-General, the Head of State. Arguably, this amendment will bring no radical change to the status quo since constitutional provisions[58] generally require the Governor-General, in the exercise of his functions, to act in accordance with the advice of the political directorate (the Cabinet) or of a minister having Cabinet's authority. *Prima facie*, the situation for board appointments in Jamaica contrasts with the position in Trinidad and Tobago where CBTT and TTSEC board appointments are made by the President, the Head of State.[59] The Governor and up to two Deputy Governors must be appointed to the CBTT's board but the President is also conferred the power to appoint these officers in their substantive roles. It appears though that in relation to the TTSEC, appointments having been made by the President, it is the Minister's prerogative to select a Deputy Chairman of the Commission.[60] The appointment of *ad hoc* Commissioners is by the President and expressly 'on the advice of the Minister'.[61]

In Jamaica then, there is, in large measure, a concentration of the power of appointment in the minister, the political representative. In Trinidad and Tobago, this direct political influence in the appointment process appears to be mitigated with formal neutrality being achieved via an appointer (the President) who is, arguably, a less

52 For example, (Ja) Financial Administration and Audit Act 1959, the Public Sector Procurement Regulations 2008; (T&T) Exchequer and Audit Act 1959.

53 For example, (Ja) Corruption (Prevention) Act 2001; (T&T) Prevention of Corruption Act 1987, Integrity in Public Life Act 2000.

54 FSC Act, First Schedule, para 1, 3, and 4; BOJ Act, s 6.

55 BOJ Act, s 6(2)(b).

56 BOJ Act, s 6(2)(a).

57 BOJ Act, s 6(2) and (8).

58 Constitution of Jamaica, s 32.

59 (T&T) Central Bank Act, s 7(1); Securities Act, s 10(2).

60 (T&T) Securities Act, s 10(3A).

61 (T&T) Securities Act, s 10(7).

partisan, more collective representative.[62] However, this apparent neutrality must be seen in the context of a constitutional provision[63] which requires the President, in the exercise of functions conferred on him by the constitution or any other law, to act in keeping with the advice of the Cabinet or a minister. In relation to the TTSEC, the law attempts to claw back some of the formal presidential powers of appointment by allowing direct ministerial involvement in the selection of a Deputy Chairman. Jamaica's, and arguably Trinidad and Tobago's, model of appointment power concentration in the political representative is often criticised on the ground that it facilitates cronyism. This, in turn, may negatively affect the selection of competent persons and thus undermine the effectiveness of the regulatory agency.[64] But the minister's power of appointment in the Jamaican situation must be viewed in the context of other legal requirements for board appointments which may operate to constrain absolute ministerial discretion. Similar legal constraints are also applicable for directorial appointments to the boards of the financial regulators of Trinidad and Tobago.

A bar on appointments of members of parliament, members of local authorities, as well as directors, officers, employees of, and persons with a material ownership interest in the relevant regulated entities is typical.[65] This is an attempt to insulate the regulator from direct influences which may be exerted by these elected officials or by persons with interests in the regulated entities. The appointer must also have regard to professional or academic qualifications of potential directors. The more recent Securities Act of Trinidad and Tobago appears to be the most explicit in relation to the fetter that it places on the appointer's discretion in this regard. Unlike the other enabling statutes, it requires firstly that an attorney of at least ten years' standing be a member of the TTSEC.[66] It also requires that most directors or commissioners have at least

62 Under the Constitution of Trinidad and Tobago (ss 22–31), the president is elected by an electoral college consisting of the members of the lower and the upper house. This must be viewed, however, in the context of the quorum requirements for the electoral college as well as the vote threshold for election of the president (candidate receiving the greatest number of votes). These factors may affect the degree of bipartisan consensus around the election of the president and thus impact adversely on the notion of the president being a collective representative.

63 Constitution of the Republic of Trinidad and Tobago, s 80(1).

64 L Enriques and G Hertig, 'Improving the Governance of Financial Supervisors' (2011) *European Business Organization Law Review* 357, 373.

65 See, FSC Act, First Schedule, para 2, which sets a conservative disqualifying shareholding threshold of 5% of any class of shares in a regulated entity; BOJ Act, Schedule, para 2. A new amendment to this Schedule via the pending Banking Services Act 2014 will plug the current gap in the law which does not expressly exclude persons with a proprietary interest in regulated entities but it should be noted that under s 34C of the BOJ Act, the officers and other employees of the Supervisory Department of the Bank are obliged to disclose any direct or indirect shareholdings they may have in institutions regulated by the Bank upon which they may be required to dispose of such shares; (T&T) Central Bank Act, s 9 which bars completely shareholders of regulated entities; (T&T) Securities Act, s 11 which appears not to contain the expected exclusion of elected political representatives.

66 (T&T) Securities Act, s 10(1).

five years' post-qualification experience[67] in specified professions or disciplines (law, finance, business, economics, accounting, securities, investment, and management). The language of the corresponding provisions in the other statutes under consideration appears to allow the appointer comparatively more flexibility and room for discretion in this regard.[68] The provisions, particularly those of the Securities Act of Trinidad and Tobago, while not preventing cronyism, safeguard against the risk of sacrificing competence for politically aligned board appointees.

Equally important as the qualifications for appointment are the bases upon which one's appointment will be terminated which also double as bars to appointment. Bases for termination that are common to all statutes are bankruptcy, mental incompetence, a sentence of imprisonment, and conviction for offences involving fraud or dishonesty.[69] These grounds apply as well to the Inspector of Financial Institutions,[70] an officer of the CBTT. Uniquely, the Securities Act of Trinidad and Tobago includes the ground of suspension or bar from practice of a professional director by the relevant professional regulating council. The foregoing grounds, for the most part, would likely arise from matters concerning conduct unconnected with one's directorship. But the statutes also stipulate grounds for termination which are related to one's performance *qua* director. Under the BOJ Act and FSC Act, these grounds are captured in the general language of 'fail[ing] to carry out any of the functions conferred or imposed'[71] on a director under the Act. The Trinidad and Tobago statutes under consideration legislate what may be referred to as a minimum performance standard by including absence of a director, without board permission,[72] from a specified number of meetings over a given period of time as a ground for termination. There is thus an implicit statutory duty on directors of the TTSEC and CBTT to attend board meetings habitually.

---

67 (T&T) Securities Act, s 10(3). These required qualifications contrast with the position for corporate directors for whom there is no minimum academic qualification or standard.

68 The language of the (T&T) Central Bank Act, s 8(2) states that the ordinary directors (ie those other than the executives of the Bank and the compulsory appointments from the public service) 'shall be selected from amongst persons drawn from diverse occupations appearing to the President to be qualified by reason of their experience and capacity in matters relating to finance, economics, accountancy, industry, commerce, law or administration'. This is largely comparable to the corresponding provision in Jamaica's FSC Act, First Schedule, para (1)(b). There appears to be no corresponding provision in the BOJ Act.

69 The FSC Act also includes the conviction of an offence involving 'moral turpitude' as a basis for the termination of one's directorship. The term appears to be used rather synonymously with dishonesty (see, for example, language in *Dudley Ernest Felix v General Dental Council* [1960] AC 704, 721 and in *Twinsectra Ltd v Yardley* [2002] UKHL 12 para 125). However, in US law the term has the status of a formal legal standard and has been defined as 'conduct that is inherently base, vile, or depraved, and contrary to the private and social duties man owes to his fellow men or to society in general' (*Navarro-Lopez v Gonzales* 503 F3d 1063, 1068 (9th Cir 2007)) which has captured a range of conduct extending beyond dishonesty. See J Simon-Kerr, 'Moral Turpitude' (2012) 2 *Utah Law Review* 1001.

70 (T&T) Financial Institutions Act, s 7(6)(a), (b) and (c).

71 BOJ Act, Schedule, para 5(e); FSC Act, First Schedule, para 7(f). The (T&T) Central Bank Act, s 12(g) reflects similar language.

72 (T&T) Central Bank Act, s 12(f). The (T&T) Securities Act, s 12(4)(b) adds 'without reasonable cause'.

Beyond this, the Trinidad and Tobago statutes expressly incorporate directorial misconduct. The Securities Act and the Central Bank Act use the broad term 'misconduct' in connection with one's duties as a director[73] as a basis for termination of appointment. The Central Bank Act, in addition, identifies specific conduct which would lead to termination – a director's failure to adhere to the conflict of interest disclosure requirements contained in the Act[74] as well as breach of 'any prescribed Code of Ethics in respect of which [a director] is liable to termination of his appointment'.[75] The precise scope of the term 'misconduct' is uncertain though useful as a catch-all for the contemplated, and indeed unforeseen, types of activity or conduct in which a director may be implicated. It is reminiscent of, and probably intended to draw on the common law offence of misconduct in public office which, while potentially spanning a wide range of conduct, is itself vaguely defined, notwithstanding the isolation of the ingredients of the offence by the English Court of Appeal in the relatively recent case of *Attorney General's Reference (No 3 of 2003)*.[76] As McKoy[77] demonstrates, it is difficult to predict the kind of conduct that will be caught by the offence. In addition, the offence should be reserved for the most egregious conduct and so may not be judicially countenanced as being appropriately deployed where the behaviour does not so deviate from 'acceptable standards as to amount to an abuse of the public's trust in the officeholder'.[78] Given these factors, there is considerable merit in the approach adopted in the Central Bank Act of identifying at least one particular type of conduct – that of a director's failure to comply with the conflict of interest disclosure requirements – as a basis for termination. In addition to this, specific types of conduct prohibited or discouraged under the relevant code of ethics may provide cause for termination. The common law offence is further discussed below within the context of the legal liability of directors of regulatory agencies. It is interesting to note, though, that the misconduct ground in the Trinidad and Tobago statutes is confined to the director's behaviour in relation to his/her duties as a board member of the agency. The language appears not to contemplate termination of one's directorship on the basis of improper conduct in other public service arenas in which a director may be involved.

The absence of similar language in the relevant Jamaican statutes does not exclude the indirect operation of misconduct in public office as a ground for termination of a director's appointment. As noted above, the FSC and BOJ Acts both provide for

---

73 (T&T) Securities Act, s 12(4)(c); Central Bank Act, s 12(c); Financial Institutions Act, s 7(6)(e) in relation to the office of Inspector of Financial Institutions.

74 (T&T) Central Bank Act, s 16(1) which outlines the need and procedure for disclosure in circumstances where a conflict of interest arises for a director.

75 (T&T) Central Bank Act, s 12(fb).

76 [2004] EWCA 868. The ingredients of the offence of misconduct in public office are specified by Pill LJ at para 61. It must be established that the officer wilfully neglected to perform his duty and/or wilfully misconducted himself to such a degree as to amount to an abuse of the public's trust in the officeholder.

77 D McKoy, *Corruption: Law, Governance and Ethics in the Commonwealth Caribbean* (Hansib 2012) 96–100.

78 *Attorney General's Reference (No 3 of 2003)* [2004] EWCA 868, para 56.

termination where a director has been convicted of an offence and sentenced to a term of imprisonment. This would capture at least some situations where a director has been found guilty of misconduct in public office since the sentence for such a conviction may involve a term of imprisonment.[79] While the absence of a clear misconduct ground for termination is perhaps a deficiency in the Jamaican statutes, it is important to ask whether the apparent weight of reliance on the common law offence across some statutes serves the governance purpose associated with such disqualifications. This issue will be addressed below.

The tenure of directors and officers, particularly of the head of the regulatory agency, is also important in regulatory governance as it plays a role in underpinning the independence component. In Jamaica, FSC directors may hold office for a period 'not exceeding five years'.[80] They are eligible for reappointment. A similar provision[81] governs the term of office for the BOJ Governor but a forthcoming amendment provides for a minimum seven-year tenure which may be renewed.[82] The Senior Deputy Governor (and Deputy Governors, if any) may be appointed for periods not exceeding five years[83] but all other BOJ directors, save one,[84] may hold office for a maximum term of three years which is renewable. With the exception of the tenure of the BOJ Governor under the upcoming new dispensation, the legislation merely provides an upper limit for tenures but the actual term of appointment is left to the discretion of the appointing minister. The provisions for tenure in the Jamaica statutes largely contrast with those in the relevant statutes of Trinidad and Tobago where terms are fixed in the legislation.[85] The language of these statutes is marked with the mandatory auxiliary, 'shall' in relation to specific tenure periods, leaving apparently no discretion for the President except in relation to the deputy governors whose term 'shall be for such period as the President may fix in the appointing instrument'.[86] The absence of a mandatory fixed term in the Jamaican statutes lends itself to manipulation particularly in the context of the appointer being a political representative who may make tenures considerably shorter than the statutory maximum thresholds. This risk has, in

79 D Lusty makes the point that there is a judicial tendency to impose deterrent sentences which typically involve terms of imprisonment. 'Revival of the Common Law Offence of Misconduct in Public Office' (2014) 38 Crim LJ 337, 350. As exemplified in the Eastern Caribbean case of *R v Williams* (1986) 39 WIR 129, fines may also be imposed.

80 FSC Act, First Schedule, para 5.

81 BOJ Act, s 6(8).

82 The Banking Services Act in its Tenth Schedule indicates amendments to the BOJ Act which will provide for this increased tenure in s 6A(3).

83 BOJ Act, s 6(8). See, too the pending s 6D of the BOJ Act in the Tenth Schedule of the Banking Services Act.

84 A forthcoming amendment to the BOJ Act will extend the maximum board tenure for the Financial Secretary to five years. See, BOJ Act, Schedule, para 1 as amended by the Banking Services Act.

85 (T&T) Central Bank Act, s 7(2) and (4) requiring a five-year term for the Governor and a three-year term for other directors; Securities Act, s 12(1) requiring a three-year term for commissioners (save for temporary commissioners whose individual term may not exceed one year). All terms may be renewed.

86 (T&T) Central Bank Act, s 7(3).

all likelihood, informed the pending change in the BOJ Governor's tenure, but there appears to be a reluctance on the part of Jamaica's law-makers to strengthen directorial independence by providing generally for minimum long-term tenures.

In Jamaica, the relevant statutory provisions confer on the minister the role of determining the remuneration for board directors.[87] This reflects the trend in Jamaica, already seen in the discussion above, whereby power is legislatively concentrated in the minister regarding directors' appointments and tenure. In contrast to the position in Jamaica, directors' remuneration for the CBTT and the TTSEC is determined by the board of the central bank and the President of Trinidad and Tobago respectively.[88] In relation to the chief executive officer of the TTSEC, the minister is given an approval function regarding the terms and conditions of his/her employment, suggesting some ministerial control over the remuneration of this officer.[89]

Board structure

To a certain extent, legislation also dictates board structure. The FSC and the TTSEC share the feature of a clear separation in the roles of board chair and the chief executive of the institution. The FSC Act, however, makes the chief executive of the regulatory institution an *ex officio* member of the board,[90] while the chief executive of the TTSEC is not a part of its board.[91] Both these scenarios are in sharp contrast to the position regarding the BOJ and the CBTT where the respective governors are both the chief executive and the chair of the board.[92] The resulting power emanating from the roles being combined in a single person is consolidated by the statutory provision which allows the chair of the central bank boards to have a casting vote at board meetings.[93] Corporate governance literature discourages this practice of a combined chief

87 BOJ Act, Schedule, para 8; FSC Act, First Schedule, para 12. The FSC Act, s 4 confers on the Commission the responsibility for appointing and employing the executive director who is an *ex-officio* board member. Particularly in the context of the much more explicit language used in s 4(3) which gives the Commission the power to employ and determine the remuneration of other officers/employees, it is unclear whether the Commission has the authority to determine the executive director's remuneration. Additionally, it appears that ministerial approval would be required for the remuneration of the executive director whose appointment and remuneration is likely to be caught by the terms of the s 4(3) proviso.

88 (T&T) Central Bank Act, s 14; Securities Act, s 12(5).

89 (T&T) Securities Act, s 22(2).

90 FSC Act, First Schedule, para 1.

91 (T&T) Securities Act, s 22(1).

92 The BOJ Act, s 6(4) provides that the Governor (or in his absence, the Senior Deputy Governor or a Deputy Governor appointed by the Minister) has day-to-day management and control of the Bank's operations. Similar language is retained by the pending amendment to the BOJ Act which addresses the functions of the Governor (see Banking Services Act, Tenth Schedule). The Schedule to the BOJ Act, para 7(2) stipulates that the Governor (or in his absence, the Senior Deputy Governor) should also preside at Board meetings. Trinidad and Tobago's Central Bank Act is explicit in relation to the Governor's roles. Section 10 states that the Governor 'shall be the chief executive officer of the Bank' and s 15 expressly makes this officeholder the chairman of the board.

93 BOJ Act, Schedule, para 7(3); (T&T) Central Bank Act, s 16(6).

executive and chairman on two main bases. The first is the need for a clear separation of the directorial and the managerial functions especially since the former includes supervision and monitoring of the latter. The second relates to power concentration and the impact of this on the extent to which other board members, particularly executive directors, can effectively fulfil their role. It is notable that notwithstanding the considerable authority given to the respective governors of the CBTT and the BOJ for institutional management, they are explicitly made answerable to their boards for their decisions and actions.[94] This requirement baldly presents difficulties and conflicts for these CEO-chaired boards in relation to the general administration of the institution. The question also arises as to whether this model, which is fairly typical for several central banks universally,[95] presents any difficulties for regulatory governance where the regulatory function is also discharged by the central bank as occurs in the jurisdictions under discussion.

With the exception of the FSC Act, all statutes provide for the appointment of persons holding a substantive office in the public service (public sector directors) to the agency's board.[96] These persons are senior civil servants in the ministries responsible for finance and economic planning. As indicated in the above discussion, with the exception of TTSEC, the various statutes require that certain executive officers of the regulating institutions be members of its board. As a consequence of these two factors, several directors of the regulatory agencies will be employed in the government. It should be noted too that, with the exception of the board of the CBTT,[97] there seems to be no statutory bar on the appointment of other public service employees to the boards. This means that the actual number of board appointees who are also employed in government institutions may be above that demanded by the legislation. Direct employees of the regulating agency are of course classic executive directors, but it may be argued that other directors who are employed in the wider government bureaucracy are notionally equivalent to executive directors. This argument is perhaps stronger where these other public sector directors have their substantive positions in the finance ministry. Even if this position is extreme, public sector directors who are not executives of the regulatory institution would not be considered independent in the traditional corporate governance sense. This has implications for regulatory governance and is developed below.

Organisational governance models increasingly support the establishment of a number of board committees to supervise certain organisational functions.[98] Audit committees have become a standard feature of boards of public listed companies[99]

94 (T&T) Central Bank Act, s 10; BOJ Act, s 6(4) and pending amendment, s 6B.

95 T Lybek and J Morris, 'Central Bank Governance: A Survey of Boards and Management' (2004) IMF Working Paper WP/04/226, 25–26, available at <http://www.imf.org/external/pubs/ft/wp/2004/wp04226.pdf> accessed November 2013.

96 BOJ Act, s 6(2)(b); (T&T) Central Bank Act, s 8(2A); Securities Act, s 10(1)(b).

97 The T&T Central Bank Act, s 5 stipulates that two directors may be public sector directors.

98 For example, *King Report (III) on Governance for South Africa* (2009) para 125–130.

99 The strong recommendation by the Cadbury Report (1992) for audit committees and the endorsement of that recommendation by the subsequent Hampel Report (1998) contributed significantly to widespread establishment of such committees.

in the monitoring of the finance and audit function and, in some instances, are now statutorily required for some financial regulatees.[100] The public sector has followed suit.[101] In Jamaica, this aspect of board structure for statutory agencies is shaped by provisions of the Public Bodies Management and Accountability Act (PBMA Act). It establishes the general rule that public sector boards must set up and maintain audit committees consisting of at least three directors.[102] This legislation also requires that the majority of the audit committee be persons who are not employed by the particular agency[103] and that at least one member be a registered public accountant or have expertise in finance.[104] The BOJ and FSC, being statutory bodies which are included in the definition of public bodies, are entities to which the PBMA Act is applicable. Thus, the provisions of the PBMA Act to which reference has just been made have an impact on the exercise of the Minister's discretion in constituting the boards of these institutions. The Trinidad and Tobago Securities Act contains a similar provision to the PBMA Act requiring at least a three-member sub-committee of the board of TTSEC to oversee the audit function[105] but it does not address details regarding the sub-committee's composition. It appears, though, that the board of the CBTT is under no statutory imperative to have an audit committee.

Jamaica's PBMA Act, by requiring that the majority membership of the audit committee be non-employees of the particular agency, attempts to achieve a measure of compliance with corporate governance recommendations. These advocate that the audit committee consist of non-executive directors, the majority being independent of management having no relationship with the company which may compromise their judgment.[106] Indeed, the current best practice is that all audit committee members should be independent non-executives.[107] The statutory requirement, which insists only on a majority of non-executives, is itself at odds with the current best practice. Furthermore, in the context of the suggestion made above that persons in the employ of government generally, but particularly those employed in the finance ministry, may be notionally considered as executive directors, it is arguable that the statutory requirement regarding composition of the audit committee falls short of setting an appropriate governance standard for constituting the audit committee of the regulatory agencies. The Securities Act of Trinidad and Tobago, by failing to stipulate details regarding the composition of the audit committee, leaves open the potential for audit committee members to be public sector directors who may not bring the degree of

---

100 Note, for example, (Ja) Insurance Regulations, 2001, r 73 and (T&T) Financial Institutions Act, s 36.

101 In Jamaica, for example, there is now a legal requirement for government *departments* to have audit committees which are supervised by an Audit Commission. See (Ja) Financial Administration and Audit Act, s 33.

102 PBMA Act, s 8(1).

103 PBMA Act, s 8(3).

104 PBMA Act, s 8(7).

105 (T&T) Securities Act, s 31(8).

106 See, for example, Cadbury Report 1992, para 4.35(b).

107 See, King Report 2009, Principle 2.18(66) and Sir Robert Smith Report on Audit Committee Combined Code Guidelines 2003, para 3.1.

independence, actual or perceived, recommended by governance codes. This creates a risk for the proper functioning of the committee.

Responsibilities and duties of the boards of directors

This part deals with the nature of the responsibilities borne by the board of directors of the selected regulators. It examines their role as stewards for the general administration of the respective institutions, the scope of their duties in discharging the regulatory function, explores their relationship with the political representative in charge of the ministry under whose auspices the regulatory agency falls, and ends by outlining their duty of loyalty and the level of competence expected of them.

Institutional stewardship

It is convenient perhaps to begin this examination of the functions and duties of the boards by referring to the BOJ Act which summarises the board's role as being 'responsible for the policy and general administration of the affairs of the Bank'.[108] In support of this function, the BOJ board is given a power to make, with the minster's approval, by-laws for the good order and management of the bank.[109] The language of the Trinidad and Tobago Central Bank Act differs somewhat from that of the BOJ Act. The Trinidad and Tobago statute provides that the 'Bank shall be managed by [the] Board of Directors' which suggests a hands-on involvement on the part of the board in the institution's operations. This statutory provision should be seen, however, in the context of the provision of the Act which confers on the CBTT Governor the responsibility for executive management, 'with the authority to act in the conduct of the business of the Bank in all matters which are not by this Act or by the Rules and Regulations made thereunder, specifically reserved to be done by the Board'.[110] Given this and the fact that only a few matters are specifically reserved for the board of the CBTT, the board's role must be conceived as being more in the nature of a monitoring board with oversight for management. This is in line with modern corporate governance thinking which recognises that the role of a board of directors in large public corporations is to provide leadership in setting the overall aims of the organisations, to supervise the strategies involved in achieving the aims, and to assess the performance of the managers as they work to realise the aims. The language of Jamaica's BOJ Act is perhaps more reflective of this role since it confers on the board the responsibility for policy and general supervision of the institution's affairs. The provision of the Trinidad and Tobago statute appears to mimic the traditional wording of model company articles regarding the functions of the directors.[111] This language is arguably

108 BOJ Act, s 6(1).

109 BOJ Act, s 45. In the (T&T) Central Bank Act, s 60(2), an equivalent power is conferred on the bank and not directly on the board.

110 (T&T) Central Bank Act, s 10.

111 Despite being a fairly recent statute, Jamaica's Companies Act 2004, First Schedule, carries model articles (art 86 of Table A) which contain language similar to the provision in the (T&T) Central Bank Act under discussion.

inappropriate given not only the evolution in corporate governance thinking which makes a clear distinction between directorial and management functions, but also in view of the fact that the Governor of the CBTT is statutorily responsible for the management of the Bank. Despite the linguistic imprecision in the Central Bank Act of Trinidad and Tobago, it seems clear that the boards of the BOJ and the CBTT have overall stewardship for the administration of the respective institutions. This responsibility for general administration of the institution is distinguished from the technical regulatory/supervisory function of the institutions which is discussed below.

The FSC Act and the Trinidad and Tobago Securities Act are perhaps less explicit than the central bank legislation of both Jamaica and Trinidad and Tobago regarding the responsibility of the boards for the overall administration of the respective institutions. In relation to the TTSEC, this function may perhaps be inferred from section 22(3A) of the Trinidad and Tobago Securities Act. This provision states that the CEO is responsible to the Commission for the execution of its policy and the management of its affairs. Support for this inference comes in the nature of some of the tasks assigned by the statute specifically to the board of Commissioners, such as, the appointment of the CEO[112] as well as other officers and staff.[113] These tasks may be regarded as typical prerogatives of boards of directors who should ensure the adequacy of competent staff to accomplish the institution's objectives.[114] There seems to be an absence of language in Jamaica's FSC Act which would readily imply the board's responsibility for general administration and stewardship of the institution. This gap, however, is plugged by the PBMA Act which charges the boards of public bodies to 'take such steps as are necessary for the efficient and effective management'[115] of the particular institution.

Drawing on Jamaica's PBMA Act, it is apparent that a board's oversight for general administration involves setting institutional objectives, ensuring appropriate systems for the control of the institution's assets, resources and risk exposure, contracting, on the minister's approval, with the chief executive, as well as advising the minister on general policy issues relating to the management of the institution.[116] The FSC board is expressly conferred the power to employ staff on such terms as it considers fit.[117] In fulfilling its role as steward of the institution, a board is required to formulate a yearly corporate plan[118] which should identify the agency's objectives, the activities to be undertaken in pursuit of those objectives, how performance will be measured, among several other factors.[119] The plan is submitted to the minister for his/her endorsement

112 (T&T) Securities Act, s 22(1).

113 (T&T) Securities Act, ss 23 and 24.

114 See, J du Plessis, A Hargovan and M Bagaric, *Principles of Corporate Governance* (2nd edn, CUP 2011) 77.

115 PBMA Act, s 6(1)(a).

116 PBMA Act, s 6.

117 FSC Act, s 4(3). This power is, however, subject to the board operating within the emolument rates set by the Minister or to ministerial approval for remuneration in excess of such rates. See too, PBMA Act, s 20.

118 PBMA Act, s 7.

119 PBMA Act, First Schedule.

and is tabled in Parliament for approval. There appears to be no statutory equivalent in Trinidad and Tobago of Jamaica's PBMA Act and perhaps, consequently, an absence of the detailed statutory itemisation of board responsibilities in relation to the function of planning and strategy which have just been discussed in relation to the Jamaican institutions. The enabling statutes appear short on directives for the board of the CBTT and the TTSEC regarding this function. However, the Exchequer and Audit Act of Trinidad and Tobago, which applies to the TTSEC but not the CBTT,[120] does require some financial planning and projection on the part of statutory bodies. By virtue of this Act, the TTSEC would be obliged to submit to the minister, for his approval, a capital expenditure as well as an income and expenditure budget prior to the start of its financial year.[121] This introduces a critical aspect of a board's responsibility for general administration of the institution's affairs – the board's oversight of the finances of the entity.

Financial oversight typically includes the board's duty to appoint an external auditor, though ministerial approval of the selected auditor is required.[122] In Jamaica, by virtue of the PBMA Act, the FSC and BOJ boards are obliged to advise the Auditor-General and the minister of a recommendation on their part not to renew the external auditor's appointment and to provide reasons for their recommendations.[123] Beyond this responsibility for the prudent selection and appointment of external auditors, the board of a public body is also charged with the timely delivery to the minister of the annual reports which must include the audited financial statements.[124] In Jamaica the PBMA Act requires a directors' report[125] which should also comment on the proposals outlined in the corporate plan. The board, via its audit committee, is obliged to review the institution's financial statements and the auditor's report.[126] It is ultimately the board's responsibility to ensure that proper accounts are maintained by the institution. This responsibility is expressly stated in respect of the both the TTSEC under the Securities Act, and the FSC under the FSC Act.[127] The fact that Jamaica's

120 (T&T) Central Bank Act, s 62.

121 (T&T) Exchequer and Audit Act, ss 33 and 34. It is noted that the responsibility for submitting the financial projection is placed on the statutory body and not directly on boards.

122 BOJ Act, s 43, FSC Act, s 12(2); (T&T) Central Bank Act, s 52(1), Securities Act, s 31(5).

123 PBMA Act, s 13(3).

124 PBMA Act, s 3(2); FSC Act, s 13(1). The BOJ Act, s 44(1) places the duty to deliver the annual report inclusive of the audited accounts on the institution and not specifically on the board but this provision must be seen in the context of the PBMA Act, s 27 which states that provisions of this statute would trump provisions in other enactments in the event of inconsistencies. In Trinidad and Tobago, under the Central Bank Act, s 53, the duty to deliver the annual report along with the audited financial statements is also placed on the institution. It is the duty of the TTSEC, which consists of the board members or commissioners, to ensure the preparation of the annual report and audited accounts of the institution, but the Commission's Secretary is specifically charged with ensuring that these documents are submitted to the Minister ((T&T) Securities Act, s 31(4)(5) and (6)).

125 PBMA Act, Second Schedule, para 3.

126 PBMA Act, s 9(1)(b) and (d). A similar obligation is placed on the audit committee of the TTSEC under s 31(9) of the (T&T) Securities Act.

127 (T&T) Securities Act, s 31(1); (Ja) FSC Act, s 12(1).

PBMA Act allows a board to co-opt persons with relevant expertise to enable the audit committee to perform its functions[128] tends to suggest that the responsibility to review financial statements may not be perfunctorily discharged by a board. This suggestion is underscored by the fact that the PBMA Act provides for sanctions for default in the performance of the functions of the audit committee, including this review function. While audit committee directors may have special responsibility regarding financial statements, there is a duty on all directors to advise the auditor of any errors or omissions contained in the statements accompanying the auditor's report.[129] The degree of care that ought to be taken by the directors in considering financial statements will be discussed below. In addition to the duty to review the financial statements, the PBMA Act assigns other responsibilities to the audit committee of the board. These include, among others, advising the board on systems which may enhance productivity, the extent to which the aims of the institution are being accomplished, and supervising the internal audit.[130] The directors then are under a duty to inform themselves of, deliberate on, and make decisions regarding these issues.

In Trinidad and Tobago, the enabling statutes confer particular responsibilities on the boards regarding finance and accounts. Under the Central Bank Act, for example, the board must approve an increase in the Bank's authorised capital.[131] The TTSEC board must ensure compliance with the statutory provisions regarding the handling of monies paid to and by the Commission,[132] and the location at which the institution's accounts are to be maintained.[133] The TTSEC board and senior officers should also ensure the institution's compliance with those provisions of the Exchequer and Audit Act which are made especially applicable to statutory bodies such as the need for ministerial approval for borrowing money.[134] A similar condition regarding borrowing governs the FSC of Jamaica under the PBMA Act,[135] as well as the BOJ, but the provision does not, of course, extend to the activities undertaken by the latter in the performance of its monetary policy function.

Boards are assigned other non-regulatory functions, such as appointing certain officers which has already been outlined above. The Central Bank Act of Trinidad and Tobago expressly requires the CBTT board to approve certain prosecutions regarding the improper issue and circulation of bills of exchange.[136] Jamaica's PBMA Act places a duty on public bodies to adhere to government procurement rules and guidelines.[137] While this duty is not specifically placed on the board, it is arguably part of the board's responsibility to ensure that appropriate institutional systems are in place to achieve

128 PBMA Act, s 8(6).
129 PBMA Act, s 16.
130 PBMA Act, s 9.
131 (T&T) Central Bank Act, s 34.
132 (T&T) Securities Act, s 30.
133 (T&T) Securities Act, s 31(3).
134 (T&T) Exchequer and Audit Act, s 36.
135 PBMA Act, s 5.
136 (T&T) Central Bank Act, s 28.
137 PBMA Act, s 6A.

compliance with the rules and guidelines. Executive officers, particularly the chief executive, as well as the officer with charge of the financial administration of the institution, and procurement officers, should be acutely aware of the relevant regulations on procurement,[138] especially the functions assigned to them, and the ethical norms[139] which should be observed in the procurement process. These ethical standards include rules regarding conflicts of interest and offers of gifts and favours by prospective contractors. Directors who may be asked to serve on procurement committees must be informed of these regulations and standards.

The legislative framework regarding procurement in Trinidad and Tobago is undergoing reform.[140] It appears that the proposed new legislation will apply to statutory bodies like the CBTT and TTSEC, requiring them to comply with the new procurement rules and guidelines, when put into effect. As suggested is the case for the BOJ and the FSC in Jamaica, the prospective legislation for Trinidad and Tobago is likely, at the very least, to imply a duty on the directors of the CBTT and TTSEC to ensure the implementation of institutional systems that support compliance with the procurement rules. In addition, the bill contains clauses which, if enacted, will directly regulate the conduct of directors and officers of public bodies in the procurement process.[141] The current centralised system for tendering via the Central Tenders Board does not extend to many statutory bodies, including the CBTT and the TTSEC.[142] The result is that these institutions operate their own regimes, ungoverned by special statutory procurement rules. However, the disclosure requirements in the Central Bank Act for directors in situations of conflict, obliging them to excuse themselves from the decision-making process,[143] would be applicable to procurement procedures undertaken by the CBTT board. These provisions, though, are weakened by a power given to the board to direct that the disclosing director remain present in the decision-making forum.[144]

As part of their role as institutional stewards, directors should also ensure that appropriate systems are established to satisfy obligations placed on their institutions under other statutes. For example, both the BOJ and the FSC are included in the list of

138 In Jamaica, the main regulations are the Public Sector Procurement Regulations 2008, made under the Contractor-General Act 1983.

139 See (Ja) the Public Sector Procurement Regulations, 2008, rr 36 and 38 and the First Schedule to these Regulations.

140 The Parliament of Trinidad and Tobago is deliberating the Public Procurement and Disposal of Public Property Bill 2014 which is expected to rescind the current procurement regime under the Central Tenders Board Act and the attendant regulations.

141 For example, clause 59(3) of the Public Procurement and Disposal of Public Property Bill, forbids members and officers of procuring institutions from accepting gifts or offers of any value in connection with a procurement and clause 59(4) prohibits procurement of goods and services from persons who have 'direct influence on the decision of a procuring entity'. Persons having such influence are also required to declare any interest they have in a bid and to recuse themselves from the relevant procurement procedure (clause 59(6)).

142 Neither statutory body appears in the First Schedule to the (T&T) Central Tenders Board Act which specifies the bodies to which the Act applies.

143 (T&T) Central Bank Act, s 16.

144 (T&T) Central Bank Act, s 16(2).

'prescribed persons' under Jamaica's Protected Disclosures Act 2011. Consequently, the agencies are responsible for receiving and investigating information disclosed to it, in accordance with the provisions of the Act, concerning improper conduct of employers. This requires that systems be established for the execution of this function. Statutes providing for public access to information on governmental activity[145] also tend to require that public authorities have certain systems in place to facilitate prompt attention to requests for information. Good stewardship demands appropriate board oversight of these statutory requirements for effective systems.

Responsibilities may also arise by virtue of anti-corruption statutes which may oblige directors and senior officers to file statutory declarations regarding their assets, liabilities and income with the relevant integrity commissions. Based on the nature of Jamaica's statutory provisions which generally relieve from filing persons receiving less than a certain threshold of emoluments from the office he or she performs, it is unlikely that non-executive board members of the BOJ and the FSC will be under a duty to submit these filings.[146] Senior officers, though, would, in all likelihood, be obliged to comply with the filing requirements. Trinidad and Tobago does not appear to have statutory provisions under its integrity legislation which carve out similar filing exemptions which would be applicable to board members of its financial regulators.

Regulatory remit

Save for making regulations, the FSC and the TTSEC are conferred full responsibility for the gamut of regulatory/supervisory functions catalogued in the statutes they administer.[147] This is evidenced by the content of the statutes which indicates that these Commissions are vested with licensing/registration, supervisory and enforcement powers. The Commissions are constituted by their boards[148] so it is the boards of directors who ultimately exercise regulatory/supervisory powers though the statutes allow the Commissions to delegate their functions with minimal restriction on this delegation power.[149]

145 For example, (Ja) Access to Information Act 2002; (T&T) Freedom of Information Act 1999. The CBTT, however, is an exempt authority in respect of this Act.

146 (Ja) Corruption (Prevention) Regulations 2003, r 3(1) provides that public servants 'in receipt of total emoluments of less than two million dollars per annum' are not obliged to furnish declarations required under s 4(1) of the Corruption (Prevention) Act. The stipend or honoraria generally paid to non-executive directors of Jamaica's financial regulators do not usually exceed this prescribed threshold. See, for example, the Financial Services Commission Annual Report 2012–2013, 31 which reflects the honoraria paid to the non-executive commissioners for the period.

147 The power to make regulations involves the relevant minister. Under the FSC Act, s 18, the Commission makes regulations but must do so with the minister's approval. Under the (T&T) Securities Act, the power to make regulations (by-laws) is reserved to the minister who acts on the Commission's recommendations.

148 See FSC Act, s 3(2) coupled with the Act's First Schedule; (T&T) Securities Act, s 10.

149 FSC Act, First Schedule, para 11; (T&T) Securities Act, s 8.

The sweeping regulatory/supervisory remit possessed by the boards of the FSC and TTSEC contrasts with that of the boards of the BOJ and CBTT. The CBTT is given responsibility for administering the Financial Institutions Act (FI Act) and the Insurance Act.[150] An officer of the CBTT, the Inspector of Financial Institutions, is appointed by the President under the FI Act[151] and is conferred with a range of supervisory functions under this Act as well as the Insurance Act. While the Inspector of Financial Institutions has general powers of supervision of licensees under these statutes, there are a few regulatory functions that are explicitly reserved to the board of the CBTT. These functions concern decisions involving severe enforcement action including licence suspension and revocation, the issue of directions regarding the scope of business that may be undertaken by a licensee at risk of having its licence suspended or cancelled,[152] and the suspension or winding up of the business of a licensee which is insolvent.[153] These regulatory functions must be carried out by the CBTT directors because, though they may be delegated, the FI Act confines such delegation to at least a three-member sub-committee of the board.[154] Although the CBTT recommends regulations, the rule-making power lies with the minister[155] who also performs a few other regulatory/supervisory functions.[156]

In relation to the BOJ, it appears that the directors have no or only marginal regulatory/supervisory responsibilities. A statutory department of the BOJ[157] is charged with the supervision of financial institutions. The minister is responsible for making financial regulations governing licensees,[158] but this function is to be carried out by a new statutory entity, the Supervisory Committee, with the minister's approval, when the new Banking Services Act takes effect. Under the current regime, the board of the bank is merely given the authority to appoint the executive officers for this department, notably, the Supervisor[159] and the Deputy Supervisor, the latter being directly in charge of the supervisory operations.[160] Beyond this task, which itself is subject to ministerial approval, the BOJ's board has no functions relating to regulation

150 (T&T) FI Act, s 5(1); Insurance Act, s 4.

151 (T&T) FI Act, s 7. The appointment of the Inspector of Financial Institutions is subject to conditions similar to those for the Governor and his/her appointment may be terminated on grounds similar to those for the directors of the CBTT.

152 (T&T) FI Act, ss 23–29; Insurance Act, s 25.

153 (T&T) FI Act, s 63; Insurance Act, s 68.

154 (T&T) FI Act, s 15. There appears to be no similar delegation power under the (T&T) Insurance Act in relation to these functions.

155 (T&T) FI Act, s 9; Insurance Act, s 214; Central Bank Act, s 60(1).

156 See, for example, (T&T) FI Act, ss 4(1), 21; Central Bank Act, ss 44B(2), 44F(5).

157 The Department of Supervision of Banks and Financial Institutions. BOJ Act, s 34A.

158 BOJ Act, s 34F.

159 The BOJ Governor is typically appointed the Supervisor. This convention is to be statutorily formalised under the new dispensation being brought about by the Banking Services Act (see meaning of 'Supervisor' under s 2(1) and Tenth Schedule which indicates the new s 34B of the BOJ Act).

160 BOJ Act, s 34B; Banking Act 1992, ss 29A–29G. The BOJ's role as regulator is shared with the minister who not only has the power to make regulations but also to carry out a number of other critical activities.

and supervision and, strictly, ought not to be regarded as a regulatory board. In this context, it is unsurprising then that the BOJ board, unlike the other boards being discussed, has no powers of delegation. Unlike the other institutions under discussion, the regulatory function is discharged by the BOJ's executive to the exclusion of the board, with the Governor being conferred the role of the banking supervisor.

The pending Banking Services Act will modify this structure. While the new enactment will not assign regulatory functions to the board of directors, it establishes a five-member Supervisory Committee which is charged with a wide range of regulatory functions.[161] Decision-making will thus lie in a panel of executives and non-executives. This contrasts with the current situation where supervisory decisions are made largely by the Bank's executives, almost exclusively by the Supervisor/Governor or the Minister. The Supervisory Committee is to be chaired by the Supervisor (the Governor). Its other members are the Deputy Supervisor, a senior executive of the bank with responsibility for oversight of financial system stability, and two non-executive members who are to be appointed by the Head of State on the minister's advice after consultation with the Supervisor.[162] This model, notwithstanding its committee structure, arguably perpetuates power concentration in the Governor/Supervisor, a view which seems to be bolstered by the requirement for the Committee to 'take into account the assessments and recommendations of the Supervisor' in carrying out its functions.[163] It is generally expected that decision-making bodies, as opposed to individuals, arrive at positions after discussion of the various perspectives put forward and careful evaluation of each perspective. In corporate situations, a board would give serious consideration to executive proposals and would be expected to provide compelling reasons for not adopting such proposals.[164] Given this, the statutory imperative for the Supervisory Committee, the regulatory/supervisory decision-making organ, to take into account the Supervisor's positions is perhaps remarkable. The presence of such a provision could suggest a paramountcy of the Supervisor's (Governor's) position which, in the absence of strong non-executive members, may dampen enquiry, debate and robust appraisals of the positions advanced by the Supervisor. It is also noted that the majority of the Supervisory Committee will be executive officers of the bank, answerable to the Governor, whether as CEO of the bank or as Supervisor. This, arguably, weakens the effectiveness of these Committee members as impartial and disinterested reviewers of the Supervisor's positions.

Although the non-executive members of the Supervisory Committee may not be BOJ board directors, they will be an important part of Jamaica's regulatory governance structure. They will thus be included in this discussion of the legal position of persons possessing leadership roles in regulatory institutions. Non-executive members of the Supervisory Committee will be subject to statutory (dis)qualifications which are

161 (Ja) Banking Services Act, ss 6 and 7.

162 (Ja) Banking Services Act, Second Schedule, para 1.

163 (Ja) Banking Services Act, s 7(3).

164 Sir Geoffrey Owen makes the point that it is difficult for non-executive directors to turn down proposals advanced by CEOs: 'The Role of the Board' in Ken Rushton (ed), *The Business Case for Corporate Governance* (CUP 2008) 26.

similar to those which govern BOJ directors. These Committee members must also satisfy the fit and proper requirements applicable to directors and officers of regulated entities.[165] While some of these requirements overlap with the grounds for disqualification, there are elements of the fit and proper test which would impose additional qualifying conditions[166] on these Supervisory Committee members.

In the new scheme to be introduced by the Banking Services Act, the BOJ board will continue to perform a peripheral regulatory-related function. It will appoint the Deputy Supervisor. It will also be responsible for terminating the tenure of this officer (a) if s/he becomes liable for disqualification by virtue of the statutory bars[167] discussed above, or (b) for cause, but only 'on the recommendation of the Supervisor'. The BOJ board will also have the statutory duty to appoint other officers of the Supervisory Department.[168]

Based on the descriptions of the regulatory scope of the boards under discussion, it is clear that the FSC board comes closest to being an encompassing regulator. Unlike the other boards, the FSC board is vested with all regulatory and supervisory functions, with the exception only of the need for ministerial approval in the making of financial regulations under the statutes it administers. This partial rule-making function distinguishes the FSC board from the TTSEC board which has no legal power to make financial regulations. The CBTT board possesses some regulatory responsibilities while the BOJ board effectively has no duties in this regard. In Jamaica, the banking supervision function is completely hived off from the board of directors, a model that is not reflected in any other institution under study. There is thus a varying scale of oversight responsibility for regulation/supervision across the boards being studied. The data indicate that where the central bank is also a regulator/supervisor, there is a tendency to concentrate the supervisory function in specially assigned executive officers of the bank. The imminent introduction in Jamaica of a Supervisory Committee does not negate this observation, given the majority executive membership of the Committee, the fact that it is presided over by the chief executive of the central bank/ Supervisor, and the statutory implication that the Committee take the counsel of the chief executive/Supervisor.

A duty concomitant with the supervisory function is that of confidentiality in respect of information regarding licensees known by directors and officers as a result of their position within the regulatory institution. This duty, with certain exceptions carved out, appears in the enabling statutes under discussion.[169] This includes the BOJ Act which, despite the fact that the BOJ board has no practical regulatory function,

165 (Ja) Banking Services Act, Second Schedule, para 2(2) and s 3(1).

166 This includes compliance with tax and other statutory payments imposed on the income of individuals as well as not having been convicted of a range of offences related to financial crimes, drug and arms trafficking, certain offences under the Sexual Offences Act 2009, among others. See Banking Services Act, s 3(a).

167 BOJ Act, Schedule, para 5.

168 (Ja) Banking Services Act, Tenth Schedule will introduce a new s 34B of the BOJ Act which addresses this role of the BOJ board.

169 FSC Act, ss 15 and 16; BOJ Act, s 34D; (T&T) Securities Act, s 14; Central Bank Act, s 56.

contemplates the possibility of disclosure of the affairs of licensees to the board.[170] Supervisory Committee members will also have this duty of confidentiality.[171] It should be noted too that there is generally a duty of secrecy on directors and officers of regulatory agencies regarding information concerning the affairs of the agency itself which is acquired as a result of their relationship with the agency.[172]

Minister's relationship with the board and senior officers

An important feature of three of the enabling statutes under discussion, the FSC and BOJ Acts and the Trinidad and Tobago Central Bank Act, is that the minister has a power to give general directions in writing to the respective institution.[173] It is expected that, in practice, these ministerial directions would be given to the board or the chief executive officer. The provision of the Central Bank Act of Trinidad and Tobago specifically requires that the ministerial directives 'be necessary to give effect to the monetary and fiscal policies of the government'. Although there may be a connection between monetary policy and prudential regulatory policy,[174] this provision in the Trinidad and Tobago statute appears to circumscribe the scope of ministerial directives to the monetary policy function of the central bank rather than to its supervisory function. Trinidad and Tobago's FI Act, a statutory centrepiece for financial regulation in this jurisdiction, does not appear to carry a provision allowing for ministerial directions to the central bank in its regulatory capacity, though it places a duty on the Governor to keep the minister abreast of all financial sector activities.[175] It would seem then that in Trinidad and Tobago ministerial intervention by way of general policy directions to the regulator is not statutorily permissible. This should, however, be seen in light of the fact that the minister is actively involved in regulatory matters, whether by way of ministerial approvals of regulatory actions or because of the need for the supervisor to consult with the minister prior to making certain regulatory decisions.[176]

The language of the relevant provisions in the FSC and BOJ Acts differs. Under the BOJ Act, ministerial directions to the Bank should be 'of a general nature as appear to the Minister to be necessary in the public interest'.[177] *Prima facie*, this appears to give the

170 BOJ Act, s 47(1).

171 (Ja) Banking Services Act, s 9(1).

172 BOJ Act, s 47(3); (T&T) Central Bank Act, s 56(1); Securities Act, s 14. Jamaica's FSC Act does not seem to have an equivalent provision.

173 FSC Act, s 7; BOJ Act, s 41; (T&T) Central Bank Act, s 50.

174 See S Cecchetti and L Li, 'Do Capital Adequacy Requirements Matter for Monetary Policy?' (2008) 46 *Economic Inquiry*, 643, available at <http://onlinelibrary.wiley.com/doi/10.1111/j.1465-7295.2007.00085.x/abstract>.

175 (T&T) FI Act, s 5(4).

176 By way of examples, see (T&T) Central Bank Act, s 44F(5) under which the Bank is obliged to consult the Minister before acting on any of its powers of intervention in respect to a troubled institution and also obliged to comply with any directions given by the Minister regarding its intervention; (T&T) FI Act, s 73 which requires that mergers involving licensees be approved by the Minister; (T&T) FI Act, s 21(1) which states that the Bank must consult the Minister before approving or refusing applications for banking licences.

177 BOJ Act, s 41.

minister very wide discretion in terms of the matters in respect of which he/she may issue directions and, unlike what appears to be the case in Trinidad and Tobago, may apparently extend to regulatory matters. In this regard, it is noted that the Supervisory Committee under the new Banking Services Act is obliged to 'consult with the Minister on matters relating to the national interest'[178] in relation to their decisions regarding licensing of financial institutions, establishment of branches and representative offices, mergers, acquisitions and corporate restructuring. This requirement for consultation opens the door to ministerial influence, if not directions, in these matters.

The FSC Act permits general ministerial directions on the policy to be adopted by the Commission 'in the performance of its functions in matters appearing to the Minister to concern the public interest'.[179] This form of words appears to restrict the nature of directions which may be lawfully issued to the regulator. A provision under Jamaica's Telecommunications Act drafted in substantially similar language was considered by the Judicial Committee of the Privy Council in *Mossell (Jamaica) Ltd v Office of Utilities Regulations*.[180] The issue was whether the direction issued by the Minister was within his powers as contemplated by the provision. It was held that the terms of a direction must allow a regulator to perform its functions and duties. Consequently, directions which purport to disable the regulator in this regard may not lawfully be made by the minister.[181] It is clear then that the statutory mechanism for ministerial directions may not be used to restrain the regulator in the carrying out of its functions under statute. Directors of the FSC are thus protected in the discharge of their statutory functions from ministerial intervention which is not lawfully permitted. The Privy Council appeared to have been guided by the specific language of the provision. The language of the corresponding provision in the BOJ Act diverges from that of the provision in the FSC Act, and it is thus questionable whether the *Mossell* interpretation would extend to the provision under the BOJ Act. This elevates the concern raised above regarding the room for permissible intervention by the minister in both institutional and regulatory affairs of this banking regulator.

Duties of competence and loyalty

Jamaica's PBMA Act[182] outlines the duty of care required of directors and officers of public bodies such as the BOJ and the FSC. The provision mirrors the standard of skill and care required of corporate directors under Jamaica's Companies Act.[183] Thus, a director's or officer's decisions will be measured against an objective standard of what a 'reasonably prudent person' would do in comparable situations, as well as against a subjective standard by which the knowledge and experience of the particular director in question is to be taken into account in determining the competence level expected

178 (Ja) Banking Services Act, s 7(6).
179 (Ja) FSC Act, s 7.
180 [2010] UKPC 1.
181 [2010] UKPC 1, para 37.
182 PBMA Act, s 17(1)(b).
183 (Ja) Companies Act 2004, s 174.

of him/her. In elaborating on the nature of a director's or officer's duty of competence, the PBMA Act explains that a director/officer would have satisfied the statutory test if he/she 'reasonably relied, in good faith, on documents relating to the affairs of the public body, including financial statements, reports of experts or on information presented by other directors or, where appropriate, other officers and professionals'.[184] Directors are thus, by virtue of this provision, allowed to rely on and trust experts and professionals in carrying out their functions. But the provision also appears to signal that there is an onus on directors to advise themselves appropriately on matters in order to discharge the duty of care imposed on them under the statute. This is so notwithstanding the exercise of their power to delegate.[185]

The degree of diligence required of directors is arguably high. Indicative of this is the provision in the PBMA that a director who was absent from a meeting at which a resolution was passed in favour of a particular course of action will be deemed to have agreed with the resolution unless he/she advises of his/her dissent in accordance with the statute.[186] This demands a reasonable degree of attention to and participation in the affairs of the agency well beyond the intermittent nature of the duty which had been traditionally espoused at common law.[187] In support of this view is the assertion by the court in the Canadian case of *Peoples Department Stores Inc (Trustee of) v Wise*[188] that the provision in Canadian companies legislation,[189] similar in language to the objective standard component of the duty of care in the PBMA Act, 'requires more of directors and officers than the traditional common law duty of care'.[190] If this interpretational approach is judicially adopted for the objective standard component of the PBMA Act, then directors of public bodies, including financial regulatory agencies, would be under a duty to act prudently and must ensure that their decisions are reasonably informed by relevant available data. The subjective dimension of the duty is likely to be important for directors of Jamaica's financial regulatory agencies. This is because, as discussed above, professional qualifications and experience in disciplines such as law, accountancy and finance are factors which must inform directorial appointments. The

184 PBMA Act, s 19(3). It should be noted too that s 19(1) indicates that a director/officer will not be regarded as having failed to discharge his/her duty of competence if he/she has relied on professional reports in making his/her decisions.

185 The corporate law principle outlined in *Re Barings plc (No 5)* [1999] 1 BCLC 433, 487 that company directors remain obliged to monitor and oversee the delegated functions seems eminently transferrable to public sector directors.

186 PBMA Act, s 18.

187 Cases such as *Re City Equitable Fire Insurance Company Ltd* [1925] Ch 407 and *Re Cardiff Savings Bank* [1892] 2 Ch 100 allude to the notion that a director need not devote continuous attention to a company's business. The Jamaica Companies Act does not appear to have a provision equivalent to the PBMA Act provision requiring notice of dissent by a director which seems indicative of an elevation in the degree of diligence required of directors. A Burgess, however, argues that the duty of competence as formulated in modern Commonwealth Caribbean companies statutes, like Jamaica's, calls for elevated standards of diligence: *Commonwealth Caribbean Company Law* (Routledge 2013) 267–268.

188 2004 SCC 68 (CanLII), available at <http://canlii.ca/t/1j0wc> accessed December 2014.

189 Canada Business Corporation Act, s 122(1)(b).

190 2004 SCC 68, para 62.

implications of this are that directors possessing such qualifications and experience will be adjudged by a standard of care commensurate with their personal knowledge and experience. The question for a court assessing if a director were in breach of this subjective standard of care would be whether the director, having the knowledge, skills and experience he/she does, has acted in a reasonably prudent way. Thus, an elevated, more demanding duty of care should be factored into the nature of the standard of care required of directors holding professional qualifications versus other directors who will be adjudged by the standard of care that is expected of the average prudent person.

It is perhaps important in discussing the standard of care imposed on directors of regulatory agencies to make a distinction between their decisions *qua* financial regulator versus their decisions as stewards for the agency's administration. In the case of the BOJ, this distinction equates to some extent with a physical distinction between the department/body charged with regulatory decisions and that with responsibility for the general stewardship of the Bank.[191] This physical bifurcation contrasts with the situation regarding the FSC whose board carries out regulatory functions as well as makes general management decisions regarding the institution. Regulatory decisions are of course subject to the usual benchmark principles applied by the courts in cases of judicial review and/or those applicable in statutory appeals which are permitted in a gamut of decisions made by financial regulators. Regulators, though, have not, at law, been made subject to a duty of care to users of financial services in connection with their supervisory decisions and actions.[192] In light of this, it may be argued that, although the language of the statutory duty of care under the PBMA Act is all-embracing, it has special applicability to non-regulatory decisions and functions such as those described above.[193] It is noted, however, that the statutory duty of care, even if applicable to all kinds of decisions, is enforceable only by the Attorney General[194] as the nominal party to litigation in which the government is a party. While the imposition of the duty may inure to the benefit of all stakeholders in the regulatory environment by promoting high standards in the decision-making process, its breach is not intended to be actionable by the regulated entities or users of financial services.

Despite the more stringent standard of care which seems to be demanded by statute versus the common law, directorial decisions are, perhaps, unlikely to be second-guessed by courts which tend to defer to decisions reasonably made in the context of

191 As discussed above, the board of the BOJ has no regulatory functions. These are largely carried out by a department within the Bank. The new Banking Services Act establishes a Supervisory Committee which will make regulatory decisions.

192 *Yuen Kun Yeu v Attorney General of Hong Kong* [1988] AC 175.

193 Judicial review measures a regulatory decision on the basis of reasonableness/rationality while directorial care in decision-making is assessed on the statutory tests of diligence and reasonable prudence. Despite the distinction in linguistic formulations, it is arguable perhaps that these tests overlap to some extent. Both include an attempt to determine the quality of the decision-making process. Common to the inquiry under both tests will be whether the decision-maker made an informed decision, taking into account the relevant available material.

194 PBMA Act, s 25(1).

the prevailing circumstances.[195] This judicial approach to corporate directorial decisions is arguably analogous to the inclination exhibited by courts in general to defer to decisions made by a regulator in cases of judicial review. This author has shown elsewhere, however, that Commonwealth Caribbean courts are not averse to examining regulatory decisions with a view to ensuring that the requisite high standards of care have been applied.[196] Courts may thus not be reluctant to extend this level of scrutiny to non-regulatory decisions. This is particularly likely in view of the fact that financial regulators are themselves governance watchdogs for the licensees of whom increasingly high standards of governance have come to be expected or required. Besides, a breach of the duty of competence owed by directors of financial regulatory institutions could be an attendant breach of failure to comply with express statutory responsibilities of stewardship. In this regard, it is noted that Jamaica's PBMA Act lists several key responsibilities of the audit committee.[197] This includes, among other things, the duty to review the auditor's annual report and the financial statements which will form part of the agency's annual report. A director's failure to fulfil these statutory responsibilities may also amount to breaches of the duty of competence.[198]

In Trinidad and Tobago, it does not appear that directors of the financial regulatory institutions are statutorily made subject to a duty of competence which is equivalent in nature to that which governs corporate directors. The enabling statutes, though, indirectly impose, at the very least, an obligation to attend board meetings regularly,[199] which arguably implies a duty to devote reasonable attention to directorial functions.

The statutory formulation of the duty of loyalty applicable to directors of financial regulatory agencies in Jamaica is cast in terms reminiscent of a fiduciary duty imposed on directors at law which is itself reflected in companies legislation in both Jamaica and Trinidad and Tobago.[200] The PBMA Act imposes on every director and officer of a public body the duty to act honestly and in good faith in the best interests of the public body.[201] The PBMA Act provides little or no guidance as to the nature of this duty and, despite its formulaic similarity with the common law, it is difficult to transpose the nature of the common law duty on corporate directors to public sector directors. First, the cases have interpreted the common law duty to mean that directors must act in

195 *Peoples Department Stores Inc (Trustee of) v Wise* 2004 SCC 68, paras 64 and 65.

196 See *Lascelles v Black Sand*, Jamaica Supreme Court [2011] HCV 05965, delivered 30 November 2011 discussed in C Blake, 'Judicial Oversight of Financial Regulatory Action in the Commonwealth Caribbean' (2012) 41 *Common Law World Review* 354–379.

197 PBMA Act, s 9.

198 This seems to be in line with the Australian case of *ASIC v Healey* [2011] FCA 717 which indicated that corporate directors must carefully read and apply their minds to the contents of the company's financial statements that they are required to approve. Directors in this case were found to be in breach of the statutory objective duty of care for having approved inaccurate accounts into which they ought to have enquired.

199 (T&T) Central Bank Act, s 12(f); Securities Act, s 12(4)(b).

200 See (Ja) Companies Act, s 174(1)(a); (T&T) Companies Act, s 99(1)(a). Trinidad and Tobago law does not seem to impose on the directors of the Central Bank and the TTSEC the specific duty to act *bona fide* in the interests of the institution.

201 PBMA Act, s 17(1)(a).

the interests, not of the commercial entity, but of the body of shareholders.[202] This is unhelpful in the context of statutory regulatory agencies which are not, in all respects, conceptually equivalent to a corporate entity. The statutory mandate under the PBMA Act to act in the best interests of the public body appears to contemplate the statutory body itself as an institution discharging the functions it is required to perform.

Another dimension to the interpretation of the common law duty is that directors should act for a proper purpose, not for a collateral one. The circumstances of the cases that provide an insight into the nature of this aspect of the duty are very uniquely corporate in nature[203] and consequently offer little practical insight into how this dimension of the duty could impact directors of the agencies under study. If the common law interpretation is at all instructive for directors of financial regulatory institutions in Jamaica, it would suggest that, in discharging their functions, they should not be motivated by purposes besides those for which they have been given the power. Permitted purposes may perhaps be extractable from the list of functions which tend to be itemised in modern statutes establishing regulators, such as Jamaica's FSC Act.[204] These functions, though, relate specifically to the agency's regulatory remit which will typically attract judicial review. It may be, then, that the duty to act in the interests of the public body, like the duty of competence, is particularly relevant to the directors' functions of general stewardship of the institution.

Directors and officers of all the regulatory institutions[205] under discussion are subject to disclosure requirements in connection with personal conflicts of interest which may arise in the course of their directorship. Invariably, the legislative provisions[206] oblige them not to be present or take part in the board discussions relating to the matter over which the conflict arises. As already discussed, fundamental conflicts of interest involving proprietary or other interests in the regulated entities generally constitute grounds for disqualification.

The law in Jamaica has sought to replicate corporate directorial duties in the public sector. This course has not been taken in Trinidad and Tobago where there is no general formulation of a duty of care for the directors of financial regulatory agencies. The law in this jurisdiction displays a preference for the more readily assessable duty of attending board meetings from which a duty of diligence may be inferred. The precise reach and value of the duty of care in Jamaica is yet to be judicially tested and determined. The discussion has indicated that some difficulties seem to inhere in the transposition of the corporate law fiduciary duty to act in the interests of the company, *mutatis mutandis*. The law in both jurisdictions, though, is emphatic in relation

202 The case of *Greenhalgh v Arderne Cinemas* [1951] Ch 286 is normally cited for this proposition.

203 The circumstances typically surround the directors' powers regarding the allotment of shares.

204 FSC Act, s 6.

205 This includes the members of the Supervisory Committee under Jamaica's new Banking Services Act.

206 See FSC Act, First Schedule, para 13; in the absence of a disclosure of interest provision in the BOJ Act for its directors, they seem to be governed in this regard by the PBMA Act, s 17(2); Jamaica's new Banking Services Act, Second Schedule, para 11, governs the members of the Supervisory Committee; (T&T) Central Bank Act, s 16; (T&T) Securities Act, s 18; (T&T) Integrity in Public Life Act, s 29.

to the no-conflict rule, demanding full disclosure where conflicting interests arise for directors.

SCOPE AND NATURE OF LIABILITIES

Statutory immunity and its limits

Directors and officers of financial regulators enjoy a general immunity from suit by virtue of statutory provisions in their enabling statutes.[207] The basic thrust of these provisions is that no proceedings may be brought against the regulator's directors or officers personally for acts done (or omitted) *bona fide* in the execution of the statute. While this offers considerable protection from liability in damages, it does not offer absolute immunity. It does not extend to acts involving bad faith as shown by *Three Rivers District Council v Governor and Company of the Bank of England*,[208] in which the House of Lords held that officials with oversight for financial regulation could be sued in the tort of misfeasance in public office which imports *mala fides*. In a prior hearing of this case,[209] the House of Lords was asked to review the law on this tort and to specify its nature and ingredients. It was characterised as a species of abuse of power which applies where the holder of the public office does not honestly believe that his act or deliberate omission is lawful. The critical ingredient is the state of mind of the public officer and in this regard, the court addressed the nature of the mental states that could give rise to liability. The first, labelled 'targeted malice', involves conduct specifically intended to harm someone. It satisfies the bad faith requirement because it is the use of public power for an ulterior or improper motive. The second type of mental state, sometimes described as 'untargeted malice', involves knowledge on the part of the public officer that he/she has no power to do the act in question, as well as knowledge that the act will probably harm the claimant. This latter dimension of the second type of mental state was described by the court as 'reckless indifference' because the officer wilfully ignores the risk of harm that his/her intended act or deliberate omission may cause. The second type of mental requirement is thus less exacting than the first since it does not demand a naked intention to harm. This perhaps provides some manoeuvrability for claimants by expanding the room for operation of the tort,[210] despite its still stringent requirements. The result is an increase, even if small, in the risk of personal liability of directors and officers of financial regulators. It is worth noting that the *Three Rivers* requirements for the tort of misfeasance in public office have been adopted and applied in Jamaican law[211] though not in respect of persons involved in financial regulation.

207 FSC Act, First Schedule, para 14; BOJ Act, ss 6(4) and 34E; Banking Services Act, s 8; (T&T) Central Bank Act, ss 3(4) and 44H; Securities Act, s 13.

208 [2001] UKHL 16.

209 *Three Rivers District Council v Governor and Company of the Bank of England* [2000] UKHL 33.

210 This point is made as well by M Adenas and D Fairgrieve who argue that there are additional factors which make the tort attractive to potential claimants. See, 'Misfeasance in Public Office, Governmental Liability, and European Influences' (2002) ICLQ 757, 776–778.

211 See *Wong Ken et al v National Investment Bank of Jamaica Ltd et al* [2012] JMSC 32.

Another case which indicates limits on the statutory immunity for financial regulators is *Gulf Insurance Ltd v Central Bank of Trinidad and Tobago*.[212] The Judicial Committee of the Privy Council considered that the provision in the Central Bank Act[213] should be restrictively applied and held that it did not extend to 'acts which *purported* to be in performance of functions conferred by the Act but which were in fact outside the powers which it conferred'.[214] The result was that the Bank, despite the absence of recklessness and bad faith, was held to be liable in damages for disposing of the assets in which the claimant had an interest without having the price of those assets determined by an independent valuer as required by the statute. It seems clear that good faith will not shield acts which are beyond the statutory powers of the directors and officers of the financial regulatory agency.

Gulf Insurance, a judicial review case, involved a failure by the regulator to observe a statutory requirement. This raises the possibility of liability under the tort of breach of statutory duty. The approach by the courts in this regard is a general reluctance to provide a right of private action for such breaches since, among other things, the duties involve the exercise of discretion which is subject to judicial review. This judicial approach effectively protects directors and officers to a considerable degree, even if the statute contained no immunity provisions. Courts, however, have carved out a small window via which liability for breach of statutory duty may arise for public officers or bodies. The test is whether Parliament intended to provide a right of action for the members of the class for whose benefit or protection the statutory duty was imposed.[215] This intention may be suggested, for example, if there is no other remedy available for the breach of duty. This, theoretically, provides a gateway for liability of directors and officers of regulatory agencies, though the statutory immunity provisions would likely foreclose such actions.[216] It should be noted too that Jamaica's PBMA Act provides an additional safety net for directors and officers by allowing for a public body, in certain circumstances, to indemnify their directors and officers in respect of suits against them by reason of their office with the body.[217]

---

212 [2005] 66 WIR 297.

213 (T&T) Central Bank Act, s 44H which, so far as is relevant to this discussion, provides that no liability will attach to the Bank, its directors and officers 'for anything done or omitted in the discharge or purported discharge of the functions of the Bank . . . unless it is shown that the act or omission was reckless or in bad faith'.

214 [2005] 66 WIR 297, 311.

215 See *X (Minors) v Bedfordshire County Council* [1995] 2 AC 633, 731 per Lord Browne-Wilkinson.

216 An action for breach of statutory duty was successfully appealed in *Kirvek Management and Consulting Services Ltd v AG of Trinidad and Tobago* [2002] UKPC 43. This case did not involve a financial regulator but it is also instructive to note that the court adopted a strict interpretation of the section under the State Liability and Proceedings Act 1966 providing immunity for judicial officers in connection with the discharge of their duties in the judicial process.

217 PBMA Act, ss 19A, 19B and 19C. The conditions under which indemnities may be provided include the requirement that the director has acted in good faith in the interests of the institution and, in regard to criminal or administrative proceedings for which there is a pecuniary penalty, that the director or officer had reasonable grounds for believing his conduct was lawful. Further conditions for indemnification include substantial success on the merits and that the director or officer is fairly and reasonably entitled to the indemnity.

Criminal liability: misconduct and anti-corruption

As alluded to earlier, the common law offence of misconduct in a public office presents another basis of potential liability for directors and officers of financial regulators. Pill LJ, in *Attorney General's Reference No 3 of 2003*,[218] observed that in relation to the mental element required to establish the crime, there is some resemblance to the tort of misfeasance in public office.[219] Despite this similarity, he was reluctant to use the term 'bad faith' which he suggested was more appropriate to commercial dealings[220] which are typically involved in misfeasance actions where material loss must be shown by the claimant. The misconduct alleged must amount to an abuse of the public's trust in the defendant and must have been done without reasonable cause or justification.[221]

The nature of the default or misconduct must be very serious if the offence is to be established. The court in *Attorney General's Reference No 3 of 2003* suggested that in assessing whether the alleged misconduct attained this threshold for establishing the crime, it could consider the consequences of the misconduct. If the consequences were insignificant, it would be unlikely that the necessary threshold would be achieved, though it may be that a comparable default having grave consequences would meet the threshold. The high threshold required arguably diminishes the degree of exposure of directors and officers of financial regulators to liability under this head. Compensating for this perhaps is the fact that the crime of misconduct in public office may span a very wide range of circumstances and is thus versatile in its application. McKoy argues, however, that these factors make its practical application unpredictable.[222] Interestingly though, there appears to have been a resurgence of its use in several Commonwealth jurisdictions.[223] Given this and notwithstanding difficulties in its application, it poses a risk of criminal liability for directors and officers of financial regulatory agencies as well as disqualification from office which is expressly made a consequence of directorial misconduct under the Central Bank and the Securities Acts of Trinidad and Tobago. In the Jamaican context, as suggested earlier, a conviction for the offence is also likely to trigger indirectly disqualification from directorial office under the BOJ and FSC Acts.

In addition to their exposure to liability at common law, directors and senior officers of financial regulatory agencies face possible liability for corrupt activities connected

218 [2004] EWCA 868 [53].

219 The mental element required for misconduct in public office is wilful neglect/wilful misconduct which has been particularised as 'deliberately doing something which is wrong knowing it to be wrong or with reckless indifference as to whether it were wrong or not'. See *A-G's Reference No 3 of 2003* [2004] EWCA 868 [28].

220 [2004] EWCA 868 [63] and [48].

221 Despite the itemisation of the elements of the offence in *A-G's Reference No 3 of 2003,* in a subsequent case, *R v Belton* [2010] EWCA Crim 2857 [29], it was noted that there is no exhaustive definition of the offence.

222 D McKoy, *Corruption: Law, Governance and Ethics in the Commonwealth Caribbean* (Hansib 2012) 96–97.

223 D Lusty, 'Revival of the Common Law Offence of Misconduct in Public Office' (2014) 38 Crim LJ 337.

with their office. While non-executive directors of the financial regulatory agencies in Jamaica are not generally obliged to file declarations of assets and liabilities under anti-corruption legislation, they are subject, as are executive officers, to the provisions which proscribe acts of corruption.[224] These involve receipt of benefits in exchange for doing or refraining from doing acts in the execution of their functions, improper use, for their benefit or for a third party, of confidential information available to them as a result of their office, and illicit enrichment. Illicit enrichment is *prima facie* established where the public servant owns assets disproportionate to his lawful earnings and offers no or no satisfactory explanation. The onus is on the officer to show that he acquired the assets lawfully. McKoy points out that this shifting of the burden of proof to the defendant, while not unknown to Commonwealth Caribbean law, is untypical and raises questions of constitutionality yet to be judicially determined.[225] Uncovering a case of illicit enrichment tends to be facilitated by asset/liability disclosure in statutory declarations. The fact that non-executive directors of financial regulatory agencies in Jamaica are typically relieved from this filing obligation perhaps dilutes the potency of the illicit enrichment offence and concomitantly reduces their exposure to criminal liability under the anti-corruption legislation. Jamaica's legislation imposes scales of maximum prison terms and/or hefty fines for convictions of the offences it has created.[226] Where executive officers fail to file statutory declarations as required, the anti-corruption commission in Jamaica merely reports the matter to the relevant body as well as to the Director of Public Prosecutions who may take action as he/she sees fit.[227] This contrasts with the position under the Trinidad and Tobago Integrity in Public Life Act which expressly criminalises defaults in filing the statutory declaration.[228]

Trinidad and Tobago has largely comparable offences under its Prevention of Corruption Act, 1987. This statute is supplemented by provisions of the Integrity in Public Life Act.[229] The Prevention of Corruption Act, however, stipulates more draconian penalties for its contravention than its Jamaican counterpart. In addition to imprisonment and fines, the Act provides for disgorgement of the benefit received in respect of the corrupt activity, permanent disqualification from a public office as well as the loss of any right to a pension paid by the public body.[230] It is noted, though, that the conduct prohibited under the Integrity in Public Life Act does not appear to attract similar harsh sanctions.[231]

---

224 (Ja) Corruption (Prevention) Act, s 14.

225 D McKoy, *Corruption: Law, Governance and Ethics in the Commonwealth Caribbean* (Hansib 2012) 147–148.

226 (Ja) Corruption (Prevention) Act, s 15.

227 (Ja) Corruption (Prevention) Act, s 12.

228 (T&T) Integrity in Public Life Act, s 21(1).

229 (T&T) Prevention of Corruption Act, ss 3(1), 4(a), 5 and 7; Integrity in Public Life Act, ss 24–28 which include prohibitions regarding the use of one's office or confidential information acquired as a result of one's office for private gain and advancing one's personal interests, use of office to influence decisions for personal benefit, and receipt of gifts in connection with the performance of one's functions in the relevant office.

230 (T&T) Prevention of Corruption Act, s 6.

231 (T&T) Integrity in Public Life Act, s 31 provides for the reporting by the integrity commission of breaches of the provisions proscribing certain conduct to relevant authorities and the Director of Public Prosecutions.

Directors and officers of financial regulatory agencies are also exposed to criminal liability for breach of their duty of confidentiality.[232] Where, as may occur in Jamaica, they serve on procurement committees, they are also exposed to criminal and civil liability for contraventions of the procurement regulations.[233]

Sanctions for failure to carry out statutory responsibilities and duties

In Jamaica, under the PBMA Act, directors and senior officers of the regulatory agencies are liable to pecuniary penalties[234] if they fail to comply with several of the responsibilities with which they are charged under this statute. Among the defaults which may attract a pecuniary penalty are failure to deliver to the Minister the requisite corporate plan, failure on the part of audit committee members to perform their statutory duties including the responsibility to review the agency's financial statements for inclusion in the annual report, failure on the part of directors or officers to provide information required by external auditor, as well as breach of the duties of competence and loyalty. The court, in imposing a penalty for such breaches, should consider the nature of the default, whether anyone has suffered loss on account of the default, the circumstances of the default, and whether the defendant has already been found in breach of the Act.

Although loss suffered by a third party is a consideration for the court, it is the Attorney General who is empowered to make the application and it appears that such a third party has no right of action under the statute. The question arises as to who, in a practical sense, would drive such an application. One possibility is a third party who alleges loss as a result of the default. Given the nature of the actionable defaults under the Act, it is uncertain whether there is, realistically, a potential pool of persons who routinely stand to suffer loss and who may thus have an interest in pressing for legal action by the Attorney General. Two other persons who may be uniquely placed to drive legal action for breaches of the PBMA are the external auditor of the agency and the Auditor-General, an independent public officer under the Constitution with responsibility for the scrutiny of the use of public funds. Under the current framework of the Act, the external auditor of a public body is already charged with reporting to the board any contravention by directors or officers of the PBMA Act or any relevant statute.[235] Given this, the auditor's independence, and his statutory relationship with the Auditor-General[236] who retains a residual power to audit entities governed by the Act,[237] it is suggested that they are positioned to facilitate the initiation of action in the name of the Attorney General against defaulting directors and officers. This suggestion may require appropriate

232 BOJ Act, ss 34D(2) and 47(1); FSC Act, s 15(3). Both Acts provide for fines or terms of imprisonment. (T&T) Central Bank Act, s 56(2); Securities Act, s 14(5) provide for fines and imprisonment.

233 Public Sector Procurement Regulations, rr 39 and 40.

234 PBMA Act, s 25(2). The court may also grant an injunctive remedy.

235 PBMA Act, s 14(3)(c).

236 See PBMA Act, ss 13C(b), 14(5), and 16(3).

237 PBMA Act, s 13.

legislative underpinning but the absence of such a facilitator appears to present a hiatus in the enforcement of contraventions of the Act.

The Trinidad and Tobago Central Bank Act and the Securities Act impose criminal liability by way of fines and imprisonment on directors and officers of the CBTT and the TTSEC respectively for failure to declare their interest in matters in which they are conflicted which come before the board for determination.[238] A director of the TTSEC who acquires a material beneficial interest in an entity regulated under the Act by way of gift or on transmission and who does not disclose and dispose of the interest or does not resign will also be exposed to criminal sanction.[239] Directors of the Trinidad and Tobago financial regulators who contravene the statutory duty to attend board meetings are liable to be removed from office.[240] The Central Bank Act also makes it a criminal offence where a director knowingly verifies or delivers any materially false statement, account or report.[241]

Evaluation of exposure

While the presence of a general statutory immunity may be comforting for directors of the financial regulators under study, it is clear that they remain legally exposed under various heads of liability. There appears, though, to be a gap between this legal risk and a realistic assessment of the likelihood of liability. Notwithstanding the restrictive approach adopted by courts to immunity provisions, the operative scope of these provisions is still likely to protect directors in a wide range of circumstances. Secondly, although the use of misfeasance and misconduct in public office seems to be on the rise in some Commonwealth jurisdictions, the rigorous standard required to establish the *mens rea* component depresses their utility value. In addition, the apparent deficiency in the practical enforcement of the duties of competence and the duty to act in the best interests of the public body in the Jamaican law weakens their impact even if the conceptual hurdles pertaining to how they actually work in the context of the public sector are overcome. The fact too that Jamaica's anti-corruption regime carves out, indirectly, an exemption for non-executive directors in relation to the duty to file statutory declarations arguably erodes possible exposure and affirms the arguably over-protectionist tendency in the law towards such directors.

In Trinidad and Tobago, the statutory bifurcation of the anti-corruption regime appears to have the effect of creating two different degrees of exposure. There are robust sanctions under the Prevention of Corruption Act but relatively mild exposure under the Integrity in Public Life Act which contains a critical set of proscribed abuses. Additionally, with a limited array of other statutory heads of liability in the Trinidad and Tobago law, it is perhaps fair to conclude that the actual risk of exposure for directors and officers of the financial regulatory agencies in this jurisdiction is also low.

238 (T&T) Central Bank Act, s 16(3); Securities Act, s 18(5).
239 (T&T) Securities Act, s 11.
240 (T&T) Central Bank Act, s 12 and Securities Act, s 12(4).
241 (T&T) Central Bank Act, s 57.

IMPLICATIONS FOR REGULATORY GOVERNANCE

This part attempts an evaluation of the extent to which the matrix of laws governing the directors and senior officers of financial regulatory agencies contributes to the main principles of good regulatory governance – independence, accountability, transparency, integrity. In doing so, it draws on some of the relevant criteria used by Quintyn, Ramirez and Taylor[242] (Quintyn *et al*) in their determination of the degree to which the principles are exhibited in the financial regulatory agencies they studied.

Minimising or preventing political interference and industry capture is the primary goal of the principle of independence in the governance of financial regulatory agencies. The appointment procedure, the make-up of the board, the tenure of board members and senior officers and the bases for their termination are important factors for independence. In the two studied jurisdictions, Jamaica and Trinidad and Tobago, directorial appointments are made either by the relevant minister of government or on his/her say-so. This is not the procedure preferred by the independence criteria used by Quintyn *et al* which favour parliamentary approval before government appointment.[243] As discussed above, ministerial power in the appointment process must be viewed in the context of the legal requirements imposed on the exercise of the minister's discretion concerning who may be appointed. In this regard, the law in both jurisdictions supports directorial independence from the regulated industry and, particularly in respect to the TTSEC, secures professional skills on the boards. This arguably protects objective decision-making since it is likely that even if the appointed board members are sympathetic to the minister and the political directorate, professional reputation and integrity constitute a strong countervailing force. An additional safeguard which the law should consider as a means of insulating appointees from the risk of political or industry influence is that appointees should not have held positions in the political directorate or in regulated entities for a prescribed period prior to appointment. A similar restraint period post-service to a regulatory agency should be considered for directors and senior officers who demit office. It is recognised, however, that in small jurisdictions like Commonwealth Caribbean territories where the resource pool for potential appointees tends to be limited, such a requirement may not be feasible.

---

242 M Quintyn, S Ramirez and M Taylor, 'The Fear of Freedom: Politicians and the Independence and Accountability of Financial Supervisors in Practice' in D Masciandaro and M Quintyn (eds), *Designing Financial Supervision Institutions: Independence, Accountability and Governance* (Edward Elgar 2007) 61, 103–106 (Table 3A.2).

243 Enrique and Hertig argue that such a process guards against cronyism and appointments which are merely political which jeopardise competence. See, 'Improving the Governance of Financial Supervisors' (2011) *European Business Organization Law Review* 357, 374–375. The UK experience indicates perhaps that an appointment process involving parliamentary confirmation hearings may not find favour with Westminster parliamentary-style democracies. See, A Page, 'Regulating the Regulator – A Lawyer's Perspective on Accountability and Control' in E Ferran and C Goodhart (eds), *Regulating Financial Services and Markets in the Twenty-first Century* (Hart 2001) 127, 134. It is this style of government which has been largely adopted in the Commonwealth Caribbean.

A concerning trend, seen in Jamaica, which may have an impact on independence is the way in which the tenures of directors are generally determined. The relatively short maximum periods provided in the law for non-executive directors[244] open a door to political control and political interference. In addition, particularly for boards having a regulatory remit such as the FSC and the new Supervisory Committee, short discretionary terms tend to militate against directors developing and sharpening their competence, and hence, the quality of their regulatory decisions and supervision. The fixed term approach adopted in Trinidad and Tobago law is thus more desirable.

Termination bases and procedures are as important as tenures to directorial and institutional independence. While the statutes indicate clear bases for termination of directors and senior officers, they are unclear as to whether the termination and disqualification bases highlighted constitute the only grounds for dismissal. In Jamaica, the termination by the Minister in 2009 of the then Governor's contract for reasons other than the statutory grounds[245] indicated, though perhaps dubiously, that these grounds were not exhaustive and illustrated the susceptibility of the Governor's appointment to political whim. This gives practical context to the independence criterion insisted upon by Quintyn *et al* that the law should have clearly defined bases for dismissal of the chief executive of a financial regulatory agency. It is interesting that an amendment to the BOJ Act which coincides with the Banking Services Act appears to legislate the vulnerability of the Governor's appointment by providing that the Governor may be removed from office on advice given by the Cabinet if 'the Cabinet is satisfied that the Governor should be removed for cause'.[246] This is in addition to the grounds for termination/disqualification which were already contained in the Act. The amendment also provides that the Cabinet is at liberty to give such advice irrespective of whether the board has proposed that the Governor's appointment be terminated. The new provision raises the question of the nature of the matters in respect of which the provision may be successfully invoked. It is presumed that dismissal for *reasonable* cause is implicit and it is suggested that this should only contemplate activities or conduct on the part of the Governor which, being unlawful or unethical, make him/her unfit to continue in the office. The language, 'if the Cabinet is satisfied' contained in the provision is also unsettling, and the lack of specificity in the provision, as a whole, appears to undercut the principle of independence via security of tenure without a compelling concomitant gain or trade-off in respect of any of the other principles of good governance. In fact, it has the potential as well to reduce transparency in the governance

244 This includes non-executive members of the Supervisory Committee under Jamaica's new Banking Services Act.

245 Termination was said to be on the basis that the 'government found unacceptable, embarrassing and repugnant the interpretation and application of certain provisions of the Governor's contract of employment'. 'Statement by the Prime Minister, Hon. Bruce Golding on the Dismissal of BOJ Governor Derrick Latibeaudiere' (3 November 2009), available at <http://jis.gov.jm/statement-by-the-pm-hon-bruce-golding-on-the-dismissal-of-boj-governor-derick-latibeaudiere-and-resignation-of-commissioner-of-police-hardley-lewin/> accessed November 2014.

246 (Ja) Banking Services Act, Tenth Schedule which contains the amendment in s 6C.

arrangements of the agency, thus exposing the agency to suspicion and diminishing its legitimacy in the eyes of its stakeholders and the wider public.

The tendency, if not the requirement to appoint to the boards, public sector officers, particularly officers employed at the ministry of finance or at agencies under the purview of that ministry, is arguably problematic for independence. This is not so much in relation to lack of autonomy on account of one's political affinity. The potential threat to their independence in decision-making is linked to the fact that these officers, in their substantive positions, report directly or indirectly to the Minister. This could be a factor which, consciously or unconsciously, affects their perspectives and may, in some cases, bring about conflicts.

A delicate issue in the governance arrangements of financial regulators located within or annexed to the central bank is the dominance of the Governor who occupies the positions of chief executive and chairman of the bank as well as Supervisor, and in Jamaica, chair of the Supervisory Committee under the new Banking Services Act. From a governance point of view, this makes the Governor's role of being answerable to the board for his/her actions and decisions awkward. It may negatively affect the degree of accountability expected of the Governor and the ability of the other directors to demand it in their role as stewards of the institution. The constituency of public service officers on the board of central banks is also unlikely to present a satisfactory counterbalance to the considerable power concentrated in the Governor. Regulatory governance is likely to be affected given the statutory authority of the Governor as the Supervisor and, in Jamaica, as chair of the Supervisory Committee. A criterion used by Quintyn *et al* discourages single-person decision-making in supervision in favour of a board or commission. In Jamaica and to a lesser extent in Trinidad and Tobago, the board/committee structure for decision-making seems compromised. The preponderance of central bank executives on Jamaica's Supervisory Committee arguably buttresses the Governor's/Supervisor's power and authority. The minority status of the non-executive membership of this Committee is further weakened by what appears to amount to a statutory control valve on the exercise of their judgment.[247] In Trinidad and Tobago, only a small set of decisions is reserved for the board. Many supervisory decisions then are essentially matters for executive officers.

In Trinidad and Tobago, and in Jamaica with the Banking Services Act, the Minister retains limited residual regulatory and supervisory functions, the main functions being delegated to the regulatory agencies. This generally bodes well for the principle of independence in regulatory governance. Judicial authority suggests that the statutory power possessed by the Minister to give general directions to the institution may not interfere with the statutory mandate and functions of a regulatory agency. Provisions permitting ministerial directions then, ought not perhaps to be interpreted as posing a real threat to the independence principle.

A critical independence criterion is the existence of legal immunity for acts done in good faith. The idea is that the regulator's decision-making process and judgment would be impaired if carried out under the weight of potential liability. All directors

247 See (Ja) Banking Services Act, s 7(3) discussed above.

and officers of the regulatory agencies under study have the benefit of this protection. The immunity provisions, however, do have an impact on the principle of accountability of directors and officers. The law appears to be grappling with the hazard of over-protection at the expense of accountability by strictly interpreting and applying statutory immunity provisions. This approach demands more caution on the part of decision-makers who stand albeit limited risk of being held accountable by way of liability in damages. While indemnity provisions play a part in diminishing the sense of personal risk and accountability, the reputational risk of liability for flawed regulation and supervision may be a significant incentive for directors and senior officers to take the required care in their decision-making and actions. It should be noted that indemnity provisions are especially important for non-executive directors who receive nominal remuneration for carrying out their functions.

In Jamaica in particular, the law is, *prima facie*, strong in its demand for personal accountability in the discharge of directorial functions by imposing duties of competence and loyalty, breach of which exposes directors and officers to pecuniary sanctions. A number of factors, however, appear to weaken the apparent value of these duties as a mechanism for personal accountability. These include the low prospect of enforcement given the nature of the current PBMA Act apparatus, some uncertainties as to precisely how these duties operate in the context of the public sector, and a general judicial caution or reluctance regarding court scrutiny of directorial decisions. The Trinidad and Tobago model, however crude, of requiring attendance at board meetings with the risk of termination for absence, provides a useful starting point for demanding diligence and accountability of directors. In Jamaica, directors are specifically made to account to the minister and the Auditor-General where they have decided not to renew the appointment of the external auditor. This is a check on capricious decision-making regarding a critical board function. Directors also play a key role in contributing to institutional accountability and transparency by their direct involvement, via the audit committee, in the keeping of proper accounts and their duty to review the financial statements. Personal accountability in this process via an effective duty of care could enhance the quality of the review process and the diligence brought to bear by directors in it, thereby strengthening the overall governance of the institution.

The secrecy obligation on directors and officers, important though it is to the supervisory process, is inimical to the transparency and accountability principles. Lack of transparency is compounded by the fact that a financial regulator has a virtual monopoly on the aggregate information it acquires. It may be that the scope of confidentiality provisions has to be maintained for supervisory integrity. Given, however, the increasing pressure by the public for disclosure and transparency in the affairs of government in general, it might be useful to start interrogating whether the reach of the secrecy provisions could be contracted, and to assess the efficacy of a regulators' regulator as a governance watchdog in the public interest.

Institutional integrity depends a great deal on the personal integrity of the institution's stewards and senior officers. Integrity safeguards are contained in the qualifications for appointments and bases for the termination of appointment. The trend in more recent statutes is to insist on even higher standards of probity. In Jamaica, the fitness and propriety requirements applicable to the non-executive members of the Supervisory Committee under the Banking Services Act is an example of this more rigorous standard relating to integrity. In Trinidad and Tobago, disqualification based on professional misconduct leading to disbarment from practising one's profession is another example. These are buttressed by the common law of misfeasance and misconduct in public office, conflict of interest provisions for directors and senior officers, as well as a battery of anti-corruption laws. While misfeasance and misconduct in public office are useful, given the demanding legal standards required to establish them, governance frameworks ought not to rely too heavily on them to deter or capture dishonest or unethical behaviour on the part of directors and senior officers. Thus, the thrust towards statutory anti-corruption laws becomes very important. It is unfortunate that a primary anti-corruption strategy, that of requiring disclosure of personal assets and liabilities, has bypassed the usual governance framework applicable to non-executive directors of the financial regulatory agencies in Jamaica. This is arguably a remarkable exception in the context of their role in and/or proximity to the licensing and registration of entities providing financial services, the investigation and enforcement of financial regulatory breaches by these entities along with the fact that they receive nominal remuneration for performing these duties. This combination of factors makes the position held by non-executive directors vulnerable to corruptive influences. That they are made to fall outside of the requirement for disclosure of assets in the normal course undermines transparency inasmuch as it weakens the systems for uncovering unethical conduct on the part of the directors. It is notable that the position under the counterpart statutes in Trinidad and Tobago presents a marked contrast to the situation in Jamaica. Lame sanctions, however, in respect of activity outlawed under Trinidad and Tobago's Integrity in Public Life Act give the impression of a half-hearted effort to intensify anti-corruption measures and underpin the integrity principle particularly in financial regulatory agencies.

CONCLUSION

This chapter has provided a comprehensive description of the nature of the laws governing directors and senior officers of institutions bearing responsibility for financial regulation/supervision in Jamaica and Trinidad and Tobago. The study shows that in addition to the regulatory functions they perform, directors also have oversight for the management of the institution and its resources. In the case of the directors of the Bank of Jamaica, this latter function comprises the full scope of their role. A key factor, which has emerged, is the dominance of central bank governors. This contrasts sharply with the governance model in the other regulatory institutions studied. With the exception of the FSC in Jamaica, the reliance on public sector non-executives is another salient feature of the governance structure. Both these factors impinge on independence in decision-making, though they are not centrally related to autonomy from political and industry influence, a main concern of regulatory governance.

While there are several features of the law which underpin independence in the context of regulatory governance, there are weaknesses in the provisions relating to tenures, sharply exemplified in the Jamaican laws. This potentially undermines security of tenure, a crucial feature of the independence principle in regulatory governance. Particularly in Jamaica where the PBMA Act provides a statutory foundation for governance across the public sector, directors of financial regulatory agencies are required to play a role in the arrangements for institutional accountability. Perhaps the centerpiece of the legal provisions supporting personal accountability is the statutory duties of care and loyalty in the PBMA Act. The viability of these duties in the public sector context is yet to be determined, but more importantly, their effectiveness as an accountability measure appears uncertain given the apparent gap in the mechanism for their enforcement. Directorial immunity from suits may frustrate legal mechanisms for personal accountability for faulty regulatory decisions, but this is a trade-off in support of the principle of independence. The courts, however, appear to be vigilant regarding the boundaries of statutory immunity. This judicial stance guards the principle of accountability in the regulatory process, and attempts to strike an appropriate balance between the need for regulatory/supervisory efficiencies and the importance of accountability and transparency.

Provisions in the law abound in support of the principle of integrity. This sends a crucial signal in relation to regulatory governance – that governance watchdogs are prepared to hold themselves to standards equal to, or even more rigorous than those governing regulated persons. But the intensity of this signal is somewhat diminished by virtue of the improbability of actual liability for improper conduct on the part of directors and officers, whether on account of weak sanctions, difficulties in establishing the ingredients of the relevant causes of action, or exceptions in the law for some directors.

BIBLIOGRAPHY

Adenas, M and Fairgrieve, D, 'Misfeasance in Public Office, Governmental Liability, and European Influences' (2002) ICLQ 757

Armour, J, Hansmann, H and Kraakman, R, 'Agency Problems, Legal Strategies and Enforcement' (2009) Oxford Legal Studies Research Paper 21/2009 (http://papers.ssrn.com/sol3/papers.cfm?abstract_id=1436555)

Arnone, M, Darbar, S and Gambini, A, 'Governance in Banking Supervision: Theory and Practices' in D Masciandaro and M Quintyn (eds), *Designing Financial Supervision Institutions: Independence, Accountability and Governance*, 2007, Edward Elgar 150

Blake, C, 'Judicial Oversight of Financial Regulatory Action in the Commonwealth Caribbean' (2012) 41 *Common Law World Review* 354

Burgess, A, *Commonwealth Caribbean Company Law*, 2003, Routledge

Cadbury Report, *Report of the Committee on the Financial Aspects of Corporate Governance,* 1992, Gee

Carmichael, J, 'Public Sector Governance and the Finance Sector' in R Litan, M Pomerleano and V Sundararajan (eds) *Financial Sector Governance: The Roles of the Public and Private Sectors*, 2002, Brookings Institution

Cecchetti, S and Li, L, 'Do Capital Adequacy Requirements Matter for Monetary Policy?' (2008) 46 *Economic Inquiry* 643

Cheema, G S, 'A Governance Approach to Development: New Role for Development Co- operation' in H A Hye (ed), *Governance: South Asian Perspectives*, 2000, The University Press 513

Das, U and Quintyn, M 'Crisis Prevention and Crisis Management: The Role of Regulatory Governance' (2002) IMF Working Paper WP/02/163 (http://www.imf.org/external/pubs/ft/wp/2002/wp02163.pdf)

Das, U, Quintyn and Chenard, K, 'Does Regulatory Governance Matter for Financial System Stability? An Empirical Analysis' (2004) IMF WP/04/89

Department of Trade and Industry (UK), Higgs Report, *Review of the Role and Effectiveness of Non-executive Directors*, 2003

du Plessis, J, Hargovan, A and Bagaric, M, *Principles of Corporate Governance*, 2nd edn, 2011, CUP

Enriques, L and Hertig G, 'Improving the Governance of Financial Supervisors' (2011) *European Business Organization Law Review* 357

Farrar, J, *Corporate Governance: Theories, Principles and Practice*, 3rd edn, 2008, OUP

Ferlie, E, Ashburner, L, Fitzgerald L and Pettigrew, A, *The New Public Management in Action*, 1996, OUP

Global Reporting *Initiative, Sustainability Reporting Guidelines*, Version 3.1, 2000–2011, 10. https://www.globalreporting.org/resourcelibrary/G3.1-Guidelines-Incl-Technical- Protocol.pdf

Goodhart, C, 'Regulating the Regulator – An Economist's Perspective on Accountability and Control' in E. Ferran and C Goodhart (eds), *Regulating Financial Services and Markets in the Twenty-first Century*, 2001, Hart Publishing 151

Hampel Report, *Committee on Corporate Governance, Final Report*, 1998, Gee

Hüpkes, E, Quintyn, M and Taylor, M, 'The Accountability of Financial Sector Supervisors – Principles and Practice' (2005) *European Business Law Review* 1575

Jamaica, 'Corporate Governance Framework for Public Bodies in Jamaica' (2011) (http://www.mof.gov.jm/sites/default/files/public/Corporate_Governance_Framework_September_2011.pdf)

Jensen, M and Meckling, W, 'Theory of the Firm: Management Behaviour, Agency Costs and Ownership Structure' (1976) *Journal of Financial Economics* 305

Kerr, V L, *Effective Corporate Governance*, 2005, GovStrat

King Report, *King Report on Governance for South Africa*, 2009, IOD

Lastra, R and Shams, H, 'Public Accountability in the Financial Sector' in E Ferran and C Goodhart (eds), *Regulating Financial Services and Markets in the Twenty-first Century*, 2001, Hart Publishing 165

Lusty, D, 'Revival of the Common Law Offence of Misconduct in Public Office' (2014) 38 Crim LJ 337

Lybek, T and Morris, J, 'Central Bank Governance: A Survey of Boards and Management' (2004) IMF Working Paper WP/04/226 (http://www.imf.org/external/pubs/ft/wp/2004/wp04226.pdf)

Masciandaro, D and Quintyn, M (eds), *Designing Financial Supervision Institutions: Independence, Accountability and Governance*, 2007, Edward Elgar

Masciandaro, D, Quintyn, M and Taylor M, 'Financial Supervisory Independence and Accountability – Exploring the Determinants' (2008) IMF Working Paper WP/08/147 (https://www.imf.org/external/pubs/ft/wp/2008/wp08147.pdf)

McKoy, DV, *Corruption: Law, Governance and Ethics in the Commonwealth Caribbean*, 2012, Hansib

Mulgan, R, *Holding Power to Account*, 2003, Palgrave Macmillan

Oliver, D, Prosser, T and Rawlings, R, *The Regulatory State*, 2010, OUP

Owen, G, 'The Role of the Board' in K Rushton (ed), *The Business Case for Corporate Governance*, 2008, CUP 26

Page, A, 'Regulating the Regulator – A Lawyer's Perspective on Accountability and Control' in E Ferran and C Goodhart (eds), *Regulating Financial Services and Markets in the Twenty First Century*, 2001, Hart 127

Quintyn, M, 'Independent Agencies: More than a Cheap Copy of Independent Central Banks?' (2009) 20 *Constitutional Political Economy* 267

Quintyn, M, Ramirez, S and Taylor, M, 'The Fear of Freedom: Politicians and the Independence and Accountability of Financial Supervisors in Practice' in D Masciandaro and M Quintyn (eds), *Designing Financial Supervision Institutions: Independence, Accountability and Governance*, 2007, Edward Elgar 61

Quintyn, M and Taylor, M, 'Robust Regulators and their Political Masters: Independence and Accountability' in Theory in D Masciandaro and M Quintyn (eds), *Designing Financial Supervision Institutions: Independence, Accountability and Governance*, 2007, Edward Elgar 1

Robert Smith Report, *Audit Committees Combined Code Guidance*, 2003, (Financial Reporting Council)

Ryan, S, 'Good Governance: Old Wine in New Bottles?' in S Ryan and A Bisessar (eds), *Governance in the Caribbean*, 2002, SALISES 7

Ryan, S and Bisessar, A (eds), *Governance in the Caribbean*, 2002, SALISES
Scott, C, 'Accountability and the Regulatory State' (2000) 27(1) *Journal of Law and Society* 38.
Sutton, P, 'The Public Sector Reform in the Commonwealth Caribbean: A Review of Recent Experiences' Caribbean Paper No. 6, Centre for International Governance Innovation 2008 (http://www.cigionline.org/sites/default/files/6.%20Public%20Sector%20Reform%20in% 20the%20Commonwealth%20Caribbean.pdf)
Young, A, 'Frameworks in Regulating Company Directors: Rethinking the Philosophical Foundations' (2009) *Company Lawyer* 355

CHAPTER 6

PUBLIC SECTOR GOVERNANCE

Change, crisis and dysfunction

Derrick McKoy

INTRODUCTION

Stripped of fanciful theories and reduced to its essential elements, governance is about decision-making. This is as true for agencies and authorities in the public sector as it is for companies in the private sector. It is as true for the board of directors of a private company as it is for the board of governors of a trade union. In short, it is not possible to have an administrative structure without having governance. One is a necessary adjunct to the other. The critical questions are, in our organisations, how should we go about decision-making processes? Who and what should we take into consideration? What issues should we consider? In some circumstances, the concern may well be what issues should definitely not be considered as a part of the decision-making process. While all organisations require governance, not all must go through the same decision-making process. A governance system that works well for one organisation may be quite unsuitable for another. The decision-making processes that should govern the conduct of, say, the governors of the Bank of Jamaica cannot be appropriate for the management of a hair salon.

PUBLIC SECTOR GOVERNANCE

Decision-making in the public sector, or public sector governance, may be more complicated and more demanding than private sector governance. This is true even when we confine our concerns only to the corporate level. There are many more stakeholders that must be taken into account in the public sector than in the private sector. Stakeholder management is a challenging responsibility for any organisation, but even with the most liberal interpretation of that responsibility, private sector stakeholding can be defined with reasonable precision. Most importantly, private sector executive officers can with some confidence define those who are not stakeholders. In the public sector, on the other hand, we all have a stake in the governance of the public enterprise. Our interests are not defined by ownership, contract or even citizenship, but by the mere fact that we share the public sector neighbourhood. Our very existence in the polity gives us a stakeholding in the management of public resources.

Administrative structures are generally managed by agents. This is so for most of the private sector, but necessarily so for all of the public sector. In relation to the governance of public resources in Jamaica, the Crown does very little in the personality of Her Majesty but does a great deal in governing the state through the host of agents representing the Crown. A commonly held assumption is that the public sector governance structures in developing economies like Jamaica's are inadequate for the numerous responsibilities that public sector agencies must discharge. This belief applies to all sectors of public services, but especially so to new emerging executive agencies and private companies now used to discharge public functions. As Thomas Sowell asserted: 'Some things are believed because they are demonstrably true. But many other things are believed because they are consistent with a widely held vision of the world – and this vision is accepted as a substitute for facts.'[1] So it is that public sector governance is considered to be generally defective because so often it is asserted that it is.

PUBLIC BODIES AND PUBLIC OFFICE

Although there is some debate as to what a public body is or who holds a public office, it must be acknowledged that a broad range of persons are subject to the public sector rules. The question is particularly vexing when it is considered that, in what is now described as the new public management, more private individuals and firms are engaged to do the work of public officers.[2] In *R v Bowden*[3] the Court of Appeal in England had held that the common law offence of misconduct in a public office is not limited to being committed by officers or agents of the Crown, but applies generally to every person who is appointed to discharge a public duty. In *Bowden*, the appellant was the chief building maintenance manager of a city council works department and his responsibilities included, in addition to the management of subordinate employees, ensuring that the department's activities were within the approved budget. While engaged in this capacity, the appellant dishonestly used the council's employees to refurbish premises that he let to one of his friends. Bowden was convicted in the Crown Court on the charge of misconduct in a public office. On his appeal, Bowden unsuccessfully contended that his appointment as chief building maintenance manager to the city council was not a public office and as such he was not subject to the rules that governed the public services.

The case of *Bowden* raised some interesting questions on the responsibility of officers of the new executive agencies introduced in consequence of the new public management now being pursued by some Commonwealth Caribbean states. In the *Bowden* case, the department was a direct labour organisation, set up under Part III of the UK Local Government, Planning and Land Act 1980. Under Bowden's contract of employment with the council, he was responsible for management and direction of subordinate employees, accountable for the handling of money, and ensuring that his department's activities were within budget.[4] In addition, it is also the statutory responsibility for each local authority to ensure that its revenue from construction or maintenance works show such positive rate of return on the capital employed for carrying out the works as the Secretary of State may direct.[5] Bowden was not taken to task

1 T Sowell, *Economic Facts and Fallacies* (Basic Books 2008) vii.

2 See, eg, P Aucoin, *The New Public Management: Canada in Comparative Perspective* (IRPP 1995); E Ferlie and others, *The New Public Management in Action* (Oxford University Press 1996).

3 [1996] 1 WLR 98.

4 ibid 100–101.

5 Local Government, Planning and Land Act 1980, s 16.

for failing to do any of these, or even for doing them badly. Indeed, it may have been argued that Bowden had discharged these contractual responsibilities well. However, as someone engaged in the public service, Bowden was held to a higher standard.

This question arose in a different context in the Commonwealth Caribbean. Here, Moe JA specifically adopted the meaning enunciated in *Whittaker*[6] that a public office at common law is '. . . a person who discharges any duty in the discharge of which the public are interested, more clearly so if he is paid out of a fund by the public'. Among the earliest authorities to be found in support of this principle is the statement of Lord Mansfield CJ in *Bembridge*,[7] where the position was put in this manner:

> . . . a man accepting an office of trust concerning the public, especially if attended with profit, is answerable criminally to the King for misbehaviour in his office; this is true, by whomever and in whatever way the officer is appointed.[8]

So too, relying on *R v Whitaker*, the Court of Appeal of Jamaica in *R v Rhoden and Thomas*[9] agreed that 'A public officer is one who discharges any duty in which the public is interested, and more particularly if he receives public money'.[10] In *Rhoden and Thomas*, the appellants, members of the Island Special Constabulary Force, were charged and convicted before the Resident Magistrate on two counts. The first was a count of conspiracy to pervert or defeat the course of public justice, and the second was a count of bribery at common law. The evidence was that the appellants had asked for and had accepted a bribe from the vendor of illegal gambling tickets to refrain from prosecuting him. The Court of Appeal reserved judgment on the appeal on the count of bribery. The question that provoked the court was whether a special constable had a public duty to prosecute, in the same manner that regular constables do. The Court of Appeal accepted that special constables, whether or not they had the exact duties and privileges of regular constables, were nevertheless public officers.

In other cases there was no doubt that the accused were public officers. Herst LJ, who delivered the judgment of the court in *R v Bowden*,[11] surveyed the cases, beginning with *Bembridge*,[12] and concluded that an accountant in the office of the Receiver and Paymaster-General of the Forces,[13] the mayor and burgesses of Lyme Regis,[14] bishops, clergymen, lords of the manor, officers of the Bank of England,[15] an overseer for the poor,[16] the commanding officer in charge of renting the regimental canteen,[17] a county

6 [1914] 3 KB 1283.
7 (1783) 3 Doug 327.
8 ibid 331–332.
9 (1953) 6 JLR 259.
10 (1914) 10 Cr App Rep 245, 252.
11 [1996] 1 WLR 98, 103.
12 (1783) 3 Doug 327.
13 *R v Bembridge* (1783) 3 Doug 327.
14 *Henly v Lyme Corporation* (1828) 5 Bing 91. This was a civil action and not a criminal case for misbehaviour in public office.
15 ibid.
16 *R v Hall* [1891] 1 QB 747.
17 *R v Whitaker* [1914] 3 KB.

court registrar[18] and a constable,[19] were public offices. So too, a police chief is a public officer.[20] In *AG's Ref (No 3 of 2003)* it was very clear that the term applied to the police officers who had been charged with an offence.[21]

What are public offices, or who are public officers, are often defined and clarified by the several examples of legislation in the Commonwealth Caribbean. In the case of Belize, the Criminal Code in defining a public officer focuses on how the officer is appointed and generally means any person appointed by some other public functionary or authority.[22] Interestingly, a minister of religion is also a public officer for purposes of performing functions that may ultimately be recorded in a public registry.[23] The language in the provisions under the Bahamas Penal Code is almost the same language.[24] In the Commonwealth Caribbean legislation,[25] public officers are usually defined by the fact that the person holds a public office. For example, '. . . any member, officer, or servant of the Government or of a public body'[26] and 'public office' has been defined to mean '. . . any office or employment of a person as a member, officer or servant of such public body'.[27] This includes not only person employed directly to the public service, but also those employed in municipal or parochial services, statutory bodies and authorities, and government-owned companies.[28] Naturally, it also included any official of the state or its agencies, and anyone appointed, selected, elected or engaged to perform a public function.[29]

In some cases, local legislation may avoid the term 'public officer' completely, as the term is so closely associated with the formal officers of the government.[30] Instead, new legislation simply refers to 'public servants' which is defined in the broadest sense, to include employees of 'Government Companies'.[31] 'Government Company' is also given a broad meaning. In one jurisdiction it has been defined to mean a 'company registered under the Companies Act being a company whose policy the Government or an agency of Government, whether by the holding of shares or by financial input,

18 *R v Llewellyn-Jones* [1968] 1 QB 429.
19 *R v Dytham* [1979] QB 722. See also Wooding CJ in *Bates v James* (1964) 7 WIR 203, 204, holding that constables are persons serving under the Crown and consequently fall within the meaning of the anticorruption legislation.
20 *R v Boulanger* [2006] 2 SCR 49. Here the office police chief is designated the 'director of public security', and an 'official' under the law.
21 *AG's Reference (No 3 of 2003)* [2004] EWCA Crim 868.
22 Criminal Code, s 299(1) (Bel).
23 ibid s 299(2). This was one of the professions that Herst LJ in *R v Bowden* [1996] 1 WLR 98, 103, identified as a public office.
24 Penal Code, s 6 (Bah).
25 Public Bodies Corrupt Practices Act 1889 (UK), Prevention of Corruption Act 1906 (UK), and Prevention of Corruption Act 1916 (UK).
26 Prevention of Corruption Act 2000 (Bel), s 3(1).
27 ibid s 2.
28 Corruption (Prevention) Act 2001 (Ja), s 2.
29 ibid.
30 See, eg, Corruption (Prevention) Act 2001 (Ja), First Schedule, para 13(2).
31 ibid s 2(1).

is in a position to influence'.[32] Because of Caribbean governments' extensive participation in the private sector, adding members to private sector boards or providing financial support, many employees of private companies may find themselves classified as public servants and thus subject to the oversight that in the past was reserved for public officers in the more limited sense.

THE WAY FORWARD

Many explanations may be offered, accounting for why public sector governance structures are considered to be less desirable than those of the private sector. These may be classified under three broad headings: change, crisis and dysfunction. First, it can be asserted that changes in public management structures to make them more efficient and service oriented have introduced additional governance demands that the public service cannot readily meet. Secondly, the recent crisis of the international financial meltdown, or terrorism, or organised crime (and here we have a choice of challenges) overwhelm our public bureaucracies. Finally, there is a widely held view that corruption and malpractice are endemic to governments, and most especially those of the Third World, so that public sector governance structures are always dysfunctional. It takes little reflection to see that these explanations cannot all be true, but as Sowell observed, things are believed to be true because they are often asserted as truth.

CHANGE

The wave of public sector reforms that has swept through developed, developing and transitional countries over the last 30 years has been described as a new public management revolution.[33] Initially, these reforms were associated in the UK with the Conservative political agenda of the 1980s, but many other countries jumped on the bandwagon, and public management reform transcends a wide range of political contexts.[34] The traditional civil services in the UK and its ex-colonies have been

32 ibid. In Belize, the Prevention of Corruption Act 1927, s 2 and the Prevention of Corruption in Public Life Cap 12, 1994, s 2, both define 'public body' to '. . . include local and public authorities of all descriptions'. The latter term is also the interpretation given to public bodies in the Integrity in Public Life Act 200 (T&T). The Integrity in Public Life Act 2004 (A&B) does not define public body. It overcomes this limitation by providing a schedule with a list of 'Persons in Public Life' to whom the provisions of the Act apply. See also Contractor-General Act 1983 (Ja), s 2(1). In Belize, s 2 of the Act extends the meaning to include a company where the government owns 51 per cent or more of the shares.

33 V Desai and R Imrie, 'The New Managerialism in Local Governance: North-South Dimensions' (1998) 19 *Third World Quarterly* 635.

34 See Denhardt, JV and Denhardt, RB, *The New Public Service: Serving, Not Steering* (ME Sharpe 2011); Ewan Ferlie and others, *The New Public Management in Action* (Oxford University Press 1996); Ian Marsh, 'The Changing Ethos of Public Service' (1994) 53 *Australian Journal of Public Administration* 277; Moshe Maor, 'The Paradox of Managerialism' [1999] *Public Administration Review* 5; and DV McKoy, *The New Public Managament in Jamaica: Executive Agencies and Service Quality Delivery in Public Sector Programs* (DPhil thesis, Nova Southeastern University 2004).

transitioning from unwieldy, cumbersome and bureaucratic systems with centralised, well-established schemes of uniformed terms and conditions of service to systems with devolved responsibilities and public services delivered through quasi-autonomous agencies.[35] The declared objective was to improve the efficiency and effectiveness in the delivery of public services, to widen accountability and to promote the measurement and reporting of the performance of the public services.[36] Very clearly the new reforms required new governance measures, which would push policy advice and development back into the ministries and devolve executive functions and the delivery of public services into well-defined 'executive' agencies.[37]

THE NEW PUBLIC MANAGEMENT

Commonwealth Caribbean states have been happy fellow-travellers in this march to public administration reform,[38] as are other Commonwealth countries, including New Zealand, Australia, Canada and Malta.[39] These reforms should see executive agencies enjoying increased line autonomy from central government, with greater responsiveness to organisational performance targets, and greater capacity to develop partnerships with the private and third sectors.[40] An important component of this new theory of public management is the capacity of the new public sector agencies to negotiate with the central executive and contract for the required performance, and these 'high performance agreements' will be the vehicle for the delivery of superior public services.[41] Naturally, these reforms required legislative support. In Jamaica, the legislative foundation of the new public management is to be found in the Public Bodies Management and Accountability Act 2001 and the Executive Agencies Act 2002. The latter Act provided specifically for the establishment, management and accountability of the new executive agencies, whereas the former is more general in character and

35 Ferlie and others, ibid 6.

36 Noel Hyndman and Robert Anderson, 'Performance Information, Accountability and Executive Agencies' (1998) 18 *Public Money and Management* 23.

37 Robin Ibbs, *Improving Management in Government: The Next Steps* (HMSO 1988).

38 See Carlton Davis, 'Reforming the Cabinet Office: Strengthening the Core of Government in Jamaica' (1999) 1 *Caribbean Journal of Public Sector Management* 41; and 'Executive Agencies in Jamaica: The Story Thus Far' (2001) 3 *Caribbean Journal of Public Sector Management* 5. See also, DV McKoy, 'Applying the Agency Costs Model to the "Executive Agency" Concept in Jamaica' (2000) 2 *Caribbean Journal of Public Sector Management* 34 and *The New Public Managament in Jamaica: Executive Agencies and Service Quality Delivery in Public Sector Programs* (DPhil thesis, Nova Southeastern University 2004).

39 Moshe Maor, 'The Paradox of Managerialism' [1999] *Public Administration Review* 5; DA Sarji, *The New Public Administration: Global Challenges – Local Solutions* (Commonwealth Association for Public Administration and Management 1977).

40 Sarji, ibid.

41 Peter Aucoin, *The New Public Management: Canada in Comparative Perspective* (Cambridge University Press 1995). See also, C Davis, 'Executive Agencies in Jamaica: The Story Thus Far and the Central Management Mechanism' (2001) 3(1) *Caribbean Journal of Public Sector Management* 5; and Government of Jamaica, 'Government at Your Service: Public Sector Modernisation Vision and Strategy 2002–2012' (2003) Ministry Paper 56 of 2002.

intended to cover the range of public and private authorities now engaged in delivering public services.

In the modernisation process, the Commonwealth Caribbean governments emphasised the delivery of improved public service as a key objective, with '. . . an open and impartial public sector, which puts the public's interest first . . .'.[42] These new policies have expanded rather than introduced the use of private or devolved agencies for public service delivery. There was nothing limiting the constitutional capacity of a government in the Commonwealth Caribbean from creating a private limited liability company and assigning it some particular administrative responsibility, even if in doing so the government hoped to avoid some of the traditional controls associated with civil service departments, and it is an increasing common practice in the public services of the Commonwealth Caribbean to use private limited liability companies to carry out some of the functions traditionally carried out by civil servants. For example, the Government of Jamaica has divested some of its revenue enforcement functions to private firms. The trade board functions are exercised by the Trade Board Limited, a private limited liability company. The national irrigation regulatory functions are exercised by the National Irrigation Authority Limited, which is also a private limited liability company. The list could go on. Such agencies exist essentially at the will of the Executive and, prior to the passage of the Public Bodies Management and Accountability Act, they existed without being part of a coherent scheme or organisational structure for public management. In any event, at least for purposes of judicial review, courts tend to treat such companies as 'public bodies' if they exercise public functions.[43] The purported exercise of excessive authority, procedural irregularity and, arguably when discretion has been conferred on the public body, the exercise of that discretion in an irrational manner[44] may well provoke the supervision of the courts.

The Public Bodies Management and Accountability Act 2001 in Jamaica addresses some of the concerns arising from this new scheme of public management. The Act focuses on audit controls and on the duty of care and disclosure of directors of government-owned companies. It is significant that the new legislative scheme for the executive agencies does not leave the decision for the establishment of the agency completely in the hands of individual Ministers. Section 2 of the Act makes the distinction between the 'Minister' and the 'Responsible Minister'. The latter is the Minister with portfolio responsibility for the executive agency or relevant public body, while the former is the Minister with responsibility for the public service. Under section 4 of the Executive Agencies Act, the responsibility for designating an executive agency will be in the hands of the Minister having responsibility for the public service, not the Minister with responsibility for the agency.

The Minister with responsibility for the public service is described in the Act as 'Public Service Minister' and he is empowered by the Act to designate public bodies as

42 Cabinet Office, 'Government at Your Service: Public Sector Modernization Vision and Strategy 2002–2012' (Ministry Paper No 56, Government of Jamaica, Kingston 2002) 7.

43 See Batts J in *Robinson v National Irrigation Commission Ltd* [2013] JMSC Civil 19 [42].

44 See *Associated Provincial Picture Houses Ltd v Wednesbury Corporation* [1948] 1 KB 223.

executive agencies. Before he can promulgate such an order, however, he must first satisfy several requirements. He will be required to carry out an assessment of the functions of the Government department, statutory body or government-owned company that he contemplates may be usefully re-organised as an executive agency, identifying the most effective and efficient options for undertaking the functions of those public bodies and setting out the advantages and disadvantages of each option. He is then required to recommend the preferred option and give reasons for that option and the preferred form of organisation.

The 'Public Service Minister' and not the 'Responsible Minister' must approve a scheme of management for the new executive agency. The responsibility for drafting the scheme of management will be in the hands of the 'Responsible Minister' but it will be for the 'Public Service Minister' to approve it. The proposed scheme of management for a new executive agency will have to provide for the functions of the agency, the establishment functions and tenure of an advisory board, the appointment and tenure of the Chief Executive Officer, the application of funds of the agency, provisions for the preparation of multi-year corporate plans, annual business plans, quarterly and annual reports, performance agreements, levels of emoluments and remuneration schemes. If it is considered appropriate, the scheme for management can incorporate a framework document, a performance agreement, and strategic and operational plans.

APPOINTMENT AND TENURE

Few things in the new scheme for executive agencies have created more discomfort among current members of the traditional public service than the suggestion that the officers and staff within the new agencies will be subject to capricious methods of appointment and will lack security of tenure traditionally associated with the civil service.[45] Nevertheless, the new legislative measures address many of these concerns and should allay others. The Act in Jamaica contemplates that the Chief Executive Officer of the new executive agency will be appointed by the Head of State by instrument in writing and on the advice of the Public Services Commission, in the same manner that public officers are appointed. The appointment shall be for periods not exceeding five years in the first instance, but the Chief Executive Office may be reappointed. During the period of the appointment, the Chief Executive Officer enjoys security of tenure and is subject to removal from office only for cause.[46] The Chief Executive Officer will also be subject to removal from office for failing, without reasonable excuse, to carry out any of the functions conferred or imposed by law, the contract of employment, the

45 See generally, DV McKoy, *The New Public Managament in Jamaica: Executive Agencies and Service Quality Delivery in Public Sector Programs* (DPhil thesis, Nova Southeastern University 2004).

46 For reasons of insanity, permanent physical disability, bankruptcy, conviction and sentence to imprisonment or death, conviction of offence involving dishonesty, or has been 'proven to have brought disrepute to the Executive Agency through misconduct'. See Executive Agencies Act (Ja) 2002, s 8.

framework document or the performance agreement.[47] Review of the Chief Executive Officer's performance will not be in the hands of the responsible Minister but will be the responsibility of the Permanent Secretary in the Ministry acting on his behalf. The Permanent Secretary will have the responsibility to report to the Minister on the Chief Executive Officer's performance.

It must be contemplated that the contracts of employment of the executives in these new executive agencies will be different from those directing the traditional civil services. After all, this is the whole scheme of Aucoin's 'high performance contracts', where public management executives are expected to deliver better results for greater rewards.[48] Nevertheless, it is still to be resolved whether the contract of employment in the new executive agencies can provide for inferior terms or conditions of employment. For example, would a contract of employment for a period of five years that also provides for termination on one month's notice be consistent with the Act? On the face of it, this could not be consistent with the obvious intentions of the Act that seek so strongly to guarantee security of tenure. The proposed scheme for employing subordinate officers should satisfy some of the initial concerns. The Executive Agencies Act in Jamaica contemplates that all the other officers and employees of the Executive Agency will be public officers. The scheme assumes a delegation of responsibility by the Public Services Commission under section 127 of the Constitution. This delegation of responsibility will authorise the Chief Executive Officer on behalf of the Public Services Commission to engage, discipline and dismiss officers and other employees for the executive agency. As such, the scheme addresses one of the critical problems of the current system of public service in Jamaica: the severe restrictions imposed on existing public service managers to employ, discipline and dismiss their staff. Under the new regime, this power of the Chief Executive Officer will be subject to regulation but in any event, the fact that the subordinate officers are public officers will afford them the protection of the Public Services Commission. As such, subordinate officers in the new Executive Agencies will enjoy some security of tenure.[49]

In the absence of further regulation, the Act does not completely address the issue of who will be employed as subordinate officers. Instead, it offers some pious provisions that will require the Chief Executive Officer in filling a vacancy to '. . . give notice of such vacancy in a manner sufficient to enable suitably qualified persons to apply for the post',[50] and the Act further requires that the Chief Executive Officer '. . . will give preference to the person who is best suited to the position'.[51] Since the scheme contemplates so much independent responsibility in the hands of the Chief Executive Officer, it seems that some further provisions are required to ensure that this responsibility is not abused. It is possible that regulations under section 18 of the

47 Executive Agencies Act (Ja) 2002, s 10.

48 Peter Aucoin, 'Administrative Reform in Public Management: Paradigms, Principles, Paradoxes and Pendulums' (1990) 3 *Governance* 115; and Aucoin, *The New Public Management: Canada in Comparative Perspective* (Institute for Research on Public Policy 1995).

49 Aucoin, *The New Public Management*, ibid.

50 Executive Agencies Act (Ja) 2002, s 11(4).

51 ibid s 11(3).

Act could be used to address this issue. Regulations will specifically address the Chief Executive Officer's exercise of disciplinary control over the subordinate officers and the latter's rights to appeal disciplinary decisions, but the public services Minister will have the responsibility to make regulations generally to give effect to the provisions and purposes of the Act.

FINANCE AND TRANSPARENCY

The new scheme for executive agencies contemplates that these agencies may earn additional income from charges imposed by them in respect of the goods and services that they provide. Thus, the Act specifically provides that the agencies may, in accordance with further regulations, charge fees for their services and that those fees may be recovered as civil debts in the Resident Magistrates' Courts. These provisions open some very challenging issues, and it is contemplated that such provisions must make it possible and may even encourage public service agencies to become rent-seekers. Income earned from rent-seeking activities will not only allow the agencies to be removed from government's regular budget, but will open up opportunities for greater personal rewards for the management and staff of these new agencies.

The Act will require corporate and business plans and financial and activities reports but one questions whether this will provide adequate controls and whether there should not be more stringent political or legislative oversight. Other than provisions for gain sharing, and the general provision that public sector salaries should be competitive, the new scheme at this time does not contemplate a public sector wage and salaries policy. Such a policy may be developed in the future. However, the Commonwealth Caribbean Governments' public sector wage and salaries policies, and Jamaica's in particular, have demonstrated glaring weaknesses in the past, and this new scheme for executive agencies may create even more difficulties.

In keeping with the thrust for openness in public management, the Executive Agencies Act states that among its purposes is the establishment of appropriate mechanisms for proper management, accountability and transparency in the operations of executive agencies. Although the Act addresses the issues of management and accountability, it does not address how the transparency in public management might be achieved.

PUBLIC POLICY IMPLICATIONS OF CHANGE

We now agree that there is something to be described as the New Public Management, although we do not seem to be completely sure what that means.[52] What is beyond doubt, however, is that this term has been used to describe the changed public

52 Michael Barzelay, *The New Public Management: Improving Research and Policy Dialogue*, Vol 3 (University of California Press 2001) xi; and see Barzelay, *Breaking through Bureaucracy: A New Vision for Managing in Government* (University of California Press 1992). And See also Ewan Ferlie *et al*, *The New Public Management in Action* (Oxford University Press 1996) 10.

services that have taken place in the United Kingdom, New Zealand, Australia, Scandinavia, North America and the Commonwealth Caribbean over the last 30 years, with new administrative structures and new views of the role of the public administrator and the nature of the profession of public administration.[53] This move to what has been described as 'entrepreneurial governance'[54] in the public sector has important policy implications. Earlier in this chapter, it was argued that governance in the public sector, including corporate governance, is complicated by the large number of stakeholders that must be accommodated. Indeed, Bozeman argues that the relationship between structural change and benefit in the public organisation is complicated precisely because there is need to consider the rights and responsibilities of all the stakeholders.[55]

To be sure, the new reforms import into public management many of the initiatives on planning, directing and rewarding in an organisational culture; but the new challenges cannot be addressed simply by importing only the private sector governance rules. In the public sector, there are important political implications of the independence and accountability of the agencies that need to be addressed. In the new public service, new agencies replace existing one where the senior civil servants had security of tenure. The new model replaces the system of public administration where the senior civil servant is reasonably free from political control to one where he need not be. On the other hand, in some cases, political and administrative controls over some agencies have been reduced. The implication of this latter development has yet to be fully explored, although this concern was articulated almost 20 years ago.[56] One implication of political executives losing control over the implementation of their policy may be a desire for greater control over the bureaucracy; similarly, senior civil servants who are removed from policy-making and thus supposed to be less political find their positions becoming more insecure due to the political executives' desire for more control.[57]

Corporate governance principles culled from the private sector will not address these concerns. Quite simply, private sector principles are not always useful since public management presents peculiar problems that cannot be solved by analogy to the private sector firm. Quite apart from a more demanding set of public sector stakeholding, the public sector enterprise usually has no conveniently measured equivalent of profit to serve as an ultimate end, as there is in the private firm, and the purpose of organisation design in the public sector, at least from a public interest standpoint,

53 Robert Denhardt and Janet Denhardt, 'The New Public Service: Serving rather than Steering' [2002] 60 *Public Administration Review* 549.

54 David Osborne and Ted Gaebler, *Reinventing Government: How the Entrepreneurial Spirit is Transforming the Public Sector* (Addison-Wesley 1992).

55 Barry Bozeman, 'Organization Design in the Public Bureaucracy' (1981) 15 *The American Review of Public Administration* 107; see also Barry Bozeman and Stuart Bretschneider, 'The "Publicness Puzzle" in Organization Theory: A Test of Alternative Explanations of Differences between Public and Private Organizations' (1994) 4 *Journal of Public Administration Research and Theory* 197.

56 Moshe Maor, 'The Paradox of Managerialism' [1999] *Public Administration Review* 5.

57 See generally, Maor ibid.

should not be the aggrandisement of the organisation.[58] On the other hand, the discipline of public administration has not yet developed the theories or conceptual tools to address these issues.[59]

CRISIS

If the international Press is to be believed, the Global Financial Crisis of 2007 and 2008 was the worst since the Great Depression of the 1930s.[60] This opinion is also shared by very eminent scholars.[61] Commonwealth Caribbean countries, like the rest of Latin America, are mainly on the periphery of the international finance system,[62] but sufficiently closely integrated into that system to be badly affected by the global meltdown. One view is that that the Global Financial Crisis was so severe that it undermined the dominant models of state–society relations.[63] Another competing view is that the crisis simply allowed some states to continue the transitional structures of the New Public Management.[64] As most countries have recovered or seem to be recovering from the global crisis, perhaps it is now safe to say that the heavens did not fall and that our public management systems have been able to cope with the challenges. The same can be said of international terrorism. The portents are dire, but somehow our public management structures have survived.

The latest international threat is organised crime. In pursuit of the now popularly characterised state action, 'the war against drugs', Commonwealth Caribbean states have introduced legislation to allow the state to forfeit the proceeds derived from illegal dealing in drugs. One example of this was the Tracing and Forfeiture of Proceeds of Drug Trafficking Act, now the Proceeds of Crime Act 2000 of the Bahamas.[65] In the

58 See Barry Bozeman and Stuart Bretschneider, 'The "Publicness Puzzle" in Organization Theory: A Test of Alternative Explanations of Differences between Public and Private Organizations' (1994) 4 *Journal of Public Administration Research and Theory* 197; and Barry Bozeman, 'Organization Design in the Public Bureaucracy' (1981) 15 *The American Review of Public Administration* 107. See also, P Aucoin, *The New Public Management: Canada in Comparative Perspective* (Institute for Research on Public Policy 1995).

59 Vandana Desai and Rob Imrie, 'The New Managerialism in Local Governance: North-South Dimensions' (1998) 19 *Third World Quarterly* 635.

60 See, eg, David Pendery, 'Three Top Economists Agree 2009 Worst Financial Crisis Since Great Depression; Risks Increase if Right Steps are Not Taken' (Reuters 2009) <http://www.reuters.com/article/2009/02/27/idUS193520+27-Feb-2009+BW20090227> accessed 8 March 2015.

61 J Crotty, 'Structural Causes of the Global Financial Crisis: A Critical Assessment of the "New Financial Architecture"' (2009) 33(4) *Cambridge Journal of Economics* 563; José Antonio Ocampo, 'Latin America and the Global Financial Crisis' (2009) 33 *Cambridge Journal of Economics* 703.

62 José Antonio Ocampo, *International Asymmetries and the Design of the International Financial System* (CEPAL – Sweie Temas de coyuntura No 15, United Nations, Santiago 2001).

63 Carlo Ruzza, 'The Ideology of New Public Management, Associational Representation and the Global Financial Crisis' [2014] *Partecipazione e Conflitto* 490–508, 490.

64 Andrew Massey, 'Nonsense on Stilts: United Kingdom Perspectives on the Global Financial Crisis and Governance' (2011) 11(1) *Public Organization Review* 61–75, 61.

65 Chapters 86 and 93, Bah.

language of Henry P of the Bahamian court of appeal, the purpose of the act is '. . . to ensure that persons who lay up for themselves treasure derived from their activities in relation to trafficking in dangerous drugs do not continue to enjoy the fruits of these activities'.[66] The *Re Lehder-Rivas* case is authority for the proposition that the court may make a restraint order under section 10 of the Tracing and Forfeiture of Proceeds of Drug Trafficking Act 1986 in respect of assets held by companies, even where there is no evidence that the companies had been improperly used by the defendant.[67] Nevertheless, there is increasing insecurity that our public bureaucracies cannot cope with these new demands.

DYSFUNCTION

Commonwealth Caribbean public management systems must not only accommodate a demanding body of stakeholders, the uncertainty of administrative change and reform, international crises and complicated measures of success and failure, but also the fact that many of the decision-making processes that would be acceptable in the private sector would be open to allegations of corruption if they were applied in a public sector setting. No example better demonstrates this than the case of *CO Williams Construction Ltd v Blackman*.[68] Commonwealth Caribbean countries have developed many schemes for public sector procurement. Some schemes are set out in legislation and regulations, whereas others are based on administrative structures. In Barbados, the Financial Administration and Audit Act delegates to Cabinet the authority to regulate the public procurement regime,[69] and the prescribed rules provide that public invitations to tender should be issued for contracts above a predetermined value. The rules also required that the received tenders are first to be examined by a specially constituted tenders committee.[70] The rules also provide that the committee shall make its recommendations on the award to the head of department, who in turn is required to submit the recommendation to the Minister. The Minister is not required to accept the recommendation, but then he must pass it on to the Cabinet for final decision.[71] In *CO Williams Construction Ltd v Blackman*,[72] the applicant submitted the lowest tender to construct a road and was recommended by the committee for the award of the contract. The Minister did not accept the recommendation but instead advised Cabinet to accept the higher tender of a competitor. The Cabinet accepted the Minister's advice. The applicant challenged the decision of the Cabinet, asserting the principle that when a governmental function is regulated by legislation then that function can only

66 *Re Lehder-Rivas, International Dutch Resources Ltd v A-G* (1990) 56 WIR 1, 3.
67 ibid.
68 (1994) 45 WIR 94.
69 Section 39.
70 *CO Williams Construction Ltd v Blackman* (1994) 45 WIR 94, 97–98.
71 Rule 148.
72 (1994) 45 WIR 94.

be exercised in accordance with that statute.[73] That principle should only support the applicant if there is also a necessary construction of the regulations that where a public tender is invited, the government must accept the lowest valid tender. It is difficult to see how this construction would arise in a private sector organisation. The typical invitation to tender, in both the private and the public sector, carries the provision that the person inviting the tender need not accept the lowest or any offer. In the private sector, that limitation means what it says. In the public sector, however, applying that principle may well be regarded as corruption. In *CO Williams Construction Ltd*, the Judicial Committee of the Privy Council accepted that in the public sector it is possible for the court to review the government decision, even where the decision is ultimately made by the Cabinet.[74] The power given to the Minister to accept or reject the advice of the Committee, and the inherent power of the Cabinet to accept or reject the advice of the Minister seemed not to count. Put another way, Lord Reid's injunction in *Anisminic Ltd v Foreign Compensation Commission and Another*[75] that, '. . . if a tribunal has jurisdiction to go right, it has jurisdiction to go wrong',[76] for some inexplicable reason does not apply to public procurement in the Commonwealth Caribbean. Governments may try to reduce this dysfunction by specifically setting out the public procurement regime in legislation,[77] but judging from the experiences of Barbados as demonstrated in the *CO Williams Construction Ltd* case, this does not always avoid the difficulty.

Jamaica has a modified public procurement scheme that is based both on legislation and on special administrative arrangements but this regime presents two sets of problems. First, there is apparent conflict between the two acts governing public procurement and, secondly, there is some doubt as to the enforceability of the current administrative arrangements. In 1992, amendment to the Financial Administration and Audit Act introduced new provisions on regulating governing contracts[78] which required that agreements for public procurement shall be on such terms and conditions as the Minister may prescribe in regulations.[79] Those regulations may prescribe the extent to which an officer is authorised to enter into the agreement, the procedures relating to the offer and acceptance of tenders, the signing of the agreements, the forms they may take, and the measures for executing the agreements and making payments under them.[80] Later, in 2001, the Contractor-General Act was amended to establish a National Contracts Commission also with responsibilities to promote the efficiency, transparency and equity in public procurement contracts.[81] The powers given to the new commission seem to cover the

73 ibid 99.

74 ibid 100–101.

75 [1969] 2 AC 147; [1969] 2 WLR 163; [1969] 1 All ER 208.

76 [1969] 1 All ER 208, 213.

77 For example, the Public Procurement and Disposal of Public Property 2015 (T&T); Contractor-General Act 1983 (Ja); Contractor-General Act 1994 (Bel); and Financial Administration and Audit Act 1964 (Bds).

78 Amendment introduced by Act 1/1992, s 5(a).

79 Financial Administration and Audit Act, s 19B.

80 ibid s 19B(2).

81 Contractor-General Act, s 23D.

same field as the responsibilities given to the Minister under the Financial Administration and Audit Act, and there is not clear direction as to how the conflicting responsibilities are to be reconciled.

MISCONDUCT IN PUBLIC OFFICE AS A GOVERNANCE STANDARD

In addition to legislation, regulations, directions, orders and policies on governance in the public sector, public servants are also governed by the common law. The common law on bribery, extortion and misconduct in public office are all part of the public sector governance regime, but it is the crime of misconduct in public office which covers the broadest field of misbehaviour. As Paul Finn explained:

> Unlike with the more narrow offences of bribery and extortion, official misconduct is not concerned primarily with the abuse of official position for pecuniary gain, with corruption in the popular sense. Its object is simply to ensure that an official does not, by any wilful act or omission, act contrary to the duties of his office, does not abuse intentionally the trust reposed in him.[82]

To satisfy the requirements of the offence, there must be an element of misconduct calculated to injure the public interest, and thus sufficient to call for condemnation and punishment, even if the conduct is not of such a nature as to be described as corrupt or dishonest.[83] Misconduct in public office has been used quite effectively in some jurisdictions to control the conduct of public officials.[84]

The terms, 'misconduct in public office', 'misbehaviour in public office' and 'misfeasance in public office' are often used interchangeably and the terms generally refer to the same common law offence.[85] A second view is that the term accommodates two distinct offences: misfeasance in public office and neglect in public office.[86] A third view is that misconduct in public office is an omnibus offence, with several different dimensions. Thus, Olsson J, in the Court of Criminal Appeal of South Australia, suggested that apart from '. . . specific offences termed bribery, extortion, buying and selling public offices . . .', the common law did not '. . . contemplate closed, specifically titled, categories of offences in relation to public officers'.[87] In his opinion, a public

---

82 P Finn, 'Official Misconduct' [1978] 2 Crim LJ 307.

83 *R v Dytham* [1979] 1 QB 722, 727 (Lord Widgery CJ).

84 See, eg, use of the common law offence of misconduct in public office in the anticorruption project in Hong Kong as evidenced by *Sin Kam Wah and Lam Chuen Ip v HKSAR* [2005] HKCFA 29, FACC No 14 of 2004; *Shum Kwok Sher v HKSAR* [2002] HKCFA 27, FACC 1/2002; and *HKSAR v Shum Kwok Sher* [2001] HKCA 108, CACC 3/2001.

85 Finn (n 82) suggests that the offence has been '. . . variously described as "official misconduct", "breach of official trust", or "misbehaviour in a public office"'.

86 *R v Boulanger* [2006] 2 SCR 49, [10] (where McLachlin CJ concluded that misfeasance in public office alone, and not neglect in public, was incorporated in Canada in the Criminal Code, RSC 1985, c C-46, s 122).

87 *Question of Law Reserved (No 2 of 1996)* No SCCRM 96/131 Judgment No 5674 (South Australian Supreme Court).

officer could have been indicted for any misbehaviour '. . . categorised as misfeasance, malfeasance or nonfeasance in office of a criminally culpable nature'.[88]

To be sure, the offence of misconduct in public office has been recognised in the common law for over 400 years. McLachlin CJ, in the Supreme Court of Canada,[89] identified a reference to misconduct in public office in a written judgment in 1704,[90] but other authorities argue that it is much older.[91] The charge of misconduct in public office is sometimes directed at the corrupt behaviour of public officials, but the offence does not specifically deal with corruption. At common law, the offence is directed principally at the neglect of public duty. The editors of *Russell on Crime* set out the common law offence in the following terms:

> Where a public officer is guilty of misbehaviour in office by neglecting a duty imposed upon him either at common law or by statute, he commits a misdemeanour and is liable to indictment unless another remedy is substituted by statute. The liability exists whether he is a common law or a statutory officer; and a person holding an office of important trust and of consequence to the public, under letters patent or derivatively from such authority, is liable to indictment for not faithfully discharging the office. [92]

The leading case of *R v Bembridge*[93] is generally accepted as the source of the modern law, and it is possible to interpret Lord Mansfield's statement in that case on the common law offence as accommodating two distinct types of activity. Lord Mansfield said:

> Here there are two principles applicable: first, that a man accepting an office of trust concerning the public, especially if attended with profit, is answerable criminally to the King for misbehaviour in his office; this is true, by whomever and in whatever way the officer is appointed . . . Secondly, where there is a breach of trust, fraud, or imposition, in a matter concerning the public, though as between individuals it would only be actionable, yet as between the King and the subject it is indictable. That such should be the rule is essential to the existence of the country.[94]

Thus, the public officer is criminally responsible when he misbehaves in carrying out his office; and he is also guilty if there is breach of trust or fraud in carrying out his office. In *Williams v R*,[95] when the Court of Appeal of the Eastern Caribbean States considered misconduct in public office, it relied on two cases – *R v Whittaker*[96] and

---

88 ibid. Olsson J finds support for this view in *R v Llewellyn-Jones* [1968] 1 QB 429.

89 *R v Boulanger* [2006] 2 SCR 49.

90 McLachlin CJ cited *Anonymous* (1704), 6 Mod 96, 87 ER 853 (KB), where it was held: 'If a man be made an officer by Act of Parliament, and misbehave himself in his office, he is indictable for it at common law, and any publick officer is indictable for misbehaviour in his office.'

91 See the arguments in *AG's Reference (No 3 of 2003)* [2004] EWCA Crim 868, [2005] 1 QB 73, citing *Crouther's Case* (1599) Cro Eliz 654.

92 WO Russell and JWC Turner, *Russell on Crime* (12th edn, Stevens 1964) 361.

93 (1783) 3 Doug KB 327.

94 *R v Bembridge* (1783) 3 Doug 327, 332.

95 *Williams v R* (1986) 39 WIR 129.

96 [1914] 3 KB 1283.

Walter v R.[97] Moe JA, in delivering the judgment of the Court, suggested that for the offence to exist the accused must be a public officer, he owes a duty in consequence of that office, that he has breached that duty, that his conduct was calculated to injure the public interest, that his conduct was of such a nature as to call for condemnation and punishment, and that he had an oblique or fraudulent motive.

Moe JA's last requirement, that there must be an oblique or fraudulent motive, brings misbehaviour in public office into the realm of corruption, but there is nothing in Lord Mansfield's definition that requires that the conduct be corrupt. Lord Mansfield's two alternative requirements were misbehaviour, or breach of trust or fraud in carrying out the office.[98] *AG's Reference (No 3 of 2003)*[99] did not require the existence of an oblique or fraudulent motive to constitute the offence. In this case, several police officers were charged with manslaughter and misconduct when they neglected to attend a prisoner in their custody who was in some physical distress. The prisoner died when he was left unattended. The English Court of Appeal was required to decide on the ingredients of the offence of misconduct in a public office, and whether it is necessary for the prosecution to prove 'bad faith' to establish the offence.[100] The Court of Appeal concluded that discussions of 'bad faith' were inappropriate to this case. The critical question was whether the police officers had wilfully neglected to perform their duty or wilfully misconducted themselves in looking after the prisoner.

Nevertheless, the existence of fraudulent motives or bad faith is certainly one way of constituting the offence. Abbott CJ in *R v Borron*[101] declared that '. . . dishonest, oppressive, or corrupt motive, under which description fear and favour may generally be included', was one way of grounding an indictment or criminal information. Thus, while such considerations are not always irrelevant, there are many situations where whether or not the defendant has acted in bad faith will be critical to guilt. Moreover, it is possible to characterise misconduct in public office as corruption when it is accompanied by an oblique or fraudulent motive.[102]

What amounts to misconduct in public office is not without controversy. This is because the offence is defined in such general terms, and the terms are used to cover such a wide range of wrongdoing. The problem is not completely solved by adopting McLachlin CJ's suggestion in *Boulanger*,[103] that misconduct in public office is really two distinct offences: misfeasance in public office and neglect in public office. In *Williams*,[104] the appellant was jointly charged with another with four offences, including the common law offence of misbehaviour in public office. While he was a Minister of the

97 (1980) 27 WIR 386.

98 McLachlin CJ in *R v Boulanger* [2006] 2 SCR 49, suggested the dichotomy of *non*-feasance, were the neglect of official duties, and *mis*feasance (or *mal*feasance) where there is a '. . . a corrupt, dishonest or oppressive intent'.

99 [2004] EWCA Crim 868, [2005] 1 QB 73.

100 ibid 77.

101 (1820) 3 B & Ald 432, 434.

102 ibid.

103 [2006] 2 SCR 49.

104 (1986) 39 WIR 129, 130–131.

Government and at the same time the owner of a shipping vessel, the appellant sought an overpayment for freight services provided by his ship to the government. He was convicted of the offence.

In *Walter v R*,[105] the Premier of the State negotiated in his private and personal capacity for the purchase and importation of two steel buildings, one building he sold to the government and the other he applied to his personal use. Both buildings were eventually cleared from the customs by the Public Works Department and entered the state free of duty on the assumption that both were for the use of the government. The Court of Appeal decided that the sale of the building to government at a profit was not misconduct in public office, as a critical ingredient of the offence was missing.[106] As reprehensible as the appellant's conduct may have been the prosecution failed to prove that in the sale of the building to the government the appellant acted with any 'fraudulent or oblique motive'. Thus, in the opinion of the Court of Appeal, the appellant, by this conduct, had not committed the offence of misbehaviour in public office.

The common law principles of misconduct in public office provide an additional standard for ensuring good governance of the public sector. It is a very high standard and imposes on those working as agents of the state the responsibility for ensuring that they do not act contrary to the duties of their offices and do not intentionally abuse the trust reposed in them.

PRIVATE LAW REMEDY FOR PUBLIC SECTOR MISCONDUCT

Misbehaviour by a public officer is generally regarded as the subject of the public law. If the public body has acted in a manner which is regarded as illegal, irregular or irrational it will be subject to judicial review. The modern trend is to broaden the categories of persons who may be regarded as having an interest, and thus capable of complaining in the courts in public law about the misconduct of the agency.

If the public officer's conduct is regarded as misconduct in public office, it may also be the basis of a criminal charge. Many judges identify the criminal offence of misconduct in public office as including misfeasance in public office.[107] These terms, misconduct and misfeasance, are sometimes used interchangeably to identify the same wrong. There are circumstances where misfeasance in public office may be regarded as '. . . happier and more appropriate phraseology . . .' to be applied to the criminal misbehaviour than the term misconduct in public office.[108] However,

105 (1980) 27 WIR 386.

106 ibid 393. It is likely that this conduct would now be caught by the Prevention of Corruption Act 2004, s 3(1)(e), which makes it an offence where '. . . one allows his private interest to conflict with his public duties'.

107 See McLachlin CJ in *R v Boulanger* [2006] 2 SCR 49, citing with approval the definition of misfeasance in public office, as defined by JF Stephen, in *Digest of the Criminal Law* (4th edn, Macmillan & Co 1887) 85.

108 *Question of Law Reserved (No 2 of 1996)* No SCCRM 96/131 Judgment No 5674 (South Australian Supreme Court).

the tort of misfeasance in public office is distinct from the criminal offence of misconduct in public office.[109] *Bembridge*,[110] decided in 1783, has been credited with '. . . providing the seminal formulation of the offence' of misconduct or misbehaviour in public office.[111] Bembridge, an accountant in the British army, was charged with misbehaviour in his office in that he had wrongfully, unjustly and fraudulently contrived to conceal omissions in the records to defraud the King. His defence was that the matter was a civil wrong and not indictable. Lord Mansfield dismissed Bembridge's motion on the basis that if one accepts an office of trust concerning the public, and misbehaves in his office, he is criminally liable. Lord Mansfield went on to say, '. . . where there is a breach of trust, fraud, or imposition, in a matter concerning the public, though as between individuals it would only be actionable, yet as between the King and the subject it is indictable'.[112] Thus, as the facts that ground the tort of deceit may also ground the criminal charge of fraud; so the facts that ground the tort of misfeasance in public office may also ground the criminal offence of misconduct in public office.

While the tort of misfeasance and the crime of misconduct are intimately related,[113] the former offers a clear and distinct opportunity for the victim of maladministration to pursue a private law remedy. Both the crime and the tort requires *mens rea*, wilfulness in the commission of the offence for misconduct[114] and recklessness for misfeasance,[115] meaning in the words of Pill LJ: 'There must be an awareness of the duty to act or a subjective recklessness as to the existence of the duty.'[116] On the question of the distinction between the *mens rea* for the crime and the tort, Pill LJ accepted Lord Steyn's suggestion that the nature of the tort contained '. . . a meaningful requirement of bad faith in the exercise of public powers . . .'.[117] and that '. . . the unifying element of conduct amounting to an abuse of power accompanied by subjective bad faith',[118] while for the crime, 'There must be an awareness of the duty to act or a subjective recklessness as to the existence of the duty'. Under this approach, meaningful requirement of bad faith, or subjective bad faith, appears to be a more demanding standard than awareness of the duty or subjective recklessness as to its existence. In both cases, the *actus reus* appears to be the same.

109 *Three Rivers District Council v Governor &Company of the Bank of England (No 3)* [2003] 2 AC 1. For a full discussion of misfeasance in public office see generally, DV McKoy, *Corruption: Law, Governance and Ethics* (Hansib 2012).
110 (1783) 3 Doug 327; 99 ER 679.
111 *R v Boulanger* [2006] 2 SCR 49 [10] (McLachlin CJ, citing Finn, 'Official Misconduct' [1978] 2 *Crim LJ* 307, 308).
112 (1783) 99 ER 679, 681.
113 See Pill LJ in *AG's Reference (No 3 of 2003)* [2004] EWCA Crim 868, [2005] 1 QB 73 [9], quoting the trial judge in the case.
114 ibid [28].
115 *R v G* [2003] UKHL 50.
116 *AG's Reference (No 3 of 2003)* [2004] EWCA Crim 868, [2005] 1 QB 73 [30].
117 [2003] 2 AC 1, 193.
118 ibid 191.

In *Attorney-General of Antigua and Barbuda and Others v Lake*,[119] the respondent had sought, among other types of relief, a declaration that the Prime Minister was guilty of misfeasance in public office in relation to him. The respondent was appointed a surgeon specialist at a public hospital and, except for a break of two years, worked in that hospital for 20 years. During that period he was appointed to the statutory post of medical superintendent,[120] which appointment was renewed from time to time. The Minister of Health then advised the respondent that he should not return to the hospital. It was also disclosed that the Prime Minister had written to the chairman of the Public Service Commission advising that he had instructed someone other than the respondent to act as medical superintendent.[121] It was held that in dismissing the respondent and appointing someone else in his place at the hospital, the Prime Minister had usurped the position of the services commission. While the Judicial Committee of the Privy Council was able to dispose of the matter simply as questions of constitutional law, it is significant that it specifically noted without any adverse comment the respondent's claim that the Prime Minister had been guilty of misfeasance in public office.

While the common law offence of misconduct in public office is sometimes applied to corrupt acts, the tort of misfeasance in public office hardly ever is. One reason for this is that corruption is seen more as a breach a public trust and not often as a private wrong and, as Pill LJ had suggested in *Attorney General's Reference (No 3 of 2003)*,[122] there is greater public interest in those matters that we would characterise as crimes than in those matters that we characterise as torts. There is an argument to be made, however, that where public bureaucracies, especially those charged with law enforcement, are weakly developed then greater use should be made of private rights of action to enforce public law.[123] The private action was clearly one of the options contemplated by Lord Mansfield in *R v Young*,[124] if the circumstances were serious enough to warrant it. In *Young*, the question was whether two justices of the peace were guilty of misconduct because they had '. . . arbitrarily, obstinately, and unreasonably' refused a tavern licence. Lord Mansfield put the issue thus:

> But if it clearly appears that the justices have been partially, maliciously, or corruptly influenced in the exercise of this discretion, and have (consequently) abused the trust

---

119 (1998) 53 WIR 145.

120 The Medical and Holberton Institution Act 1899 (A&B), s 4(1) provides: 'It shall be lawful for the Public Service Commission to appoint some duly qualified medical practitioner to be medical superintendent of the Holberton institution.'

121 (1998) 53 WIR 145, 153.

122 [2004] EWCA Crim 868.

123 Indira Carr, 'Fighting Corruption Through Regional and International Conventions: A Satisfactory Solution?' (2006) The Centre For Business Relationships, Accountability, Sustainability and Society Working Paper Series No 33, Cardiff University, 32, goes even further and suggested: 'It seems from the US experience that *qui tam* action has the potential to play an important role in fighting corruption.' See also, Indira Carr 'Corruption, Legal Solutions and Limits of Law' (2007) 3(3) *International Journal of Law in Context* 227. See DV McKoy, *Corruption: Law, Governance and Ethics* (Hansib 2012).

124 (1758) Burr 557; 97 ER 447.

> reposed in them, they are liable to prosecution by indictment or information; or even, possibly, by action, if the malice be very gross and injurious.[125]

The clear statement is that action is appropriate if the malice is very gross and injurious. In this particular case, Lord Mansfield refused the information as he found that there was no *mens rea*. That is, there was no '. . . clear and apparent partiality, or wilful misbehaviour'.[126] The prevailing doctrine, especially since *Rookes v Barnard*,[127] is that it is not the role of the private law to punish. Nevertheless, it is not difficult to conceive that corrupt activities by public agents are often also oppressive, arbitrary, or unconstitutional actions by the servants of government to warrant even punitive damages. However, even where punitive or exemplary damages are not justified, private action may be a useful adjunct in the anticorruption project.

CONCLUSION

There is a modern thrust to ensure that public sector companies apply the rules of corporate governance as they have been developed for the private sector, and this is a good thing. We would all agree that public sector boards must be composed by persons who are fit and proper to discharge the responsibilities of directors and governors. We require from all our directors and governors the highest standards of integrity and ethical behaviour. It is as important in the public sector as it is in the private sector that directors must ensure that the rights and interests of the several stakeholders of the enterprise are balanced and respected. Increasingly we are accepting that greater disclosures and transparency are necessary features of our governance systems. The arguments are as compelling for the public sector as they are for the private sector. Indeed, governments have taken more responsibility in promoting legislation and establishing regulatory regimes that encourage higher standards of governance for the private sector companies. It is natural and understandable that promoting higher standards for the private sector will result in similar principles being applied in the private sector.

On the other hand, public sector governance is not the same as private sector governance. There are some fundamental differences in how we go about decision-making in both areas. To be sure, some of the principles of corporate governance are the same and can be applied universally across the board. Other principles are not. Stakeholders in the public sector are not the same as private sector stakeholders. Moreover, the indices of success and failure are not the same for public sector institutions as they are for the private sector. The discipline of profit is a necessary feature of the private sector, but it is generally missing from public sector institutions. The desire

125 (1758) 97 ER 447, 450.

126 ibid. Cf, *R v Williams* (1762) 3 Burr 1317, 97 ER 851, where the information was granted against the justices who had corruptly refused to grant licences to applicants who had voted for Members of Parliament of whom they did not approve.

127 [1964] AC 1129; followed by the Jamaica Court of Appeal in *Douglas v Bowen* (1974) 22 WIR 333.

to increase value, which is a natural imperative in the private sector, will function differently in the public sector. There is little opportunity in the public sector to discount bad investments and pursue better ones, but that is a necessary feature of investment in the private sector. Simply put, while private sector views of corporate governance are useful, public sector agencies must of necessity pursue other values.

The public sector governance project should not be seen as a crusade. To be sure, the project requires the highest standards both in public administration and in the administration of justice but in this new imperative for reform we should expect a period of learning and experimentation. At the same time, we should not ignore the fact that we have had nearly 400 years of experience in the region with the common law. While it is now quite clear that the common law cannot address all that is required in the governance project, greater use can be made of the common law provisions. Where the new initiative fails to address some particular misconduct, the common law may still suffice to ensure that it is nevertheless discouraged.

BIBLIOGRAPHY

Aucoin, P, 'Administrative Reform in Public Management: Paradigms, Principles, Paradoxes and Pendulums' (1990) 3 *Governance* 2

Aucoin, P, *The New Public Management: Canada in comparative perspective*, 1995, Montreal: Institute for Research on Public Policy

Barzelay, M, *Breaking through Bureaucracy: A New Vision for Managing in Government*, 1992, University of California Press

Barzelay, M, *The New Public Management: Improving Research and Policy Dialogue*, Vol 3, 2001, University of California Press

Bozeman, B, 'Organization Design in the Public Bureaucracy' (1981) 15 *The American Review of Public Administration* 107

Bozeman, B and Bretschneider, S, 'The "Publicness Puzzle" in Organization Theory: A Test of Alternative Explanations of Differences between Public and Private Organizations' (1994) 4 *Journal of Public Administration Research and Theory* 197

Cabinet Office, 'Government at Your Service: Public Sector Modernization Vision and Strategy 2002–2012' (2002) Ministry Paper No 56, Government of Jamaica

Carr, I, 'Corruption, Legal Solutions and Limits of Law' (2007) 3 *International Journal of Law in Context* 3

Carr, I, 'Fighting Corruption Through Regional and International Conventions: A Satisfactory Solution?' (2006) The Centre For Business Relationships, Accountability, Sustainability and Society Working Paper Series No 33, Cardiff University

Crotty, J, 'Structural Causes of the Global Financial Crisis: A Critical Assessment of the "New Financial Architecture"' (2009) 33 *Cambridge Journal of Economics* 4

Davis, C, 'Executive Agencies in Jamaica: The Story Thus Far' (2001) 3 *Caribbean Journal of Public Sector Management* 1

Davis, C, 'Reforming the Cabinet Office: Strengthening the Core of Government in Jamaica' (1999) 1 *Caribbean Journal of Public Sector Management* 41

Denhardt, JV and Denhardt, RB, *The New Public Service: Serving, Not Steering*, 2011, ME Sharpe

Desai, V and Imrie, R, 'The New Managerialism in Local Governance: North-South Dimensions' (1998) 19 *Third World Quarterly* 635

Ferlie, E *et al*, *The New Public Management in Action*, 1996, OUP

Government of Jamaica, 'Government at Your Service: Public Sector Modernisation Vision and Strategy 2002–2012' (2003) Ministry Paper 56 of 2002.

Hyndman, N and Anderson, R, 'Performance Information, Accountability and Executive Agencies' (1998) 18 *Public Money and Management* 23

Ibbs, R, *Improving Management in Government: The Next Steps*, 1988, HMSO

Maor, M, 'The Paradox of Managerialism' [1999] *Public Administration Review* 5

Marsh, I, 'The Changing Ethos of Public Service' (1994) 53 *Australian Journal of Public Administration* 277

Massey, A, 'Nonsense on Stilts: United Kingdom Perspectives on the Global Financial Crisis and Governance' (2011) 11 *Public Organization Review* 1

McKoy, DV, 'Applying the Agency Costs Model to the "Executive Agency" Concept in Jamaica' (2000) 2 *Caribbean Journal of Public Sector Management* 34

McKoy, DV, *The New Public Management in Jamaica: Executive Agencies and Service Quality Delivery in Public Sector Programs*, 2004, Nova Southeastern University

Ocampo, JA, *International Asymmetries and the Design of the International Financial System*, CEPAL – Serie Temas de Coyuntura no 15, United Nations, Santiago, 2001

Ocampo, JA, 'Latin America and the Global Financial Crisis' (2009) 33 *Cambridge Journal of Economics* 703

Osborne, D and Gaebler, T, *Reinventing Government: How the Entrepreneurial Spirit is Transforming the Public Sector*, 1992, Addison-Wesley

Pendery, D, 'Three Top Economists Agree 2009 Worst Financial Crisis Since Great Depression; Risks Increase if Right Steps are Not Taken' (2009) Reuters <http://www.reuters.com/article/2009/02/27/idUS193520+27-Feb-2009+BW20090227>

Ruzza, C, 'The Ideology of New Public Management, Associational Representation and the Global Financial Crisis' [2014] *Partecipazione e Conflitto* 490–508

Sarji, DA, *The New Public Administration: Global Challenges – Local Solutions*, 1977, Commonwealth Association for Public Administration and Management

Sowell, T, *Economic Facts and Fallacies*, 2008, Basic Books

APPENDIX A

CORPORATE GOVERNANCE RECOMMENDATIONS FOR THE LISTED COMPANIES ON THE BARBADOS STOCK EXCHANGE INC.

TABLE OF CONTENTS

SECTION 1.0 INTRODUCTION

1.1 Goals of the recommendations

The qualities of corporate governance practices, as well as transparent disclosure practices of listed Companies, are increasingly important selection criteria for investors. From the perspective of investors, clearly defined corporate governance policies, procedures and practices that are consistent with international best practices are facilitating factors for Shareholders' reasoned investment decisions and for the public trust necessary to ensure efficient capital markets.

The corporate, accounting and securities markets laws, as well as the rules of the Barbados Stock Exchange Inc., contain regulations concerning the governance and disclosure practices of listed companies in Barbados. Regulations on the protection of minority Shareholders and the exercise of rights of ownership and possession are embedded in the **Companies Act CAP. 308** of the Laws of Barbados ("**Companies Act**"). In other words, the law includes detailed, compelling regulations on the right to vote, obtain information and submit proposals, as well as the scheduling of Shareholders Meetings.

The corporate governance of listed companies in Barbados is based primarily on compelling legislation and self-regulation; thus the Recommendations contained herein are designed to complement, and supplement as necessary, statutory guidelines.

The goals of the Recommendations are to (i) harmonise the practices of listed companies; (ii) improve transparency of their operations; (iii) provide a basis of consistency for information provided to Shareholders; (iv) improve the quality of disclosure; and (v) reinforce appropriate accountabilities. Accomplishing these goals will assist in increasing local and international investors' awareness of listed companies in Barbados, promote investor confidence, engender public trust in the functioning of the securities and capital markets and ensure that Corporate Governance Recommendations for listed companies on the Barbados Stock Exchange reflect a standard consistent with best practices.

1.2 Structure of the recommendations

The goals, structure and scope of implementation of the Recommendations as a whole are presented in Section 1. The individual Recommendations are presented in Sections 2–11 and the specifics concerning entry into force are presented in Section 12.

The general principles of the main subject of each Section are presented in the respective introductions. The individual Recommendations are presented in bold text and marked with consecutive numbers. An explanatory section, including the justifications for the Recommendation and some specifying aspects and guidance for companies in adopting and implementing the Recommendation, follow each Recommendation. The explanations also present examples of circumstances in which a Board, in its business judgment, may deem it reasonable to deviate from a relevant Recommendation, with the explanation for such deviation disclosed to Shareholders.

1.3 Implementation of the recommendations

The Recommendations are intended to be complied with by companies listed on the Barbados Stock Exchange, provided that doing so is not in conflict with the compelling regulations applicable in the domicile of the company, in which case such non-compliance and explanation should be disclosed. The term "company" is used in the Recommendations and explanatory sections and the terms "listed company" or "limited company" are used only where the context so requires.

Listed companies vary from each other in their ownership structure, the nature of their business and the extent of their operations. There are also significant differences in their administrative structures. The majority of companies listed in Barbados are medium or small-sized companies in international terms. It is, however, important that the Recommendations reflect the developments taking place in corporate governance, whilst reflecting the nature of the Barbados economy, its capital markets and the size and ownership patterns of companies listed in Barbados.

The Recommendations use the terms "describe," "disclose" or "report" to represent the dissemination of information to Shareholders. Unless otherwise provided, the information should, in all such cases, be disclosed either in the Annual Report or on the Internet website of the company.

The Recommendations have been prepared in accordance with the "Comply or Explain" principle, as opposed to prescriptive rules, *i.e.*, the company should comply with the entire Recommendation, and if the Board, in its business judgment, wishes to deviate from a particular Recommendation, the company should provide an explanation for doing so. The company must provide information on compliance with these Recommendations, either in its Annual Report or on its website, as directed by the Barbados Stock Exchange Inc. via the *Notices to Listed Companies.*

SECTION 2.0 THE GENERAL MEETING

The General Meeting is the highest decision-making body of a limited company through which Shareholders participate in the supervision and control of the company through exercising their rights to vote. The company must summon one Annual General Meeting during each financial year; and, in addition, an extraordinary or special meeting is to be convened when necessary.

2.1 Recommendation 1 – Advance information to shareholders

Prior to the convening of a Shareholders' Meeting, adequate information of the matters to be dealt with at the Meeting should be made available to Shareholders.

The advance information permits Shareholders to evaluate the necessity of attending the meeting, decide how they wish to vote and whether they wish to seek further information at the Meeting, and take decisions concerning their shareholdings.

2.2 Recommendation 2 – Organisation of the general meeting

The Shareholders' Meeting should be organised in a manner that permits Shareholders to exercise their ownership rights effectively.

When organising a Shareholders' Meeting, the company should strive to offer the Shareholders an opportunity to participate in the decision-making process of the Meeting in a meaningful and constructive manner, based on principles of transparency and accountability.

2.3 Recommendation 3 – Attendance of the chairman, other directors and the managing director/chief executive officer at the shareholders meeting

A majority of the Directors including the Chairman of the Board, the Managing Director/Chief Executive Officer (CEO), Chief Financial Officer (CFO), the Chairman of the Audit Committee, and the External Auditor should attend the Shareholders' Meeting.

The presence of the above parties is necessary to ensure interaction between the Shareholders and the Management of the company and to provide the opportunity for Shareholders to present questions and raise concerns.

By exercising their right to present questions, Shareholders can attain more detailed information about matters that may impact on the evaluation of the financial statements, the financial position of the company or other matters to be dealt with at the Meeting. Attendance of the Managing Director/CEO and the Directors at the Annual General Meeting is particularly important. In the case of an extraordinary/special Meeting, it may be sufficient, taking into account the nature of the issue to be dealt with, that the Chairman, Managing Director/CEO and only a portion of the Board attend the Meeting.

2.4 Recommendation 4 – Attendance of a prospective director in a general meeting

A person being proposed for the first time as Director should attend the General Meeting that determines his/her election, unless there are well-founded reasons for his/her absence.

A person proposed for the first time as Director should attend the Meeting that determines his/her election, in order to be introduced to the Shareholders.

SECTION 3.0 THE BOARD OF DIRECTORS

The Board is responsible for the supervision of senior Management and overseeing the operations of the company in their fiduciary capacity of acting with a view to the best interests of the company. The Board should adopt a written Mandate in which it explicitly acknowledges responsibility for the stewardship of the company, including responsibility for:

(a) The appointment, remuneration and dismissal of the Managing Director/Chief Executive Officer ("CEO");
(b) To the extent feasible, satisfying itself as to the integrity of the Managing Director/CEO and other executive Officers (*e.g.*, other Members of the executive Management team, as applicable) and that the Managing Director/CEO and other executive Officers create a culture of integrity throughout the company;
(c) Succession planning, including policies for the Managing Director/CEO selection and performance review and succession in the event of an emergency or the retirement of the Managing Director/CEO;
(d) Adopting a strategic planning process and approving, at least on an annual basis, a strategic plan and financial objectives which take into account, among other things, the opportunities and risks of the business;
(e) The identification of the principal risks of the company's business, and ensuring the implementation of appropriate systems to manage these risks;
(f) Oversight of the design and effectiveness of internal controls and management information systems;
(g) Adopting a communication policy for the company;
(h) Adopting measures for receiving feedback from stakeholders;

(i) Establishing Director expectations and responsibilities, including basic duties and responsibilities with respect to attendance at Board Meetings and advance review of meeting materials;
(j) Establishing Director qualification standards (see Recommendation 13);
(k) Addressing orientation and continuing education for Directors (see Recommendation 16);
(l) Facilitating Director access to Management and, as necessary and appropriate, independent advisors;
(m) Setting Director compensation, including principles for determining and reviewing the form and amount of Director compensation (see Recommendations 49–52); and
(n) Undertaking an annual performance evaluation of the Board, Board Committees and individual Directors (see Recommendation 7, 26 and 21).

The Board must also ensure that the company has duly endorsed the corporate values applied to its operations, which are typically embodied within a company's Code of Business Conduct and Ethics (see Recommendation 33).

The duty of the Board is to promote the best interests of the company. The Directors do not represent solely the interests of the parties who may have proposed their election as Members of the Board.

3.1 Recommendation 5 – Mandate of the board

The company should adopt a written Mandate for its work and describe its essential content. This Mandate should address items (a) through (n) immediately above within Section 3.0.

Efficient operation of the Board requires that the essential duties and working principles of the Board be defined in a written Mandate. The information outlined in the Board Mandate permits Shareholders to evaluate the operation of the Board.

The Board should assume overall responsibility for developing the company's approach to corporate governance, as articulated within the written Mandate of the Board. Companies may wish to consider appointing a Corporate Governance Committee to consider these issues.

The written Board Mandate should be effective, *i.e.*, detailed, clear, complete and up-to-date.

The text of the Board's written Mandate should be disclosed and accessible to Shareholders. If the Board does not have a written Mandate, the company should describe how the Board delineates its role and responsibilities.

3.2 Recommendation 6 – Meetings of the board and board committees and director attendance

The company should disclose the number of Board and Committee meetings held during the reporting year and a summary of each Director's attendance at Board and Committee Meetings of which the Director is a Member.

The information on the number of Board and Committee Meetings and rate of attendance of each of the Directors permit Shareholders to evaluate the effectiveness and contribution of the Board, Board Committees and individual Directors.

Whilst the average attendance of Directors at Board and Committee Meetings can be presented in percentage terms, calculated on the basis of the Meetings held and the number of attending Directors, it is recommended that companies disclose the attendance record of each Director for all Board Meetings and Meetings of Committees of which the Director is a Member held since the beginning of the company's most recently completed financial year.

3.3 Recommendation 7 – Performance evaluation of the board and disclosure of performance evaluation processes

The Board should conduct an annual evaluation of its performance and working methods.

To promote the effectiveness of the Board, its performance and working methods should be evaluated annually. This performance evaluation should consider the duties and responsibilities outlined within the Board's written Mandate. A performance evaluation may be conducted as an internal self-evaluation, *i.e.*, by the Board, or by the Board retaining an external evaluator.

The results of the Board's performance evaluation should be acted upon, *e.g.*, taking timely, corrective action if or when required. The company should disclose whether or not the Board, its Committees and individual Directors are regularly evaluated (Recommendations 7, 26 and 21, respectively) with respect to their effectiveness and contribution. If performance evaluations are regularly conducted, the company should describe the process used for the evaluations. If performance evaluations are not regularly conducted, the company should describe how the Board satisfies itself that the Board, its Committees, and its individual Directors are performing effectively.

3.4 Recommendation 8 – Election of the directors

The General Meeting should elect the Directors of the company.

As per **Section 66 (3)** of the **Companies Act**, the Shareholders at the General Meeting must elect the Directors. By electing the Directors, the Shareholders provide oversight of the Management and operations of the company.

3.5 Recommendation 9 – Number of directors

The Board should be composed of at least five Directors.

To ensure the effective implementation of the duties and responsibilities of the Board, the Board should be composed of at least five Directors.

The Board should consider, in its business judgment, its appropriate size, given the size and complexity of the company and the desire to facilitate effective decision-making.

3.6 Recommendation 10 – Term of the directors

The Directors should be elected for a term not exceeding three years.

To encourage the rotation of directors, a third of the Board should be subject to election on an annual basis. This affords shareholders an opportunity to regularly evaluate the activities of the directors and to exercise effective ownership control. Directors if qualified should be eligible for re-election.

3.7 Recommendation 11 – Notification of proposed director candidates to shareholders

The prospective Director candidates notified to the Board should be disclosed in the invitation to the General Meeting, provided that the candidate has given his/her written consent to the election. Candidates proposed after the delivery of the invitation should be disclosed separately.

Since the election of Directors is one of the most important decisions of the General Meeting, Shareholders must be informed of prospective Director candidates in a timely manner before the Meeting. Before disclosing the candidates, the company must ensure that the candidates have given their written consent to be elected to the Board.

3.8 Recommendation 12 – Special order of appointment of the directors

If, according to the company's Articles or By-laws, Directors are to be appointed according to a special class of rights, the company should disclose such provisions in the invitation to the General Meeting.

The Articles or By-laws may provide that Directors may be appointed following another procedure instead of election by the General Meeting. Any special appointment of Directors outside the normal scope should be disclosed in the invitation to the Meeting.

3.9 Recommendation 13 – Qualifications of the directors

A person elected as Director should have the qualifications required to discharge Directors' duties and be able to devote sufficient time and commitment to the work of the Board and its Committees.

The effectiveness of the Board will require an appropriate level of knowledge by the individuals comprising the Board of the company's strategy and operations and an understanding of the industry in which the company operates. It is imperative that the Board be composed of Directors with versatile and mutually complementing capabilities and competencies. The age mix and gender proportion should also be taken into account in shaping the composition of the Board to ensure that the necessary balance is achieved.

Every Director should render the necessary time, attention and level of engagement to matters of the company to fulfil the requirements of the role, vis-à-vis that of Management. Directors, in particular the Board Chairman and Committee Chairs, are often required to render significant input outside the formal schedule of regular Board and Committee Meetings. Factors such as the Director's main occupation, secondary occupations and simultaneous Board Memberships can impact on his/her ability to adequately fulfil the Director's obligations. Directors should promptly advise the Board on their inability to fulfil their role and responsibilities due to conflicts of interests or inadequate time due to existing or anticipated obligations.

3.10 Recommendation 14 – Position descriptions for chairman of the board, committee chairs and the managing director/CEO

The Board should develop clear Position Descriptions for the Chairman of the Board and the Chair of each Board Committee.

The roles and responsibilities of the Chairman of the Board and the Chair of each Board Committee (*e.g.*, Audit, Governance and Compensation Committees) should be delineated in the form of a Position Description.

Position Descriptions should include details on setting agendas, ensuring appropriate information is available, marshaling resources and expertise, establishing performance expectations and oversight of Management, retaining outside advisors, chairing *in camera* or executive sessions, fulfilling Board Mandate or Committee Charter responsibilities, coordinating with other Committees, providing appropriate reporting and recommendations to the Board, and ensuring the effective assessment of the Board or respective Committee.

The written Position Descriptions should be effective, *i.e.*, detailed, clear, complete and up-to-date.

The company should disclose whether or not the Board has developed written Position Descriptions for the Chairman of the Board and the Chair of each Board Committee. If the Board has not developed written Position Descriptions for the Chairman of the Board and/or the Chair of each Board Committee, the company should briefly describe how the Board delineates the role and responsibilities of each such position.

3.11 Recommendation 15 – Right of directors to receive information and the role of the company secretary

The company should provide sufficient information of the operations of the company to its Directors. It is important that the Board and Board Committees be served by an effective Company Secretary to assist in fulfilling their duties and responsibilities.

In order to discharge their duties, the Directors require information about the structure, strategy, risks, financial accounts and business operations and the industry in which the company operates that is of sufficient quality and quantity so as to enable Directors to fulfil their responsibilities effectively. A new Director must be introduced to the nature and operations of the company and the incumbent Directors must be provided with pertinent information on the operations of the company on an ongoing and timely basis.

The Board and Board Committees should receive other forms of necessary support in order to fulfill their obligations. This support may include administrative, logistical, informational and technical resources by the Company Secretary, who should provide quality agendas, minutes and papers, maintain a register of outstanding issues, and report (functionally) to the Chairman of the Board.

3.12 Recommendation 16 – Orientation and continuing education for directors

Formal orientation and continuing education programs should be provided to new and incumbent Directors that address Directors' requirements and expectations.

The Board should ensure that all new Directors receive a comprehensive orientation. All new Directors should fully understand the role of the Board and its Committees, as well as, the contribution individual Directors are expected to make (including, in particular, the commitment of time and resources that the company expects from its Directors).

Companies should briefly describe what measures the Board takes to orient new Directors regarding the role of the Board, its Committees and its Directors, and the nature and operation of the company's business.

In addition, the Board should provide continuing education and developmental opportunities for all incumbent Directors, so that individuals may maintain or enhance their skills and abilities as Directors, as well as to ensure their knowledge and understanding of the company's business remains current.

Companies should briefly describe what measures, if any, the Board takes to provide continuing education for its Directors. If the Board does not provide continuing education, the company should describe how the Board ensures that its Directors maintain the skill and knowledge necessary to meet their obligations as Directors.

DEFINITIONS for Recommendations 17 and 18:

In Recommendations 17 and 18 the following words shall have the following meaning:

(a) "affiliated entity"

"one body corporate is affiliated with another body corporate if one of them is the subsidiary of the other or both are subsidiaries of the same body corporate or each of them is controlled by the same person; and if two bodies corporate are affiliated with the same body corporate body at the same time, they are affiliated with each other."

(b) "immediate family member" means

" a wife", "a husband", "daughter or stepdaughter", "son or stepson", "mother", "father."

(c) "material relationship" means

"a relationship to the company which has been deemed by the BSE Corporate Governance Recommendation 18 as non independent."

(d) "significant shareholdings" means

"Ownership or control of 10% or more of any class of the issuer's voting securities; (b) shareholdings which would enable the holder thereof to materially affect the control of the issuer, whether alone or by acting in concert with others."

3.13 Recommendation 17 – Composition of the board and independence of directors

The Board of Directors of every company should have a cadre of independent Directors. These directors should be independent of a significant shareholding of the company.

The duties of the Board consist of supervision and control of the executive Management of the company.

For further clarity, to be affirmatively determined to be independent by the company's Board of Directors, a Director should also be independent of Management and free from any material interest and any business or other relationship which could, or could reasonably be perceived to, interfere with the Director's ability to act with a view to the best interests of the company, other than interests arising from shareholding.

3.14 Recommendation 18 – Evaluation and disclosure of director independence

The Board should evaluate the independence of the Directors and disclose (i) the identity of Directors whom the Board determines to be independent, (ii) the identity of Directors whom the Board determines not to be independent.

Despite Recommendation 17, the following persons are considered to have a material relationship with the company, *i.e.*, such persons are <u>not</u> independent:

(a) A person who is, or has been, an employee or Executive Officer of the company, unless the prescribed period has elapsed since the end of the service or employment;
(b) A person whose immediate family member is, or has been, an Executive Officer of the company, unless the prescribed period has elapsed since the end of the service or employment;
(c) A person who is, or has been, an affiliated entity of, a partner of, or employed by, a current or former Internal or External Auditor of the company, unless the prescribed period has elapsed since the person's relationship with the Internal or External Auditor, or the auditing relationship, has ended;
(d) A person whose immediate family member is, or has been, an affiliated entity of, a partner of, or employed in a professional capacity by, a current or former Internal or External Auditor of the company, unless the prescribed period has elapsed since the person's relationship with the Internal or External Auditor, or the auditing relationship, has ended;
(e) A person who has a relationship with the company (*e.g.*, with a member of its Operational Management team) pursuant to which the person may accept, directly or indirectly, any consulting, advisory or other significant compensatory fee for services or other advice, as the case may be, from the company or any subsidiary entity of the company, other than as remuneration for acting in his or her capacity as a Member of the Board of Directors or any Board Committee, or as a part-time Chair or Vice-Chair of the Board or any Board Committee, *e.g.*, if the Director works on consulting assignments for the company; or
(f) A person who belongs, or has belonged, or whose immediate family member belongs, or has belonged, to the operational Management team of another company and the two companies have a customer, supplier or cooperative relationship significant to the other company unless the prescribed period has elapsed since the end of the service or employment;

(g) A person who belongs, or has belonged, or whose immediate family member belongs, or has belonged, to the operational Management team of another company, whose Director is a Member of the operational Management in the first company (*i.e.*, interlocking control relationship), unless the prescribed period has elapsed since the end of the service or employment;
(h) A person who is, or has been, or whose immediate family member is or has been, an Executive Officer of an entity if any of the company's current Executive Officers serve on the entity's compensation committee, unless the prescribed period has elapsed since the end of the service or employment; or
(i) A person who is an affiliated entity of the company or any of its subsidiary entities.

In addition, the Board may, on the basis of its overall evaluation, determine that a Director is not independent of the company if:

(j) The Director participates in a performance-based or share-related compensation system of the company. The financial significance of the compensation system should be taken into account; or
(k) The company (including the Board) is aware of other factors that may compromise the independence of the Director or the Director's ability to be impartial.

For the purposes of subsections (a) – (h), the prescribed period is two years.

For the purposes of subsections (c) and (d), a partner does not include a fixed income partner whose interest in the Internal or External Auditor is limited to the receipt of fixed amounts of compensation (including deferred compensation) for prior service with an Internal or External auditor if the compensation is not contingent in any way on continued service.

For the purposes of subsection (e), compensatory fees and direct compensation do not include the receipt of fixed amounts of compensation under a retirement plan (including deferred compensation) for prior service with the company if the compensation is not contingent in any way on continued service.

For the purposes of subsection (e), the indirect acceptance by a person of any consulting, advisory or other compensatory fee includes acceptance of a fee by

(a) a person's spouse, minor child or stepchild, or a child or stepchild who shares the person's home; or
(b) an entity in which such person is a partner, Member, an Officer such as a Managing Director occupying a comparable position or Executive Officer, or occupies a similar position (except limited partners, non-managing members and those occupying similar positions who, in each case, have no active role in providing services to the company) and which provides accounting, consulting, legal, investment banking or financial advisory services to the company or any subsidiary entity of the company.

Despite all of the above, a person will not be considered to have a material relationship with the company solely because he or she

(a) Has previously acted as an interim Chief Executive Officer of the company, or
(b) acts, or has previously acted, as a Chair or Vice-Chair of the Board of Directors or any Board Committee, other than on a full-time basis.

3.15 Recommendation 19 – Disclosure of the background, biographical details, compensation and shareholdings of directors

The company should disclose the following information on each Director:

(a) Name and photo;
(b) Independence status of the Director, as affirmatively determined by the Board, including the basis for a determination that the Director is not independent[1] (see Recommendations 17 and 18);
(c) Education and professional qualifications;
(d) Primary occupation;
(e) Career experiences that are relevant to the Board;
(f) Date of commencement of Board membership;
(g) Membership on Board Committees (including Chairship);
(h) A summary of the Director's attendance at Board and Committee Meetings (see Recommendations 6 and 25);
(i) Identification of interlocking Directorships[2];
(j) Other Directorships that involve major time commitments;
(k) Details of aggregate fees and other benefits provided to Directors (see Recommendation 50);
(l) Details of aggregate shareholdings in the company by the Directors (see Recommendations 51 and 53); and
(m) Details of holdings and rights based on a share-related compensation system of the company (see Recommendations 52 and 53).

The above information may be conveniently displayed in a comprehensive chart format, on a Director-by-Director basis.

The information on the Board Members and their holdings permits Shareholders to evaluate their relationships to the company.

Reference notes for recommendation 19

(1) *If a Director is non-independent, a listing of the family, business or other relationships that he or she has with the company or Management should be provided.*
(2) *If a Director is presently a Director of any other company that is a listed company (or the equivalent) in a jurisdiction or a foreign jurisdiction, the company should identify both the Director and the other company.*

3.16 Recommendation 20 – Director obligation to provide information to the board

Each Director should provide the Board with full, clear and relevant information that will allow the Board to evaluate his or her independence and qualifications, and should notify the Board promptly of any changes in such information.

The independence evaluations referred to in Recommendations 18 and 19 require that the company receive full, clear and relevant disclosure of the necessary information from Directors to support such evaluations. Each Director must also supply the background, biographical and ownership information required to be disclosed in each of the sub-sections of Recommendation 19. Directors must promptly inform the company of any material changes in the information supplied by them or third parties.

3.17 Recommendation 21 – Performance evaluation of individual directors

Each individual Director should be regularly assessed regarding his/her effectiveness and contribution.

To promote the effectiveness of individual Directors, each Director's performance and contribution should be evaluated annually. This performance evaluation should consider the role and responsibilities outlined within the applicable Position Description(s) for the Director, as well as the competencies and skills each individual Director is expected to bring to the Board. A performance evaluation may be conducted as an internal self-evaluation, *i.e.*, by the Director him/herself, or a "peer" evaluation, *i.e.*, by Directors assessing one another, or in another manner that the Board deems appropriate.

The results of the individual Director's performance evaluation should be acted upon, *e.g.*, taking timely, corrective action if or when required and reporting to Shareholders on the nature of this review process in sufficient detail so as to demonstrate its effectiveness.

SECTION 4.0 COMMITTEES OF THE BOARD

Board oversight over the functioning of executive Management is essential to ensure the effective operation of a limited company. Establishing Committees comprised of independent Members of the Board serve to enhance the effectiveness of Board operations and oversight.

Directors working on the Committees have the opportunity to concentrate on matters allocated or delegated to them more extensively than the entire Board. Board Committees should be used effectively in order to support the workload of the Board (*e.g.*, the extent of the responsibilities the Board has allocated to Committees, reporting by Management to the Committees, reporting by Committee to the Board and spreading the Board's workload appropriately).

4.1 Recommendation 22 – Appointment of a board committee

Effective organisation of the duties and responsibilities of the Board are expected to require the appointment of Board Committees.

There are two principal standing Committees of a Board: (i) the Audit Committee (see Recommendations 29–32); (ii) the Governance Committee (see Recommendations 34–37).

Other standing or ad hoc Committees may be appointed, given the nature and circumstances of the company (e.g., its industry, size, complexity, maturity, risk profile and appetite and strategy) or a particular transaction, issue, investigation or risk, with due consideration by the Board, e.g., Environment, Health and Safety, Risk Management, Special Committee, etc.

It may be necessary to appoint Board committees for the supervision of financial reporting and internal control systems, the nomination of directors and director succession planning and the oversight of executive Management and compensation systems of the company. In companies that have reasonably developed or extensive business operations, Board Committees serve to increase the effectiveness of Board work.

The Committees assist the Board by addressing issues, which, due to their complexity or potential conflicts of interests, require the necessary focus, independence and skills separate from the functioning of the Board. The entire Board remains responsible for the duties assigned to the Committees and, as the Committees have no autonomous decision-making powers, *i.e.*, Committees must review, report and recommend for approval by the Board, the Board collectively makes the decisions pertaining to it. If necessary, the Board, in its business judgment, can also appoint other standing or ad hoc Committees in addition to those outlined below, combine tasks assigned to various Committees and determine that the entire Board should address a specific issue.

4.2 Recommendation 23 – Reporting by the committees to the board

Each Committee should regularly report on their work to the Board.

The reporting details and schedules required from the Committees should be determined by the Board. As a minimum, the report(s) should include a summary of the matters addressed and the measures undertaken or recommended by the Committee.

As Committees begin to develop their working methods, the Chair of each Committee should report to the Board in a timely, comprehensive, meaningful and focused manner. Committee Meeting minutes should be provided to Committee Members, other Directors if they so desire, and should be clear, accurate, consistent, complete, timely and include appropriate detail, *e.g.*, supporting materials and satisfactory diligence of the basis for the Committee's recommendation to the Board.

4.3 Recommendation 24 – Charters of the committees

The Board should approve a written Charter for each Committee's work and describe its essential content.

A written charter helps to clarify the role of the Committee in the company.

Efficient operation of a Board Committee requires that the essential duties and working principles of the Committee be defined in a written Charter. The information outlined in a Committee Charter permits the Shareholders to evaluate the operation of the Committee.

To enable effective functioning of the Committee, a Charter should clearly establish the purpose, duties, responsibilities, structure and operations (including any authority to delegate to individual Members and subcommittees), Member qualifications, Member appointment and removal, manner of reporting to the Board and evaluation of the Committee's performance. In addition, Committees should be given authority to engage and compensate any outside advisor that it determines to be necessary to permit it to carry out its duties.

A Committee Charter should be detailed, clear, complete, up-to-date and accessible to Shareholders.

4.4 Recommendation 25 – Committee meetings and director attendance

The company should disclose the number of Committee Meetings held during the reporting year and a summary of each Director's attendance at Committee Meetings of which the Director is a Member.

The information regarding the number of Meetings and the rate of attendance of each of the Members permit Shareholders to evaluate the effectiveness and contribution of the Committee and the Board as a whole and individual Committee Members.

See Recommendation 6 for additional commentary on the disclosure of attendance records of each Director for all Committee Meetings of which the Director is a Member.

4.5 Recommendation 26 – Performance evaluation of committees of the board

Each Committee should conduct an annual evaluation of its performance and working methods.

To promote the effectiveness of each Committee, its performance and working methods should be evaluated annually. This performance evaluation should consider the duties and responsibilities outlined within the Committee's written Charter. A performance evaluation may be conducted as an internal self-evaluation, *i.e.*, by the Committee, reporting to the Board, by the Board evaluating the performance of the Committee as part of the broader Board evaluation, or by the Board or Committee retaining an external evaluator.

The results of the Committee's performance evaluation should be acted upon, *e.g.*, taking timely, corrective action if or when required and reporting to Shareholders, through the Board, on the nature of this review process in sufficient detail so as to demonstrate its effectiveness.

4.6 Recommendation 27 – Appointment of members to the committees

The Board should appoint from amongst the Directors, the Members and the Chairmen of the Board Committees. If a Committee Chair is not appointed by the Board, the Committee Chair should be elected by Committee Members.

Committees work to render assistance to the Board and prepare matters which fall under their purview thus, the Board should appoint the Members of the Committees from amongst the Directors.

The capabilities, competencies and skills of Board Members should be appropriately matched with the requirements of the relevant Board Committee, including the requirements necessary to Chair the Committee.

4.7 Recommendation 28 – Composition of the committees and independence of members

The company should report the composition of each Committee.

Outlining the composition and objectives of the Committees permits Shareholders to evaluate the effectiveness of Committee work and the relationships of the Committee Members to the company.

AUDIT COMMITTEE

4.8 Recommendation 29 – Establishment of the audit committee

An Audit Committee shall be established.

The extent of the operations of the company may require some Directors to concentrate particularly on matters relating to financial reporting and control, thus requiring the establishment of an Audit Committee. The Audit Committee is therefore tasked with the role of addressing issues connected with the financial administration and control of the company enabled through oversight of External Auditors and the Internal Audit function.

4.9 Recommendation 30 – Appointment of the members of the audit committee

The Board shall appoint an Audit Committee. The Audit Committee should be composed of a minimum of three Members, who should be financially literate.

To ensure the effective implementation of the duties and responsibilities of the Audit Committee, it should comprise at minimum of three Members (except where the board is composed of five persons the minimum number of persons on the audit committee may be reduced to two) who should be financially literate. For the purpose of this Recommendation, an individual is financially literate if he or she has the ability to read and understand a set of financial statements.

4.10 Recommendation 31 – Duties and responsibilities of the audit committee

The Board should define the duties and responsibilities of the Audit Committee.

The duties and responsibilities of the Audit Committee should be defined in the Charter approved by the Board and tailored to the particular circumstances of the company. The duties and responsibilities of the Audit Committee include the following:

(a) Reviewing the financial position of the company;
(b) Assisting Board oversight of the integrity of the company's financial statements and financial reporting and public disclosure;[1]
(c) Assisting Board oversight of risk assessment and management and the adequacy and appropriateness of internal controls;
(d) Assessing and approving as appropriate Internal Audit function's plans and reports;
(e) Assisting Board oversight of the company's compliance with legal and regulatory requirements;
(f) Reviewing and recommending for approval by the Board the nomination and compensation of the External Auditor; [2]
(g) Overseeing the External Auditor and Internal Audit function, and examining and approving as necessary Auditors' reports;[3]
(h) Assisting Board oversight of the External Auditor's qualifications and independence;[4]
(i) Assisting Board oversight of the performance of the company's External Auditors and Internal Audit function;
(j) Evaluating and pre-approving all non-audit services provided by the External Auditor;[5]
(k) Reviewing with the External Auditor any audit problems or difficulties and Management's response;
(l) Reviewing and approving the company's hiring policies for partners, employees and former partners and employees of the present and former External Auditor of the company;
(m) Meeting separately, regularly, and *in camera* with Management, with Head of Internal Audit (or other personnel responsible for the Internal Audit function) and with External Auditors;
(n) Evaluating the Audit Committee's performance annually; and
(o) Reporting regularly to the Board of Directors.

The duties and responsibilities of the Audit Committee should be disclosed in accordance with Recommendation 24 (Charters of Committees). For greater clarity, the Audit Committee must have a written Charter that sets out its mandate and responsibilities. The Audit Committee Charter must clearly establish the Committee's purpose, responsibilities, Member qualifications (see Recommendations 30), Member appointment and removal, structure and operations (including any authority to delegate to individual members and subcommittees), manner of reporting to the Board and evaluation of the Audit Committee's performance.

The Audit Committee must have the authority:

(a) To engage independent counsel and other advisors as it determines necessary to carry out its duties,
(b) To set and pay the compensation for any advisors employed by the Audit Committee; and
(c) To communicate directly with the Internal and External Auditors.

The Audit Committee must establish procedures for:

(a) The receipt, retention and treatment of complaints received by the company regarding accounting, internal accounting controls, or auditing matters; and
(b) The confidential, anonymous submission by employees of the company of concerns regarding questionable accounting or auditing matters.

Reference notes for recommendation 31

(1) The Audit Committee must review the company's financial statements, Management Discussion and Analysis (or the equivalent) and annual and interim earnings press releases (if applicable) before the company publicly discloses this information.

The Audit Committee must be satisfied that adequate procedures are in place for the review of the company's public disclosure of financial information extracted or derived from the company's financial statements, other than the public disclosure referred to in the preceding paragraph, and must periodically assess the adequacy of those procedures.

(2) See Recommendation 60: Nomination and Compensation of the External Auditor.

(3) See Recommendation 57: Oversight of the Internal Audit Function by Audit Committee; and Recommendation 59: Oversight of the External Auditor by the Audit Committee.

(4) The Audit Committee must, at least annually, obtain and review a report by the External Auditor describing: the firm's internal quality-control procedures; any material issues raised by the most recent internal quality-control review, or peer review, of the firm, or by any inquiry or investigation by governmental or professional authorities, within the preceding five years, respecting one or more independent audits carried out by the firm, and any steps taken to deal with any such issues; and (to assess the External Auditor's independence) all relationships between the External Auditor and the company;

(5) The Audit Committee must pre-approve all non-audit services to be provided to the company (or its subsidiary entities if applicable) by the company's External Auditor.

The Audit Committee satisfies this pre-approval requirement if:

(a) The aggregate amount of all the non-audit services that were not pre-approved is reasonably expected to constitute no more than ten per cent of the total amount of fees paid by the company (including its subsidiary entities if applicable) to the company's External Auditor during the fiscal year in which the services are provided;
(b) The company (or the subsidiary entity of the company, as the case may be), did not recognize the services as non-audit services at the time of the engagement; and
(c) The services are promptly brought to the attention of the Audit Committee of the company and approved, prior to the completion of the audit, by the Audit Committee or by one or more of its Members to whom authority to grant such approvals has been delegated by the Audit Committee.

The Audit Committee may delegate to one or more independent Members the authority to pre-approve non-audit services in satisfaction of the above pre-approval requirement. The pre-approval of non-audit services by any Member to whom authority has been delegated must be presented to the Audit Committee at its first scheduled Meeting following such pre-approval.

The Audit Committee satisfies the above pre-approval requirement if it adopts specific policies and procedures for the engagement of the non-audit services, if:

(a) The pre-approval policies and procedures are detailed as to the particular service;

(b) *The Audit Committee is informed of each non-audit service; and*
(c) *The procedures do not include delegation of the Audit Committee's responsibilities to Management.*

4.11 Recommendation 32 – Disclosure of audit committee information

Every company must include in its Annual Report the following disclosure requirements:

The company must disclose the text of the Audit Committee's Charter on its website.

The company must disclose the name of each Audit Committee Member and state whether or not the Member is (i) independent and (ii) financially literate.

The company must describe the education and experience of each Audit Committee Member that is relevant to the performance of his or her responsibilities as an Audit Committee Member and, in particular, disclose any education or experience that would provide the Member with:

(a) An understanding of the accounting principles used by the company to prepare its financial statements;
(b) The ability to assess the general application of such accounting principles in connection with the accounting for estimates, accruals and reserves;
(c) The experience preparing, auditing, analyzing or evaluating financial statements that present a breadth and level of complexity of accounting issues that are generally comparable to the breadth and complexity of issues that can reasonably be expected to be raised by the company's financial statements, or experience actively supervising one or more persons engaged in such activities; and
(d) An understanding of internal controls and procedures for financial reporting.

If, at any time since the commencement of the company's most recently completed financial year, a recommendation of the Audit Committee to nominate or compensate an External Auditor was not adopted by the Board of Directors, the company must state that fact and explain why.

If the Audit Committee has adopted specific policies and procedures for the engagement of non-audit services, the company must describe those policies and procedures.

See Recommendation 61: Disclosure of the External Auditor's Fees, Including Fees for Non-Audit Services.

4.12 Recommendation 33 – Code of business conduct and ethics and disclosure

The Board should adopt and disclose a written Code of Business Conduct and Ethics ("Code"). The Code should be applicable to Directors, the Managing Director/CEO and members of the Executive Management team and other employees of the company. The Code should constitute written standards that are reasonably designed to promote integrity and to deter wrongdoing. In particular, the Code should address the following issues:

(a) Conflicts of interest, including transactions and agreements in respect of which a Director or Executive Officer (*e.g.* Managing Director/ CEO and other Members of the executive Management team, as applicable) has a material interest;[(1)]
(b) Protection and proper use of corporate assets and opportunities;
(c) Confidentiality of corporate information;
(d) Fair dealing with the company's shareholders, customers, suppliers, competitors and employees;
(e) Compliance with laws, rules and regulations (including insider trading laws); and
(f) Encouraging the reporting of any illegal or unethical behaviour.

The Board should be responsible for monitoring compliance with the Code. Any waivers from the Code that are granted for the benefit of the company's Directors or executive Officers (*e.g.*, Managing Director/CEO and other Members of the executive Management team, as applicable) should be granted by the Board (or a Board Committee) only.

Reference notes for recommendation 33

(1) Although companies must exercise their own judgment in making materiality determinations, regulatory authorities may consider that conduct by a Director or executive Officer which constitutes a material departure from the Code will likely constitute a "material change" within the meaning of continuous disclosure obligations to which the company may be subject. Such obligations may require every material change report to include a full description of the material change. Where a material departure from the Code constitutes a material change to the company, the material change report should disclose, among other things: (i) the date of departure; (ii) the party(ies) involved in the departure(s); the reason why the Board has or has not sanctioned the departure(s); and (iv) any measures the Board has taken to address or remedy the departure(s).

In addition, the company should disclose whether or not the Board has adopted a written Code for the Directors, Officers and employees. If the Board has adopted a written Code, the company should:

(a) Disclose how a person may obtain a copy of the Code;
(b) Describe how the Board monitors compliance with the Code, or if the Board does not monitor compliance, explain whether and how the Board satisfies itself regarding compliance with the Code; and
(c) Provide a cross-reference to any material change report (or the equivalent, as applicable) filed since the beginning of the company's most recently completed financial year that pertains to any conduct of a Director or executive Officer that constitutes a departure from the Code.

The company should describe any steps the Board takes to ensure Directors exercise independent judgment in considering transactions and agreements in respect of which a Director or Executive Officer (*e.g.*, Managing Director/CEO and other Members of the executive Management team, as applicable) has a material interest.

The company should describe any other steps the Board takes to encourage and promote a culture of ethical business conduct.

GOVERNANCE COMMITTEE

4.13 Recommendation 34 – Establishment of the governance committee

The Board must establish a Governance Committee to improve the effective handling of matters relating to the governance of the board and the company.

The Board may improve the effectiveness of Director nomination, appointment, election and succession planning through the establishment of a Governance Committee.

Identification of individuals suitable for Directorships and the analysis of the independence, competencies, skills, experience and expected level of commitment of candidate Directors prior to election are critical to ensure the balance of Board competencies and skills and an independent and engaged Board.

The Governance Committee thus promotes the transparency, rigour and systematic functioning of the election process.

4.14 Recommendation 35 – Composition of the governance committee

The Board should appoint a Governance Committee composed entirely of independent Directors. The Managing Director/CEO and other Executive Directors should not be members of the Governance Committee.

To ensure the necessary independence and disclosure, and avoid potential conflicts of interest that may arise, the Managing Director/CEO and members of the executive Management team should not be members of the Governance Committee. Nor should the Managing Director/CEO be involved in the selection of the Directors who serve on the Governance Committee.

4.15 Recommendation 36 – Duties and responsibilities of the governance committee

The Board should define the duties and responsibilities of the Governance Committee.

The duties and responsibilities of the Governance Committee should be defined in the Charter approved by the Board and should reflect the requirements of the company. The duties and responsibilities of the Nomination Committee include the following:

(a) Reviewing and advising the Board on the nomination and appointment of Directors;[(1)]
(b) Recommending for approval by the Board a proposal for election of Directors to be presented to the General Meeting;[(2)]
(c) Reviewing Directors' competencies and skills set;[(3)]
(d) Succession planning of Directors;

(e) Evaluating the Governance Committee's performance annually; and
(f) Reporting regularly to the Board of Directors.

The duties and responsibilities of the Governance Committee must be in accordance with Recommendation 24 (Charters of Committees). For greater clarity, the Governance Committee should have a written Charter that clearly establishes the Committee's purpose, responsibilities, Member qualifications, Member appointment and removal, structure and operations (including any authority to delegate to individual Members and subcommittees), manner of reporting to the Board and evaluation of the Governance Committee's performance.

If a company is legally required by contract or otherwise to provide third parties with the right to nominate Directors, the selection and nomination of those Directors need not involve the approval of an independent Governance Committee.

Reference notes for recommendation 36

(1) Prior to nominating or appointing individuals as Directors, the Board should adopt a process involving the following steps:

(a) Consider what competencies and skills the Board, as a whole, should possess. In doing so, the Board should recognise that the particular competencies and skills required for one company may not be the same as those required for another; and

(b) Assess what competencies and skills each existing Director possesses. It is unlikely that any one Director will have all the competencies and skills required by the Board. Instead, the Board should be considered as a group, with each individual making his or her own contribution. Attention should also be paid to the personality and other qualities of each Director, as these may ultimately determine the boardroom dynamic.

In carrying out each of these functions, the Board should consider the advice and input of the Governance Committee.

(2) The Governance Committee should be responsible for identifying individuals qualified to become new Board Members and recommending to the Board the new Director nominees for the next General Meeting of Shareholders.

(3) In making its recommendations, the Governance Committee should consider:

(a) The competencies and skills that the Board considers to be necessary for the Board, as a whole, to possess;

(b) The competencies and skills that the Board considers each existing Director to possess; and

(c) The competencies and skills each new nominee will bring to the Boardroom.

The Governance Committee should also consider whether or not each new nominee can devote sufficient time and resources to his or her duties as a Board Member.

4.16 Recommendation 37 – Disclosure of the nomination process for directors

The company should describe the process by which the Board identifies new candidates for Board nomination.

COMPENSATION COMMITTEE

4.17 Recommendation 38 – Establishment of the compensation committee

The Board may establish a Compensation Committee to improve the effective handling of matters relating to the appointment and compensation of the Managing Director/CEO and other executives of the company, as well as the handling of other employee compensation systems. Where no Compensation Committee is established the duties shall be performed by the Governance Committee.

The Compensation Committee can provide the necessary focus on the development of compensation systems concerning the Managing Director/CEO and other company executives. The establishment of a Compensation Committee promotes the transparency, oversight and systematic functioning of the compensation systems of the company.

4.18 Recommendation 39 – Composition of the compensation committee

The Board may appoint a Compensation Committee composed entirely of independent Directors. The Managing Director/CEO and other Executives should not be Members of the Compensation Committee.

Due to the nature of the matters addressed by the Compensation Committee, neither the Managing Director/CEO nor other executive Directors should be Members of the Committee. Nor should the Managing Director/CEO be involved in the selection of the Directors who serve on the Compensation Committee.

4.19 Recommendation 40 – Duties and responsibilities of the compensation committee

The Board should define the duties and responsibilities of the Compensation Committee.

The duties and responsibilities of the Compensation Committee should be defined in the Charter approved by the Board and should reflect the requirements of the company. The duties and responsibilities of the Compensation Committee include the following:

(a) Reviewing and approving the corporate goals and objectives relevant to Managing Director/CEO compensation, evaluating the Managing Director/CEO's performance in light of those corporate goals and objectives, and determining (or making recommendations to the Board with respect to) the Managing Director/CEO's compensation level based on this evaluation;
(b) Making recommendations to the Board with respect to non-Managing Director/CEO Officer (*e.g.*, other Members of the executive Management team, as applicable) and Director compensation, incentive-compensation plans and equity-based plans (as applicable, given the nature and circumstances of the company);
(c) Reviewing and recommending for approval by the Board the appointment of the executive Management and the identification of successors (*e.g.*, the Managing Director/CEO and others, as appropriate);

(d) Oversight of matters pertaining to the compensation systems of the company;
(e) Evaluation of the Compensation Committee's performance annually; and
(f) Reporting regularly to the Board of Directors.

The duties of the Compensation Committee must be in accordance with Recommendation 24 (Charters of Committees). For greater clarity, the Compensation Committee should have a written Charter that clearly establishes the Committee's purpose, responsibilities, Member qualifications, Member appointment and removal, structure and operations (including any authority to delegate to individual members and subcommittees), manner of reporting to the Board and evaluation of the Compensation Committee's performance.

In addition, the Compensation Committee should be given authority to engage and compensate any outside advisor that it determines to be necessary to permit it to carry out its duties.

4.20 Recommendation 41 – Disclosure of compensation oversight duties and responsibilities

The company should describe the process by which the Board determines the compensation for the company's Directors and Officers (*e.g.*, Managing Director/CEO, other Members of the executive Management team, as applicable).

If the Board has a Compensation Committee, the company should describe the responsibilities, powers and operation of the Compensation Committee.

As applicable, if a compensation consultant or advisor has, at any time since the beginning of the company's most recently completed financial year, been retained to assist in determining compensation for any of the company's Directors and Officers, the company should disclose the identity of the consultant or advisor and briefly summarize the mandate for which they have been retained. If the consultant or advisor has been retained to perform any other work for the company, the company should state that fact and briefly describe the nature of the work.

4.21 Recommendation 42 – Disclosure of other board committees

As applicable, if the Board has standing Committees other than the Audit and Compensation Committees, the company should identify the Committees and describe their function.

SECTION 5.0 MANAGING DIRECTOR/CHIEF EXECUTIVE OFFICER (CEO)

5.1 Recommendation 43 – Position description for the Managing Director/CEO

The Board, together with the Managing Director /CEO, should develop a clear Position Description for the Managing Director/ CEO, which includes delineating Management's responsibilities. The

Board should also develop or approve the corporate goals and objectives that must be met by the Managing Director/CEO

The written Position Description for the Managing Director/CEO should be effective, *i.e.*, detailed, clear, complete and up-to-date. In delineating Management's responsibilities, the Managing Director/CEO is responsible for the day-to-day management of the company, in accordance with the instructions and direction provided by the Board. The Managing Director/CEO may undertake acts which, considering the scope and nature of the operations of the company, are unusual or extensive, only with the authorization of the Board.

The Managing Director/CEO must foster a climate of effective governance within the company through instilling a culture of accountability, transparency of business processes, quality financial reporting and compliance with the applicable laws governing the company's operations. The level of integrity set by the Managing Director/CEO and other Members of the Executive Management Team must be high. In other words, Management maintains confidentiality, identifies, discloses and manages conflicts of interest, is honest, truthful and candid, acts in a manner that would withstand scrutiny, leads by example, and fosters responsible and ethical decision-making.

The company should disclose whether or not the Board and Managing Director/CEO have developed a written Position Description for the Managing Director/CEO. If the Board and Managing Director/CEO have not developed such a Position Description, the company should briefly describe how the Board delineates the role and responsibilities of the Managing Director/CEO.

5.2 Recommendation 44 – Appointment of the Managing Director/CEO

The Board is responsible for appointing the Managing Director/CEO.

The Board appoints the Managing Director/CEO of the company pursuant to the **Companies Act (Sections 58 (1) and 93)**. To ensure the essential role of the Managing Director/CEO and an effective implementation of ownership control, it is justified that the Board should appoint the Managing Director/CEO.

5.3 Recommendation 45 – Approval and disclosure of the Managing Director/CEO's service contract

The Managing Director/CEO's service terms and conditions should be understood by the Compensation Committee, or the Board, as applicable, specified in writing in the CEO's service contract and approved by the Board.

The position of the Managing Director/CEO in the company requires that terms and conditions of service are specified in writing in the form of an agreement that is understood and approved by the Board. .

In addition, the Compensation Committee (or the Board, as applicable) should fully understand, to a satisfactory level, in the Committee's (Board's) reasoned judgment, the long-term implications on contractual arrangements between the Managing Director/CEO and certain other Members of the Management Team (as applicable) and the company, and the limitations that such contracts might impose on the compensation mix.

For example, such contractual provisions may include, depending on the size and nature of the company, the following: a change-of-control agreement, deferred compensation plan, severance agreement, SERPs (Supplemental Executive Retirement Plan), benefit formulas, contractual terms or renewal provisions, as well as an understanding of key definitions or other provisions, *e.g.*, "cause," constructive termination, "good reason," change-of-control triggers, tax gross-up provisions, restrictive covenants and the company's contractual right to recover compensation in the event of certain behaviour or events, depending on the nature of the contract that the Member of Management has with the company. The advice of legal counsel is encouraged.

5.4 Recommendation 46 – Disclosure of information on the Managing Director/CEO

The company should disclose the background, biographical details, and shareholdings of the Managing Director/CEO.

Upon the appointment of the Managing Director/CEO, the company should disclose similar background, biographical details, and share ownership information as is the case for other Directors. See Recommendation 19: Disclosure of the Background, Biographical Details, Compensation and Shareholdings of Directors.

Disclosure of the shareholdings of the Managing Director/CEO should be disclosed to the Board prior to his/her appointment and annually thereafter.

5.5 Recommendation 47 – Separation and disclosure of the roles of Managing Director/CEO and Chairman of the Board

The Managing Director/CEO should not be elected Chairman of the Board. The Chairman of the Board should be an independent Director. Where this is not appropriate, an independent Director may be appointed to act as "Lead Director." However, either the independent Chairman or independent Lead Director should act as the effective leader of the Board and ensure that the Board's agenda will enable it to successfully carry out its duties.

There should be a clear division of responsibilities between the role of the Chairman of the Board and that of the CEO to ensure the effective oversight and discharge of duties and responsibilities. No one individual should have unfettered powers of decision.

The appointment of the Managing Director/CEO as Board Chairman has been restricted because the duty of the Board is to supervise the activities of the Managing Director/CEO and Executive Management Team.

The company should clearly define the areas of responsibility of the Managing Director/CEO and that of the Board Chairman, *i.e.*, Position Descriptions for both, at Recommendations 43 and 14, respectively, to ensure that all the decision-making powers of the company are in practice not vested in a single individual. Generally, this means that the Managing Director/CEO cannot be elected Board Chairman.

However, in some special circumstances, such as extensive international operations, the company's special development phase or the ownership structure of the company, there may exist justification for the combining of these two positions.

If the company determines to appoint the same person as Managing Director/CEO and Board Chairman, it must explain its decision.

The company should disclose whether or not the Chairman of the Board is an independent Director. If the Board has a Chair or Lead Director who is an independent Director, the company should disclose the identity of the independent Chair or Lead Director, and describe his or her role and responsibilities. If the Board has neither a Chairman who is independent, nor a Lead Director who is independent, the company should describe what the Board does to provide leadership for its independent Directors.

SECTION 6.0 OTHER MANAGEMENT

The Executive Management Team of the company is based on the management organisation adopted for the company. Certain Members of the Management team may have no official statutory position (*i.e.*, not be appointed as Officers), yet play a significant role in the senior management or financial reporting system of the company.

The organisation of Management is also an important reporting element of the corporate governance structure of the company.

The term "other Management" refers to the members of the Management team, other senior or financial management, or, if the company has no formal management structure, to the executives specified by the company. For example, other Management, depending on the size and complexity of the company, may include the following: President, General Manager, Chief Financial Officer (CFO), Chief Operating Officer, Management Accountant, Chief Risk Officer, Company Secretary, Legal Counsel, CIO, Tax Director, Treasurer, Controller, Vice Presidents and Divisional Heads, or their equivalents, as applicable.

6.1 Recommendation 48 – Organisation of management

The company should describe the organisation of its Management Team.

If the company has a Management Team, the company should describe the composition and duties of the Management Team and the areas of responsibility of its Members.

A description on the organisation of Management should detail the nature of the Management activities and reporting structures to supplement the statutory Management requirements of the company.

The Management Team refers to a corporate management group or another similar body that convenes regularly. The Management Team normally consists of executives of the functional areas and operational business divisions, whose principle duty is to assist the Managing Director/CEO in the achievement of company objectives.

6.2 Recommendation 49 – Disclosure of information on the management team

The company should disclose the background, biographical details, and shareholdings of the five most senior Members of the Management Team, including the most senior financial officer. If the company has no formal management structure, the company should define the other executives whose background, biographical details, and shareholdings are subject to this disclosure obligation.

The company should disclose similar background, biographical details, and share ownership information concerning the Members of the Management team as is the case for the Directors of the company and this should be reported to the Board on an annual basis. See Recommendation 19: Disclosure of the Background, Biographical Details, and Shareholdings of Directors.

SECTION 7.0 DISCLOSURE OF DIRECTOR AND EXECUTIVE COMPENSATION

An effective compensation system is an essential tool for implementation of ownership control. The purpose of the compensation system is to increase the commitment of the Board, the Managing Director/CEO and other executives in promoting and aligning the interests of the company, its Shareholders and the Managing Director/CEO and other Members of the Management team. In addition to a basic salary, depending on the size and circumstances of the company and its services agreement with the Managing Director/CEO and other Members of the Management Team, compensation systems can encompass performance-related incentive schemes, pension schemes, awards in the form of shares, and other share-related compensation systems, *e.g.*, stock options.

COMPENSATION OF DIRECTORS

7.1 Recommendation 50 – Disclosure of fees and benefits awarded to directors

The company should describe how Directors are compensated and disclose the aggregate amount of each element of the Directors' compensation.

The information on the fees and other benefits granted to the Directors permit Shareholders to evaluate the amount of compensation in relation to the contributions of the Board in promoting the interests of the company. This disclosure also facilitates comparison with the fees and other benefits paid by similar companies within the industry.

For example, companies should provide a fee schedule that includes, as applicable, the following (i) the annual Board retainer fee (ii) Committee retainer fees; (iii) Board and Committee Meeting attendance fees: (iv) Board Chair fee and Committee Chair fees; and (v) any other fees. The total fees paid to the Board as a whole should be disclosed.

The dollar value of benefits awarded to Directors should also be disclosed. Benefits awarded to Directors may include, as applicable, the following: (i) perquisites or other personal benefits; (ii) tax reimbursements; (iii) company share purchases (through deferral of fees or otherwise) at a discount from the market price; (iv) amounts paid or accrued to any Director pursuant to a plan or arrangement in connection with the resignation, retirement or any other termination of such Director or change in control of the company; (v) annual contributions to vested and unvested defined contribution plans; (vi) all consulting fees; (vii) awards under any Director charitable awards programs; (viii) the dollar value of any insurance premiums paid by, or on behalf of, the company for life insurance for the Director's benefit; (ix) the dollar value of any dividends or other earnings paid in stock or stock option awards when the dividend or earnings were not factored into the grant date fair value; and (x) any other type of benefit, incentive plan, pension enhancement or deferred compensation awarded to Directors not referred to above.

7.2 Recommendation 51 – Payment of fees awarded to directors in shares and/or deferred share units

*The Shareholdings of Directors can be increased by paying the fees or part of the fees for Board and Committee work in the form of shares of the company or Deferred Share Units (DSUs).**

* The company may have a deferred share unit plan, into which non-executive Directors may, or are required to, defer a portion of their annual retainer. Such deferrals are converted to Deferred Share Units (DSUs), each of which has a value equal to the value of one Common Share of the company. A Deferred Share Unit is an amount owed by the company to Directors, but is not paid out until such time as the Director leaves the Board, thereby providing an ongoing equity stake in the company throughout the Director's period of Board service. Upon retirement from the Board, the Director may receive payment of his or her Deferred Share Units in cash, Common Shares of the company purchased on the open market, or Common Shares issued by the company. The liability for Deferred Share Units is included in accrued payroll and related liabilities.

If Directors can choose to receive their compensation in cash and/or shares or DSUs, then the amount of each received by the Directors should be disclosed.

The provision of shares or DSUs to Directors is expected to align the interests of Directors with those of Shareholders to promote the effective oversight of the company. It is necessary however, to ensure that Director remuneration through share offerings and other share compensation schemes are in compliance with the necessary internal regulations governing the issuance of shares to company insiders.

If the company has share ownership guidelines for Directors, through which Directors are required to acquire shares or DSUs, these guidelines, as well as the level of holdings by each Director, should be disclosed. This disclosure should include the minimum, target amount of shareownership required by Directors, any time period for meeting the minimum, target amount and any other requirements (*e.g.*, Directors must take their compensation in shares or DSUs until the minimum, target amount is reached (*e.g.*, the "at risk" investment by the Director being the summation of Common

Shares and DSUs); provisions for Directors who may not be able to attain the shareownership guideline; the portion of shareownership required to meet the minimum, target amount and the date by which they are to be met, for each Director; and year-over-year changes in share or DSU holdings for each Director).

7.3 Recommendation 52 – Participation by directors in a performance-based, share-related compensation system

It is not recommended that a non-executive Director should participate in a share-related, performance-based compensation system.

The term "non-executive Director" refers to a person who has no employment relationship with, or position in, the company. Use of share-related, performance-based compensation systems (*e.g.*, Director stock option plans) to remunerate non-executive Directors is in principle not justified from the perspective of the interests of Shareholders.

There may occur a mis-alignment of interests when Directors' remuneration is based on short-term share price appreciation, as self interest by Directors may conflict with their fiduciary duty and duty of care. Both duties may be compromised, respectively, by (i) Directors not acting honestly and in good faith with a view to the best interests of the company and all of its Shareholders; and (ii) Directors not exercising the care, diligence and skill that a reasonably prudent person would exercise in comparable circumstances.

7.4 Recommendation 53 – Disclosure of the dollar value(s) of shares and share-related rights granted to directors

The company should report dollar value of the number of shares and share-related rights granted to the Directors as compensation during the reporting year.

The company must report the dollar value of the number of shares and Deferred Share Units (if applicable) granted to Directors as compensation, along with fees and the dollar value of benefits obtained in the execution of Directors' duties. Please refer to Recommendations 50: Disclosure of Fees and Benefits Awarded to Directors and Recommendation 51: Payment of Fees Awarded to Directors in Shares and/or Share Units.

7.5 Recommendation 54: Director stock options

If a Director participates in a performance-based, share-related compensation scheme (*e.g.*, Director stock option plans), any compensation granted on the basis of such systems should be reported. If applicable, the company should include details about the number of any options granted Directors, the terms of the options (*e.g.*, date granted, expiry date, exercise price, vesting provisions, including any performance criterion, and holding provisions), the number of options that have vested, the number of options that were exercised during the year, the number of options that have not been exercised, the value of options held back at the end of the year and the current market price of the stock.

COMPENSATION OF THE MANAGING DIRECTOR/CEO AND OTHER MEMBERS OF THE MANAGEMENT TEAM

7.6 Recommendation 55 – compensation system and the related decision-making procedure

The company should disclose the criteria and decision-making procedure concerning the compensation system of the Managing Director/CEO and other Members of the Management team (e.g., the five most senior Members, including the Managing Director/CEO and most senior financial officer).

Disclosure of such compensation systems should include the company describing the following in its Annual Report:

(a) The objectives of the company's compensation system;
(b) What the compensation system is designed to reward;
(c) Each element of compensation;

As part of disclosing each element of compensation, the information to be disclosed includes the present dollar value of any and all forms of all components of Members of the Management team's compensation. This includes salary levels, incentive payments, share grants (real or phantom, *e.g.*, DSUs), share-related rights (*e.g.*, stock options), pensions (including all supplemental plans) and all other components of executive compensation, as applicable depending upon the nature of the company and its compensation system, granted to the Managing Director/CEO and other executives.

While the information to be disclosed within the above description will vary depending upon the facts and circumstances of each company, examples of such information may include, in a given case, among other things, the following:

(a) The policies for allocating between long-term and currently paid out compensation;
(b) The policies for allocating between cash and non-cash compensation, and among different forms of non-cash compensation;
(c) For long-term compensation, the basis for allocating compensation to each different form of award (such as relationship of the award to the achievement of the company's long term goals, Management's exposure to downside equity performance risk, correlation between cost to the company and expected benefits to the company;
(d) What specific items of corporate performance are taken into account in setting compensation policies and making compensation decisions; and
(e) Whether the company engaged in any benchmarking of total compensation, or any material element of compensation, identifying the benchmark and, if applicable, its components (including component companies).

The company must specify the body that determines the compensation of the Managing Director/CEO and other executives (*e.g.*, the Compensation Committee recommending approval by the Board, or independent Directors of the Board, other). It is generally appropriate that the body that appointed the individual to also determine the compensation. The preparation of compensation matters may be delegated to the Compensation Committee of the Board. (See Recommendations 38–41).

SECTION 8.0 INTERNAL CONTROLS, RISK MANAGEMENT AND INTERNAL AUDIT

The purpose of quality financial reporting, effective internal controls and a comprehensive risk management system is to ensure the effective and successful operation of the company, the disclosure of reliable information and compliance with the relevant regulations and operating principles. Internal control helps improve the effective fulfilment of the Board's supervisory obligations.

8.1 Recommendation 56 – Oversight of risk management

The company should establish a sound system for risk oversight and risk management. As part of its oversight role, the Board is responsible for establishing the company's policy on risk, and developing and implementing its system of risk management and internal control. The Board should establish the risk profile of the company. It should set out the company's appetite for risk and have regard to the material business risks faced by the company as identified by the company's risk management system. The company's risk profile should be regularly updated and reviewed.

Risk management is the culture, processes and structures that are directed towards taking advantage of potential opportunities while managing potential adverse effects. A risk management system should be designed to (i) identify, assess, monitor and manage risk; and (ii) identify material changes to the company's risk profile.

Risk management is part of the control function of the company. The purpose of risk management is to ensure that the material business risks (including financial reporting risks and others) related to the business operations of the company are identified and monitored. An effective system of risk management is enterprise-wide, robust, integrated into operations, continual, culturally embedded and responds to, identifies, evaluates, monitors, controls and mitigates material business risks to the company.

Effective risk management requires a defined risk management policy. The company's risk management policy must reflect its legal obligations, commercial prudence and the expectations of the company's stakeholders.

It is important to provide Shareholders with adequate information on the company's risk management policy.

8.2 Recommendation 57 – Oversight of the internal audit function by the audit committee

Companies must maintain an Internal Audit function to provide Management and the Audit Committee with ongoing assessments of the company's risk management processes and system(s) of internal control. A company may choose to outsource this function to a third party service provider other than its External Auditor. The Internal Audit function should report directly to the Audit Committee.

The company should describe the manner in which the Internal Audit function of the company is organised. The description must include the organisation of the Internal Audit function and the essential guidelines applied to internal audits. The organisation and working methods of Internal Audit depend on the nature and scope of the company's operations, the number of personnel and other similar factors.

The quality of the Internal Audit reporting should add value to the financial reporting process, control environment and risk management process.

The Audit Committee should ensure that the assurance role of Internal Audit (*e.g.*, independent from Management and External Audit and objective reporting of factual findings) is not compromised. The Audit Committee should carefully monitor that assurance, by Internal Audit, on the company's risk management, internal compliance and control systems (*e.g.*, identifying risks and testing the design and effectiveness of controls to mitigate such risks) remains separate from Management functions or involvement. Internal Audit should not be engaged in operational duties or non-Internal Audit transactions or oversight. The Audit Committee should review and approve the Internal Audit Charter.

SECTION 9.0 INSIDER ADMINISTRATION

The disclosure of the holdings of insiders and their trading activities promotes trust and transparency in the securities markets. An effective administration of insider matters in a listed company requires that the administration is systematically and reliably organised.

9.1 Recommendation 58 – Compliance with the insider trading guidelines for listed companies on the Barbados Stock Exchange Inc.

The company should comply with the Insider Trading Guidelines for Listed Companies on the Barbados Stock Exchange Inc., and describe its essential insider administration procedures.

Compliance with the *Insider Trading Guidelines for Listed Companies on the Barbados Stock Exchange Inc.* harmonizes and improves the administration of companies' insider matters. The information on the insider administration procedures permits Shareholders to evaluate the effectiveness of the insider administration of the company.

SECTION 10.0 EXTERNAL AUDIT

The External Auditor plays an important role as a controlling body appointed by the Shareholders. The External Auditor provides Shareholders with an independent opinion of the financial performance of the company and the effectiveness of controls in monitoring this function.

The External Auditor should acknowledge that the Audit Committee is representing the Board, which reviews and approves the audit plan and engagement letter. The External Audit should clearly articulate the types and scope of matters to be reviewed, the External Auditor's responsibility to communicate with the Audit Committee, and specifically how and when all audit related matters should be reported to the Committee.

10.1 Recommendation 59 – Oversight of the external auditor by the audit committee

Every company must require its External Auditor to report directly to the Audit Committee. An Audit Committee must be directly responsible for overseeing the work of the External Auditor engaged for the purpose of preparing or issuing an Auditor's report or performing other audit, review or attest services for the company, including the resolution of disagreements between Management and the External Auditor regarding financial reporting.

As part of its oversight role, the Audit Committee may wish, from time to time, to conduct a comprehensive review of the External Auditor's performance, having regard to the following: whether the External Auditor understands the industry and has the budget, resources, access and cooperation from Management; the quality of assurance provided by the External Auditor, including the extent of control testing and the expertise of personnel and success in executing the audit plan; and the openness and transparency of the External Auditor in communicating with the Audit Committee and the Board as representatives of the Shareholders.

The Audit Committee should ensure that the External Auditor's scope or activities is not subject to undue Management influence (*e.g.*, by impeding timely access to any relevant information, system, process, explanation or personnel, supported by full, prompt, cooperation from all employees to any External Auditor enquiries; restrictions on the scope, nature, extent or timing of plans, evaluation, testing or the freedom to complete the work plan; or implying adverse effects upon the External Audit firm or any of its staff).

10.2 Recommendation 60 – Nomination and compensation of the external auditor

A proposal for the election of an External Auditor, prepared by the Board, or the Audit Committee recommending for approval by the Board, should be disclosed in the invitation to the General Meeting. The preparation for the nomination and compensation of the External Auditor can be delegated by the Board to the Audit Committee.

The election of the External Auditor is one of the most important decisions of the General meeting and Shareholders must be notified of the appointee in a timely manner before the Meeting.

The Audit Committee must recommend to the Board of Directors:

(a) The External Auditor to be nominated for the purpose of preparing or issuing an External Auditor's report or performing other audit, review or attest services for the company; and
(b) The compensation of the External Auditor.

10.3 Recommendation 61 – Disclosure of the external auditor's fees, including fees for non-audit services

The company must disclose the fees of the External Auditor during the financial year. If the External Auditor has been paid fees for non-audit services, such fees should be pre-approved by the Audit Committee and reported separately.

The information on the fees paid to the External Auditor permits Shareholders to evaluate the activities of the External Auditor. Since the External Auditor provides an external control function over the company on behalf of Shareholders, information on fees paid to the External Auditor for non-audit services should be disclosed.

For the purpose of disclosure, this Recommendation applies to companies associated within the same group of companies, who retain the same firm of External Auditors; other subsidiary companies owned by the same parent of companies, who retain the same firm of External Auditors; and other related companies who retain the same firm of External Auditor.

The company must disclose External Auditor service fees (by category):

(a) Under the caption "Audit Fees," the aggregate fees billed by the company's External Auditor in each of the last two fiscal years for audit services;
(b) Under the caption "Audit-Related Fees," the aggregate fees billed in each of the last two fiscal years for assurance and related services by the company's External Auditor that are reasonably related to the performance of the audit or review of the company's financial statements and are not reported under clause (a) above. The company must include a description of the nature of the services comprising the fees disclosed under this category;
(c) Under the caption "Tax Fees," the aggregate fees billed in each of the last two fiscal years for professional services rendered by the company's External Auditor for tax compliance, tax advice, and tax planning. The company must include a description of the nature of the services comprising the fees disclosed under this category; and
(d) Under the caption "All Other Fees," the aggregate fees billed in each of the last two fiscal years for products and services provided by the company's External Auditor, other than the services reported under clauses (a), (b) and (c), above. The company must include a description of the nature of the services comprising the fees disclosed under this category.

SECTION 11.0 COMMUNICATION AND DISCLOSURE

Effective corporate governance of a listed company requires reliable, up-to-date, full and clear disclosure practices. This objective of enhanced disclosure supports well-founded price development of securities subject to public trade and promotes trust in the securities markets. The information communicated and published by the company permits Shareholders to evaluate the functioning of the corporate governance of the company and make reasoned and informed decisions concerning their holdings.

Both the content of information and the clarity of its presentation, coupled with electronic dissemination of information, promote transparency and increase Shareholders' opportunities to obtain information.

11.1 Recommendation 62 – Disclosure of information on corporate governance (*corporate governance statement*)

The company should ensure that at least the following matters are presented within its Corporate Governance Statement on the website and in the Annual Report of the company:

(a) *Information on compliance with Corporate Governance Recommendations contained herein as well as possible deviations and their explanations;*
(b) *Notice of General*
(c) *Articles and By-laws*
(d) *Board of Directors;*
(e) *CEO and other executives;*
(f) *External Auditor;*
(g) *Shares, share capital, principal shareholders (holders of 10% or more of the issued share capital of the company) Shareholder agreements to which the company is party.*
(h) *Annual Report; and*
(i) *Other circumstances to be reported in accordance with these Recommendations.*

Clear presentation of a company's compliance with the Recommendations and corporate governance matters permits Shareholders to develop an overall picture of the operations of the company. An essential requirement is that the presentation of the company's corporate governance practices is clear, comprehensive and easy-to-find. It is recommended that the subject matters are described both on the website and in the Annual Report of the company. The presentation may include cross references to information presented elsewhere in the Annual Report or on the website of the company.

11.2 Recommendation 63 – Electronic investor information

The company should have an Internet website.

The company can improve the effectiveness of its disclosure practice by means of the Internet. Use of Internet websites provides quick and easy access to Shareholders. Electronic information is easier to update than hard copy versions, permitting Shareholders to obtain the most recent information available about the company.

11.3 Recommendation 64 – Publication of information on internet website

The company should disclose on its website all the information that has been published pursuant to the statutory obligation of listed companies to provide information.

Publication of all investor information of the company in one place facilitates easy distribution of such information to Shareholders. When all listed company releases and other information on the company are made available on the Internet, Shareholders are provided with a detailed picture of the operations and financial position of the company.

SECTION 12.0 EFFECTIVE DATE

These Recommendations come into force on the 1st of January, 2014. If the company so wishes, it may, however, implement the Recommendations immediately after publication.

Decisions that are required to be submitted to the General Meeting and the changes to the Articles and By-Laws that are deemed necessary in order to comply with these Recommendations may be made at the Annual General Meeting or a special meeting of shareholders.

APPENDIX B

FOREWORD

A MESSAGE FROM THE CHAIRMAN

The development of a Trinidad & Tobago Corporate Governance Code ("TTCGC" or "the Code") is a partnership initiative led by the Caribbean Corporate Governance Institute, the Trinidad and Tobago Chamber of Industry and Commerce and the Trinidad and Tobago Stock Exchange. It is the first of its kind in the Republic and directed primarily to those companies with public accountability.

A Working Group was established in January 2013, consisting of a diverse team of industry stakeholders, to oversee the drafting and development of the Code, with the Institute acting as the Secretariat. By November 2013, the Working Group, after many drafts, meetings and consultations with external stakeholders, arrived at what is now the Trinidad & Tobago Corporate Governance Code 2013.

The Code follows globally accepted best practices with specific consideration and much customization for the local economy and dynamics of the business society of Trinidad and Tobago. The objectives are to enhance business governance and performance, strengthen transparency and efficiency in the market, and improve the overall investment culture in Trinidad & Tobago. The Code is easy to understand, providing recommendations and guidelines for good corporate governance with a balance between costs and benefits of implementation. In this way, it provides the structure through which the company's objectives are set along with the means of attaining them and monitoring performance.

There is little doubt that strong corporate governance and transparency are critical for the success of every organization. At the highest level, it provides many benefits including:

1. Lower cost of capital:

i. In a well-governed company, performance targets, risks, and progress towards the targets are assured and reported to investors. Risks to investors are therefore reduced significantly and as a result capital can be obtained at lower costs.

2. Lower risk of scandals:

ii. Good corporate governance means that intentions of owners, the Board and Management are aligned. Capacity for taking up the roles in directing, monitoring, and communicating are there. Appropriate systems and processes for governance are in place, and the values of corporate governance, namely transparency, accountability, fairness, and corporate responsibility are alive throughout the organization. The end result is that risk of scandals is minimized or avoided altogether.

3. Higher performance of the organization. This is derived from:

i. The Board's enhanced role as a strategic contributor to business planning and risk management;
ii. decision-making authority being assigned at the right levels within the organization;
iii. delegation of authority being matched by adequate controls;
iv. improved information flows within the organization, with shareholders and the wider market;
v. alignment between shareholders, the Board, executives and employees in the pursuit of company objectives; and
vi. Increased motivation, attraction and retention of talent as good corporate governance enables the development of value-based organizations.

The standardization of best practices may be approached in various ways. One approach is on a statutory basis where companies comply or face legal sanctions. The other approach, and probably the preferred one, is by way of a voluntary code of principles and recommended practices where companies are asked to apply the recommendations or explain their reasons for deviating from them. The Code embraces the latter approach in the expectation that it will encourage voluntary adoption by those institutions to which it is directed, namely companies with a public accountability, while encouraging broader level acceptance of the spirit of each Principle and how it may further the best interests of the company.

The objective of the Code is not to replace existing legislation or regulations but rather to bolster those statutory directives and provide recommendations that are meant to fill the knowledge gaps on how best to manage an organization. By striving towards these higher aims, organizations are better equipped to succeed in an increasingly global playing field, and overall market conditions rise to reflect a more competitive outlook.

In the 2013 World Economic Forum's Global Competitive Index, Trinidad and Tobago ranked 118 out of 148 in Ethical Behaviour of Firms, 116 out of 148 in Efficacy of Corporate Boards and 111 out of 148 in Protection of Minority Shareholders' Interests.

In 2011, a report by Syntegra Change Architects Ltd. found that the majority of corporations in Trinidad and Tobago disclosed less than 40% of the items recommended by International Standards of Accounting and Reporting (ISAR). The reporting requirements, even of regulated and listed companies, were the absolute lowest of all emerging and frontier markets surveyed by UNCTAD in 2010; out of a benchmark of fifty-one items relating to corporate governance, only five were required to be disclosed. This is against the backdrop of a survey by McKinsey & Co. in 2002 that global institutional investors were prepared to pay a premium of up to 40% for corporations that apply superior corporate best practices in countries where poor corporate governance poses a high risk to investments.

The introduction of a Code of Corporate Governance is therefore long overdue.

Experience has shown that the more corporations are encouraged to have such a structure in place the greater the opportunity to attract investment and increase its competitiveness in the field. The core values of any Code therefore must be fairness, transparency, responsibility and accountability, all of which feature prominently in this Code.

In the current economic climate, it is necessary for organizations to embrace these globally accepted best practices if corporate Trinidad and Tobago is to become an efficient and competitive player in the global market.

I am indeed grateful to the three partnering organizations for galvanizing efforts and building the foundation for this initiative and to Mr. Richard Frederick, International Corporate Governance Consultant, who provided guidance on the best approaches for undertaking such a task in Trinidad & Tobago. I record my thanks and appreciation to all the members of the Working Group for devoting time and effort in the interests of improving corporate Trinidad & Tobago, without remuneration or reimbursement of expenses.

It is important to recognize all the individuals who took part in the consultations and who commented on the draft versions of the Code, including our international colleagues and those who commented at the request of the Global Corporate Governance Forum.

I thank the Caribbean Corporate Governance Institute, who, under the dedicated leadership of its Chief Executive Officer, Ms. Alex Kjorven, researched and prepared the first working draft of the Code, and convened the numerous Working Group meetings. Finally, I owe a debt of gratitude to Syntegra Change Architects Ltd. for introducing me to this project and lending their expertise and research, which catalyzed the collective effort in bringing about the transformation we are seeking.

Roger Hamel-Smith
Retired Justice of Appeal,
Supreme Court of Trinidad & Tobago

Chairman of the Trinidad & Tobago Corporate
Governance Code Working Group
November 26, 2013

OVERALL OBJECTIVES FOR THE CODE

The following objectives and key success factors have been identified and developed by the TTCGC Working Group.

1. **Enhance Business Governance and Performance**
2. **Strengthen Transparency and Efficiency in the Market**
3. **Improve the Investment Culture**

KEY SUCCESS FACTORS

1. Appropriateness for Local Markets

The Code must address challenges and market conditions unique to the local context. It is critical that companies find solutions and Recommendations that are relatable and relevant.

2. Consistent With International Standards

The Code should draw on, and embody, internationally accepted principles and best practices on corporate governance. It should not conflict directly with any international standards. However actual Recommendations may be tailored to meet other priorities of the Code.

3. High Adoption Rate

A primary indicator of success is the adoption rate of the Code amongst companies, regulators or associations. This includes adoption of Recommendations by companies with public accountability or reference and acknowledgement of the Code as standard best practice by regulatory authorities and associations.

To achieve this:

- The Code should be easy to understand.
- It should provide Recommendations and Guidance for good governance that take into consideration the balance between costs and benefits of implementation.
- Most importantly, adoption of the Code needs to be seen as a value-adding pursuit with opportunities for recognition and clear benefits for their company.

4. Increased Awareness of Corporate Governance

The development and publication of a national Code on Corporate Governance will seek to increase awareness and respect for effective governance in organizations.

This may be achieved through:

- A comprehensive and inclusive public consultation process so as to bridge the divide between companies of different sizes and ownership structures.
- The spirit of the Code should resonate across sectors beyond the initial pool of companies whom the Code initially targets.

HOW TO USE THE CODE

The proposed format of the Trinidad & Tobago Corporate Governance Code is arranged as follows:

Principles	represent high-level concepts that encapsulate the foundation of good corporate governance. Companies should always maintain consistency with the spirit of each Principle when implementing a Recommendation established in the Code.
Recommendations	are specific practices that companies are encouraged to apply as part of their governance system. Companies are expected to disclose in their annual reports whether they have applied the Recommendations set out in the Code or explain the reasons for departure.
Guidance	is provided for each Recommendation and is intended to assist companies in further understanding the practical application and benefits of adopting a Recommendation. These sections of the Code are provided as reference and/or for illustrative purposes only and are not considered specific practice against which companies are required to "apply or explain". Guidance provided is specific to companies with public accountability and may also include examples and suggestions for implementation.

SUMMARY OF KEY PRINCIPLES AND RECOMMENDATIONS

Principle one

Establish a framework for effective governance

Every company should be headed by an effective Board, which is collectively responsible for the long-term success of the company.

Recommendations

1.1 The Board should establish and make publicly available a clear outline of its roles and responsibilities, including any formal delegations to Management.

1.2 The chairperson of the Board should be a non-executive Director and preferably an independent Director. Where the chairperson of the Board is not an independent non-executive Director, the Board should appoint a lead independent Director.

1.3 The Board should demonstrate ethical leadership, which includes commitment to high ethical standards and responsible decision-making.

1.4 The Board should ensure that it is supplied with information in a timely manner, in a form and of a quality appropriate to enable it to discharge its duties effectively.

1.5 The Board should take into account the legitimate interests and expectations of all stakeholders. There should be active co-operation between corporations and stakeholders in creating wealth, employment, and the sustainability of financially sound enterprises.

Principle two

Strengthen the composition and performance of board and committees

There should be a balance of independence and diversity of skills, knowledge, experience, perspectives and gender among Directors so that the Board works effectively.

Recommendations

2.1 The Board should appoint a sufficient number of independent Directors capable of exercising unbiased judgment, particularly in tasks where there is a potential for conflicts of interest.

2.2 Directors should be selected and appointed through rigorous and formal processes designed to give the Board a balance of independence and diversity of skills, knowledge, experience, perspectives and gender among Directors so that the Board works effectively.

2.3 A Committee with a majority of independent non-executive Directors, should lead the Board's nomination process and make recommendations to the Board.

2.4 All Directors should receive induction training upon joining the Board and should regularly update and refresh their skills and knowledge.

2.5 The Board should undertake a rigorous, transparent and formal annual evaluation of its own performance and that of its committees and of the individual Directors.

2.6 The Board should ensure that the remuneration of Directors and Senior Management is transparent, fair and reasonable.

Principle three

Reinforce loyalty and independence

All Directors should act honestly and in good faith, in the best interest of the company, ahead of other interests.

Recommendations

3.1 The Board should undertake an assessment of its independence on an annual basis and disclose in the annual report each non-executive Director it considers to be independent.

3.2 All Directors should be candidates for re-election, at intervals of no more than three years, subject to continued satisfactory performance.

3.3 Members of the Board and Senior Management should disclose to the Board whether they, directly or indirectly or on behalf of third parties, have a material interest in any transaction or matter directly affecting the company.

3.4 Directors should demonstrate the capacity to commit the time needed to be fully effective in their roles.

Principle four

Foster accountability

The Board should present an accurate, timely, balanced and understandable assessment of the company's performance, position and prospects.

Recommendations

4.1 The Board should promote accurate, timely and balanced disclosure of all material matters concerning the company.

4.2 Directors should state in the annual report their responsibility towards the integrity of the financial reports. This includes a statement from Directors that these reports comply with applicable financial reporting standards and present a true and fair view of the financial affairs of the company.

4.3 The Board should, on an annual basis, report to shareholders and stakeholders on the external auditor's involvement in non-audit work and fees paid to auditors. This disclosure should differentiate between fees for audit work and fees for non-audit work.

4.4 The Board should, on an annual basis, verify that the company has appropriate processes that identify and manage potential and relevant risks.

4.5 Each company should establish an Audit Committee of the Board with responsibilities that include, but are not limited to:

a. Recommending the appointment of external auditors;
b. Assessing the suitability and independence of external auditors;
c. Following-up on recommendations made by internal and external auditors;
d. Overseeing all aspects of the company-audit firm relationship;
e. Monitoring and reviewing the effectiveness of the internal audit function;
f. Promoting integrity in financial reporting

4.6 Boards should report annually to shareholders on how the company is implementing the Corporate Governance Principles and explain any significant departure from Recommendations supporting each Principle.

Principle five

Strengthen relationships with shareholders

The Board should promote constructive relationships with all shareholders that facilitate the exercise of their ownership rights and encourage their engagement with the company.

Recommendations

5.1 The Board should facilitate the exercise of ownership rights by all shareholder groups, including minority or foreign shareholders and institutional investors.

5.2 The Board should ensure that all shareholders have the opportunity to engage with the company and participate effectively in annual and special meetings.

5.3 During the annual and special meetings, the Board should facilitate questioning of external auditors and Senior Management by shareholders, as moderated by the chairperson.

GUIDANCE

The following section provides guidance and commentary for each Recommendation offered in support of a main Principle.

Principle one

Establish a framework for effective governance

Every company should be headed by an effective Board, which is collectively responsible for the long-term success of the company.

Recommendation 1.1

The Board should establish and make publically available a clear outline of its roles and responsibilities, including any formal delegations to Management.

Guidance

Every Board should have a formal charter that sets out the responsibilities and roles of the Board and its Directors.

The Board should fulfill certain key functions, including:

a. Setting the strategic aims of the organization.
b. Reviewing and approving corporate strategy, major plans of action, annual budgets and business plans.

c. Ensuring the company has the appropriate organizational structure in place to achieve its objectives.
d. Identifying principal risks and ensuring the implementation of appropriate internal controls and mitigation measures.
e. Reviewing the adequacy and the integrity of the management information and internal control systems of the company.
f. Monitoring corporate performance and the implementation of corporate objectives.
g. Overseeing material commitments, including capital expenditures, acquisitions and divestitures.
h. Ensuring the adoption of appropriate corporate governance practices, monitoring its effectiveness and making changes as needed.
i. Monitoring and managing potential conflicts of interest of management and Board members.
j. Monitoring and managing potential misuse of corporate assets and abuse in related party transactions.
k. Selecting, compensating, monitoring and, when necessary, replacing Senior Management[1] and overseeing succession planning.
l. Approving and monitoring financial and other reporting.
m. Ensuring compliance with legal and regulatory requirements.
n. Overseeing the process of disclosure and communications with shareholders.

Recommendation 1.2

The chairperson of the Board should be a non-executive Director and preferably an independent Director. Where the chairperson of the Board is not an independent non-executive Director, the Board should appoint a lead independent Director.

Guidance

No Director of a publicly owned company should simultaneously hold the roles of chairperson and chief executive officer. Separation of these two positions helps to achieve an appropriate balance of power, increase accountability and improve the Board's capacity for decision-making independent of management bias.

Only in exceptional circumstances should the chief executive officer also serve as the chairperson, or move on to immediately become the chairperson. In this instance, the Board should consult major shareholders in advance and should set out its reasons at the time of appointment and in the next annual report.

1 For here and other parts of the code where "Senior Management" is used, see also Section 4 of the Companies Act for definition of "officer" of a company, as well as Section 4 of the Securities Act (2012 as amended) for definition of "senior officer".

Where the chairperson is not an independent non-executive Director, the Board should appoint one of the independent non-executive Directors to be the lead independent Director. His/her role would be to provide a sounding board for the chairperson and to serve as an intermediary for the other Directors, when necessary.

The lead independent Director may also be available to shareholders if they have concerns, which contact through the chairperson has failed to resolve, or for which such contact is inappropriate.

The responsibilities of the chairperson include leading the Board in the oversight of management and directing it to achieve specified longer-term results within limits stipulated by the Board. The Chief Executive Officer leads the development and execution of the Board-approved strategy for achieving specified results. This division of responsibilities should be clearly defined, set out in writing and agreed by the Board.

Recommendation 1.3

The Board should demonstrate ethical leadership, which includes commitment to high ethical standards and responsible decision-making.

Guidance

A framework for ethical conduct needs to demonstrate a commitment that goes beyond compliance with the law, which should always be a fundamental requirement.

The Board of every company should establish values and principles and ensure management adopts a written Code of Conduct that clarifies the standards of ethical behaviour required of the Board, Senior Management and employees. The Code should set the framework for the exercise of judgment in dealing with varying and potentially conflicting circumstances. At a minimum, it should set clear limits on the pursuit of private interests and measures for dealing with breaches of the Code.

The Code should include procedures for whistleblowing, which encourages individuals to disclose concerns using appropriate channels. It should include provisions that protect individuals who provide relevant information, in good faith, to the organization or to any regulatory body or authority, whether or not such information was requested.

Additionally, the Board should ensure there is a system for implementing the company's Code of Conduct, which includes company-wide training, measures for monitoring adherence to the Code and holding individuals responsible for unethical behaviour.

Companies should make the Code, or a summary of it, publicly available and make advisors, consultants and contractors aware of the expectations set out therein.

Recommendation 1.4

The Board should ensure that it is supplied with information in a timely manner, in a form and of a quality appropriate to enable it to discharge its duties effectively.

Guidance

The Board should have access to all information pertaining to the company. Management has an obligation to provide such information and Directors should seek clarification or additional support where necessary. Additionally, requests for information from Management should be channeled through the Corporate Secretary and Board Chair.

The Board may consider inviting Senior Management, who are not Board members, to participate in Board meetings where it may be more appropriate or beneficial to have information presented from individuals who may have a more intimate understanding of the matters being discussed.

The Board should ensure that Directors, especially non-executive Directors, have access to independent legal, financial, governance or other expert advice in the course of discharging their responsibilities. These services should be acquired at the company's expense through agreed procedures.

All Directors should have access to the advice and services of the Corporate Secretary, who is responsible for ensuring the integrity of Board documents and compliance with corporate governance obligations and Board-established procedures.

Recommendation 1.5

The Board should take into account the legitimate interests and expectations of all stakeholders. There should be active co-operation between corporations and stakeholders in creating wealth, employment, and the sustainability of financially sound enterprises.

Guidance

Stakeholder interests include employee, environmental, social, governance and economic matters. The Board needs to recognize that stakeholders contribute to company performance in different ways and should therefore take measures to protect their interests and respect their rights during the decision-making process. The best interests of the company should be understood within the parameters of the company being a sustainable enterprise and a responsible corporate citizen.

The Board should formalize its strategies for achieving transparency, balance and equity in stakeholder engagement. This may be done through the development of publically available policies that outline the company's relationship with major stakeholders.

Principle two

Strengthen the composition and performance of board and committees

There should be a balance of independence and diversity of skills, knowledge, experience, perspectives and gender among Directors so that the Board works effectively.

Recommendation 2.1

The Board should appoint a sufficient number of independent Directors capable of exercising unbiased judgment, particularly in tasks where there is a potential for conflicts of interest.

Guidance

For a Board to be able to exercise unbiased judgment on corporate affairs, it should strive to have a sufficient number of members who are independent of Management. Companies with public accountability[2] should ensure that the majority of the Board comprises of independent Directors.

As part of their role as a member of a unitary Board, independent Directors should challenge the performance of Management in matters sensitive to Management bias and to provide additional assurance to market participants that their interests are defended.

Examples of key responsibility areas of independent Directors include:

a. Ensuring the integrity of financial and non-financial reporting, including the external audit process.
b. The review of related party transactions.
c. Nomination, compensation and performance evaluation of Board members and the Chief Executive Officer.
d. Board remuneration.

The Board may consider establishing committees and other processes to enhance its effectiveness in dealing with subjects where there is potential for conflicts of interest. These committees should comprise entirely, or at a minimum, a majority of non-executive Directors.

The Board chairperson should conduct regular meetings with non-executive Directors in the absence of executive Directors.

Recommendation 2.2

Directors should be selected and appointed through rigorous and formal processes designed to give the Board a balance of independence and diversity of skills, knowledge, experience, perspectives and gender among Directors so that the Board works effectively.

2 An entity has public accountability under the IASB's definition if it files, or is in the process of filing, its financial statements with a securities commission or other regulatory organization for the purpose of issuing any class of instruments in a public market; or it holds assets in a fiduciary capacity for a broad group of outsiders. *http://www.ifrs. com/overview/IFRS_SMES/IFRS_SMES_FAQ.html#q2*

Guidance

Board appointments should be made on the basis of the person's probity, competence and soundness of judgment for fulfilling the responsibilities of Directors. Also consider the diligence he or she may apply towards fulfilling Directors' responsibilities, and whether the interests of shareholders, or potential shareholders may be threatened in any way by the persons considered for Board appointment.

Appointments should be made with due consideration of the existing balance of skills, knowledge and experience on the Board as well as the duration of each Director's tenure so as to maintain effective succession planning. Following such an evaluation, a description of the role, capabilities required and time commitment expected should be prepared for each appointment.

The Board should formalize its position and approach toward boardroom diversity. These policies and targets should be disclosed in the annual report along with measures taken to meet those targets.

The nomination and election process for Board members should be disclosed in the annual report.

Recommendation 2.3

A Committee with a majority of independent non-executive Directors should lead the Board nomination process and make recommendations to the Board.

Guidance

The Committee's responsibilities include:

a. Searching, assessing and recommending candidates for Board appointments to the Board.
b. Recommending Directors to Board committees.
c. Reviewing of Board succession plans.
d. Facilitating training programs for the Board and induction programs for new Directors.

The role of the Committee, including the authority delegated to it by the Board and the process it uses in relation to Board appointments, should be disclosed in the company's annual report. Where consultants are used, they should be identified and a statement made as to whether they have any connection with the company.

In smaller companies, the Committee could be appointed on an ad hoc basis.

The chairperson or an independent non-executive Director should chair this Committee; however, the chairperson should not chair the Committee when it is dealing with the appointment of a successor to the chairmanship.

Recommendation 2.4

All Directors should receive induction training upon joining the Board and should regularly update and refresh their skills and knowledge.

Guidance

The Board should allocate time and resources towards enabling Directors to acquire and retain a sound understanding of their responsibilities. This includes the facilitation of appropriate induction training for new Directors as well as assisting with ongoing professional development, as required.

Directors need to have a strong understanding of the company, the industry in which it operates as well as governance principles that allow them to perform their oversight functions effectively.

Induction programs for new Directors should cover:

a. The company's financial, strategic, operational and risk management positions.
b. Roles and responsibilities of Directors.
c. Roles and responsibilities of Senior Management.
d. Roles and responsibilities of Board committees.
e. Expectations of executive and non-executive Directors.

Professional development programs should be available to provide Directors with:

a. Understanding of governance principles and best practices.
b. Understanding financial reporting, legal, regulatory and tax requirements, especially those unique to the industry of operation.
c. Understanding of industry and market trends, and their impact on the company.
d. Subject matter expertise on specific topics relevant to their role (i.e., chairmanship, remuneration, nomination, risk management, strategy evaluation, etc.).

Recommendation 2.5

The Board should undertake a rigorous, transparent and formal annual evaluation of its own performance and that of its committees and of the individual Directors.

Guidance

Board evaluation provides an opportunity to critically assess the balance of skills, experience, independence and competency of individual Directors and the Board as a whole. It is a time for reflecting on how the Board works together and the degree to which the Board has achieved its governance objectives as well as targets for diversity and balance.

Individual evaluation of Directors should address whether each Director needs specific training, continues to contribute effectively and demonstrates commitment to the role.

The Board should state in the annual report how performance evaluations have been conducted of the Board as a whole, its committees and its individual Directors. The full Board should perform the evaluation of the chairperson.

Recommendation 2.6

The Board should ensure that the remuneration of Directors and Senior Management is transparent, fair and reasonable.

Guidance

Fair remuneration is critical to attract, retain and motivate Directors of a quality required to run the company successfully.

The Board should establish a Remuneration Committee that consists of, at a minimum, a majority of independent non-executive Directors and seeks advice from experts if necessary. Where executive Directors or Senior Management are involved in advising or supporting the Remuneration Committee, care should be taken to recognize and avoid conflicts of interest.

The Remuneration Committee's responsibilities include:

a. Recommending all remuneration for Directors and the chairperson.
b. Recommending and monitoring the level and structure of remuneration for Senior Management.
c. Establishing the policy for determining remuneration.
d. Reviewing and evaluating the appropriateness of remuneration plans on an annual basis.
e. Ensuring that the total remuneration and other benefits paid to Directors are properly disclosed.

The role of the Remuneration Committee, including the authority delegated to it by the Board, should be disclosed in the company's annual report. Where consultants are used, they should be identified and a statement made as to whether they have any connection with the company.

The Board should submit the recommendations for Board fees to shareholders in a general meeting for approval, prior to implementation and payment.

Boards should develop and disclose remuneration policy and procedures that cover Directors and Senior Management. The policy should specify the relationship between remuneration and performance and include measurable standards that protect long-term interest of the company over short-term considerations.

There should be clear differentiation between executive Director and non-executive Director remuneration to allow the company the flexibility to address the different roles and incentives. Remuneration for non-executive Directors should not include share options or other performance-related elements that may increase the risk of Directors taking a short-term approach rather than a strategic view.

In general, remuneration incentives should be compatible with Board-established risk policies and systems. Additionally, consideration should be given to the use of provisions that permit the company to reclaim variable components of remuneration plans in exceptional circumstances, such as misstatement or misconduct.

Principle three

Reinforce loyalty and independence

All Directors should act honestly and in good faith, in the best interest of the company, ahead of other interests.

Recommendation 3.1

The Board should undertake an assessment of its independence on an annual basis and disclose in the annual report each non-executive Director it considers to be independent.

Guidance

The Board should determine whether Directors are independent in character and judgment. Additionally, the Board has a responsibility to identify whether there are relationships or circumstances that are likely to affect, or could be perceived to affect, a Director's judgment.

The Nominating Committee should develop the criteria to assess independence and should include considerations for whether or not the Director:

a. Has been an employee of the company within the last three years;
b. Has, or has had within the last three years, a relationship, that is material to the Director, with the company directly, or in their capacity as a partner, shareholder, Director or senior employee of a company that has had such a relationship with the company;
c. Receives, or has received remuneration from the company (apart from Director's fees), participates in a share option or other performance-related pay program, or is a member of the company's pension program;
d. Has family ties, as defined by law, with any of the company's Directors or employees or major suppliers;
e. Holds cross-directorships or has significant links with other Directors through involvement in other companies or organizations;
f. Represents a significant shareholder, to be considered as a person who either alone or with one or more affiliates or connected parties is entitled to exercise 20%[3] (or such other percentage as may be determined relevant on a case by case basis) or more of the voting power at any general meeting of the company; or
g. Has served on the Board of the company for more than nine years from the date of their first election.

3 2008 Financial Institutions Act, Preamble

Directors should be assessed based on these criteria at time of admission to the Board, annually and whenever any new interest or relationship develops. The Board should consider disclosing its criteria for assessment in the annual report.

It is important to recognize that focus should go beyond the Director's background, economic and family relationships and consider overall whether the Director is able to bring independent and unbiased judgment to Board deliberations, especially in areas where the interests of management, the company and its shareholders may diverge.

Recommendation 3.2

All Directors should be candidates for re-election, at intervals of no more than three years, subject to continued satisfactory performance.

Guidance

All Directors should be subject to re-election by shareholders, under the condition of continued satisfactory performance. Maintaining a transparent and timely process for re-election enhances the assurance to shareholders that Directors' performance and independence are evaluated on a regular basis.

The tenure of an independent Director should not exceed a cumulative term of nine years. Non-executive Directors serving for more than nine years should be subject to re-election on an annual basis. They should be subject to particularly rigorous review that recognizes independence as being influenced, and potentially compromised by, long-term relationships being established with Senior Management and other Directors.

The names of Directors submitted for election or re-election should be accompanied by sufficient biographical details and any other relevant information to enable shareholders to make an informed decision.

Recommendation 3.3

Members of the Board and Senior Management should disclose to the Board whether they, directly or indirectly or on behalf of third parties, have a material interest in any transaction or matter directly affecting the company.

Guidance

The company should have a policy on related-party transactions and how to deal with conflicts of interest. Boards should consider making this policy publicly available and disclose it in the annual report.

Members of the Board and Senior Management have an obligation to recognize and disclose to the Board where they have a business, family or other special relationship outside of the company that could affect their judgment with respect to an existing or upcoming transaction or matter affecting the company.

Shareholders should be provided with disclosures necessary to evaluate whether the company's financial position may have been affected by the existence of related parties and by transactions or outstanding balances with such parties.

Where an individual has a material interest in a transaction or matter affecting the company, it is good practice for that individual to declare their interest in the matter and to immediately thereafter recuse from the deliberations and not be involved in any decision-making or implementation process involving the transaction or matter.

Additionally, any transaction the company has with related parties or individuals should be disclosed in the company's financial statements along with outstanding balances with such parties.

Recommendation 3.4

Directors should demonstrate the capacity to commit the time needed to be fully effective in their roles.

Guidance

Outside commitments of executive and non-executive Directors should be disclosed to the Board before appointment with an indication of the time involved. The Board should be informed of any subsequent changes to outside commitments of all Directors including any new directorships being considered.

Directors should be provided a limit, as determined appropriate by the chairperson or the Nomination Committee, on how many directorship positions they may hold in the same period.

Boards should consider disclosing in the annual report, any additional directorships held by its Directors.

Principle four

Foster accountability

The Board should present an accurate, timely, balanced and understandable assessment of the company's performance, position and prospects.

Recommendation 4.1

The Board should promote accurate, timely and balanced disclosure of all material matters concerning the company.

Guidance

Material information may be considered to be "information whose omission or misstatement could influence the economic decisions taken by users of the information."

Disclosure should include[4], but not be limited to, material information on:

a. The financial and operating results of the company.
b. Company objectives.

c. Major share ownership and voting rights.
d. Remuneration policy for members of the Board and Senior Management.
e. Information about Board members, including their qualifications, the selection process, other company directorships and whether they are regarded as independent.
f. Related party transactions.
g. Foreseeable risk factors.
h. Issues regarding employees and other stakeholders that may materially affect the company.
i. Governance structures and policies, in particular, the content of any corporate governance code or policy and the process by which they are implemented.
j. Compliance with statutory, regulatory and tax requirements.

Boards should ensure that any disclosures or announcements of material information that concern the company should be done in a timely manner and received equally by all investors and shareholders, regardless of ownership percentage or class.

Recommendation 4.2

Directors should state in the annual report their responsibility towards the integrity of the financial reports. This includes a statement from Directors that these reports comply with applicable financial reporting standards and present a true and fair view of the financial affairs of the company.

Guidance

The Board's responsibility to present accurate, fair and balanced assessments extends to all interim and other public reports, including reports to regulators as well as information compulsory to meeting statutory requirements.

All Boards should have a rigorous process for assuring Directors of the quality and integrity of the company's financial reports, including their relevance, reliability, comparability and timeliness.

Recommendation 4.3

The Board should, on an annual basis, report to shareholders and stakeholders on the external auditor's involvement in non-audit work and fees paid to auditors. This disclosure should differentiate between fees for audit work and fees for non-audit work.

Guidance

Provision of non-audit services by the external auditor can significantly compromise their independence when there is increased risk of auditing their own work. Boards are responsible for ensuring that accounting firms who provide audit services to the

4 Refer to Appendix A for list of disclosure items used in the International Standards of Accounting and Reporting benchmarks

company do not undertake any work that may impair, or be perceived to impair, their independence in the audit process.

Non-audit work[5] performed should be disclosed in the annual report along with explanation as to why this did not compromise auditor independence.

Recommendation 4.4

The Board should, on an annual basis, verify that the company has appropriate processes that identify and manage potential and relevant risks.

Guidance

Boards can only be effective if they are aware of, and can properly evaluate, the nature and magnitude of risks faced by the company. Effective risk management enables a company to operate within the limits established by the Board as acceptable for achieving its strategic objectives.

To this end, companies should develop clear policies and a framework for monitoring and managing risk.

Additionally, the Board should ensure that the integrity of a company's internal controls and risk management systems are evaluated on an annual basis and report to shareholders that such an evaluation has been conducted.

The Board should ensure that there is an effective risk-based internal audit function that reports directly to the Audit Committee. The internal audit function must have the relevant qualifications necessary to provide an assessment of the effectiveness of the company's system of internal controls in managing the risks that arise from its strategic direction.

In certain companies, especially banking and financial institutions, it may be considered necessary to establish a separate Risk Oversight Committee to oversee risk exposures and strategy in relation to credit, market, operational, compliance, legal, property, security, IT and reputational risks. Membership composition may follow those of the Audit Committee.

Recommendation 4.5

Each company should establish an Audit Committee of the Board with responsibilities that include, but are not limited to:

a. Recommending the appointment of external auditors;
b. Assessing the suitability and independence of external auditors;
c. Following-up on recommendations made by internal and external auditors;
d. Overseeing all aspects of the company-audit firm relationship;

5 The Institute of Chartered Accountants of Trinidad & Tobago recognizes and follows the IFAC Handbook of the Code of Ethics for Professional Accountants (See 2013 Edition S290.156 to S290.219 for definitions of non-assurance work provided to assurance clients)

e. **Monitoring and reviewing the effectiveness of the internal audit function;**
f. **Promoting integrity in financial reporting**

Guidance

The Audit Committee is responsible for the quality and independence of the external audit process and should, therefore, inform itself fully on the responsibilities of external auditors and be rigorous in its selection of auditors.

The Board should satisfy itself that the Audit Committee has at least three members, where at least one member is a Chartered Accountant or has another recognized form of financial expertise and that the Committee comprises a majority of non-executive independent Directors. The Chairperson of the Audit Committee should meet the Board's criteria as an independent Director. The Chairperson for the Board of the company should not be the Chairperson of the Audit Committee.

The Audit Committee should satisfy itself that there is no relationship between the auditor and the company or any related person that could compromise the independence of the auditor. The Board should require written confirmation of this from the auditor.

Similar to the recommendations on re-election of Directors and recognizing that independence is sensitive to, and potentially compromised by, long-term relationships with Senior Management and the Board, the Audit Committee should ensure that the same audit Partner should not lead the external audit for more than five consecutive years.

The Audit Committee should ensure that arrangements which facilitate whistleblowing, or which allow staff of the company and other concerned parties to raise apprehensions about possible improprieties in confidence, and without fear of repercussion, are implemented and monitored. It is the Audit Committee's responsibility to ensure that arrangements are in place for appropriate and independent investigation or follow-up of matters raised. Oversight of the whistleblowing process should be the responsibility of a non-executive Director of the Audit Committee.

Recommendation 4.6

Boards should report annually to shareholders on how the company is implementing the Corporate Governance Principles and explain any significant departure from Recommendations supporting each Principle.

Guidance

The way in which the Principles and supporting Recommendations of the Code are applied should be central to a Board's evaluation of its governance practices.

Alternative methods of following a recommendation may be justified in a particular circumstance if it can be explained, clearly and carefully to shareholders, that good governance was achievable by other means. Where deviation from a particular Recommendation is intended to be limited in time, the company should indicate in its explanation when it expects to apply the Recommendation.

Principle five

Strengthen relationships with shareholders

The Board should promote constructive relationships with all shareholders that facilitate the exercise of their ownership rights and encourage their engagement with the company.

Recommendation 5.1

The Board should facilitate the exercise of ownership rights by all shareholder groups, including minority or foreign shareholders and institutional investors.

Guidance

The Board is responsible for ensuring that a satisfactory dialogue exists with shareholders based on the mutual understanding of objectives and that all shareholders within the same class of shares should be treated equally.

Where companies have a single controlling shareholder, efforts should be made to emphasize independence from controlling shareholders or another controlling body so as to restore confidence amongst other or minority shareholders that their interests and rights are not neglected. Shareholders who individually or collectively hold at least five (5) percent of shareholdings should have the right to propose agenda items to be discussed in a meeting of shareholders, and the right to nominate candidates for Board membership.

Efforts should be made to reduce impediments to cross-border voting as a means to attract and accommodate foreign shareholders. This includes encouraging participation through the use of modern technology and ensuring that information or proxy materials are sent out in a manner that allows investors adequate time for reflection and consultation.

Recommendation 5.2

The Board should ensure that all shareholders have the opportunity to engage with the company and participate effectively in annual and special meetings.

Guidance

Companies should have clear and published policies for shareholder relations that are reviewed regularly to ensure practices are conducive to the clear communication of goals, strategies and performance of the company to all shareholders.

The Board should state in the annual report the steps it has taken to solicit and understand the views of shareholders. This may include direct face-to-face contact, analyst briefings, and surveys of shareholder opinion or investor roadshows.

The chairperson of the Board should ensure that the views of shareholders are communicated to the Board as a whole. Non-executive Directors should be offered the opportunity to attend meetings with shareholders.

All shareholders should be encouraged to take part in annual and special meetings that are held in locations and at times that are convenient. Additionally, company procedures should not make it unduly difficult or expensive to cast votes.

Notice for the annual meeting, including date, location, agenda and related papers should be sent to shareholders at least 21 days before the meeting for special resolutions and otherwise not less than 10 business days nor more than 50 days before the meeting.

Recommendation 5.3

During the annual and special meetings, the Board should facilitate questioning of external auditors and Senior Management by shareholders, as moderated by the chairperson.

Guidance

Shareholders should have the opportunity to ask questions of the Board, including questions relating to the annual external audit.

Additionally, the chairperson of the Board should arrange for all Directors and members of Senior Management to attend, and ensure that the chairpersons of the Audit, Remuneration and Nomination Committees are available to answer questions. Additionally, shareholders may be encouraged to submit questions in advance, and where appropriate, the chairperson of the Board should allow members of Senior Management to prepare responses to specific questions on matters related to their role.

INDEX

For Product Safety Concerns and Information please contact our
EU representative GPSR@taylorandfrancis.com Taylor & Francis
Verlag GmbH, Kaufingerstraße 24, 80331 München, Germany